QUICKEN® 2007 PERSONAL FINANCE SOFTWARE

QuickSteps

BOBBI SANDBERG
MARTY MATTHEWS

New York Chicago San Francisco
Lisbon London Madrid Mexico City
Milan New Delhi San Juan
Seoul Singapore Sydney Toronto

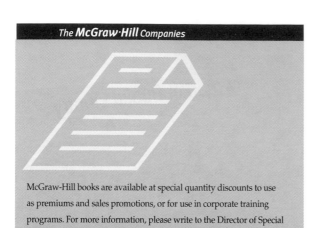

NOV 17 2006

QUICKEN® 2007 PERSONAL FINANCE SOFTWARE QUICKSTEPS

1234567890 CCI CCI 019876

ISBN-13: 978-0-07-226388-6
ISBN-10:   0-07-226388-1

SPONSORING EDITOR / Megg Morin
EDITORIAL SUPERVISORS / Jody McKenzie, Patty Mon
PRODUCTION SUPERVISOR / James Kussow
ACQUISITIONS COORDINATOR / Agatha Kim
TECHNICAL EDITOR / Marty Matthews
COPY EDITOR / Lisa McCoy
PROOFREADER / Stefany Otis
INDEXER / Valerie Perry
COMPOSITION / Apollo Publishing Services
SERIES DESIGN / Bailey Cunningham
ART DIRECTOR, COVER / Jeff Weeks
COVER DESIGN / Pattie Lee

To Judy & Margaret
Your friendship is better than gold.
Thank you for your support and nurturing
during this and every year. And always, Sandy.

Bobbi Sandberg

About the Authors

Bobbi Sandberg has been involved with computers and accounting for five decades. Her extensive background combined with her ability to explain complex concepts in plain language has made her a popular instructor, speaker, and consultant. Bobbi has been a CPA and was a geek long before it was popular. She is the co-author of *Quicken 2006 QuickSteps*. Currently semi-retired, she lives on an island surrounded by deer, chipmunks, trees—and at last count, 23 computers in various stages of operation.

Marty Matthews has used computers for over 40 years, from mainframes to the most recent PCs. He has done this as a programmer, and as the president of a software firm, and many positions in between. As a result, he has first-hand knowledge of most facets of computing. Over 20 years ago Marty and his wife Carole began writing computer books and they have now written over 70 of them, including *Windows XP QuickSteps*, *Microsoft Office Outlook 2003 QuickSteps*, and *Quicken 2006 QuickSteps*, all published by McGraw-Hill. Marty and his wife live on an island in Puget Sound.

Contents at a Glance

1
2
3
4
5
6
7
8
9
10

Contents

3 Chapter 3 **Setting Up the Other Centers** 51

4 Chapter 4 **Using Quicken Every Day** 69

7 Chapter 7 **Keeping Your Records Up to Date**............................ 139

8 Chapter 8 **Managing Your Investments** 159

Chapter 9 **Making Plans for Your Future** 181

Chapter 10 **Getting Ready for Tax Time** 201

Acknowledgments

Our book has only two names on the cover, but there were so many more involved than are shown. Were it not for the efforts of the entire team, this book would not be possible.

Megg Morin, acquisition editor at McGraw-Hill, who was there with encouragement, ideas, and help during the entire process.

Jody McKenzie, McGraw-Hill project editor, who made it happen over and over again, with her astute eye and understanding. Her suggestions improved the book every time.

Patty Mon, McGraw-Hill project editor, who caught many an error and made the book better for finding them.

Lisa McCoy, copy editor, caught widely varied inconsistencies and suggested improvements to the text that transformed it into much more readable prose.

The entire Quicken 2007 beta team at Intuit, especially Donald, who kept long hours and helped immeasurably. The team provided us with the great product from which this book stems.

Bobbi Sandberg and Marty Matthews

Introduction

QuickSteps books are recipe books for computer users. They answer the question "how do I" by providing a quick set of steps to accomplish the most common tasks with a particular operating system or application.

The sets of steps are the central focus of the book. QuickSteps sidebars show how to quickly perform many small functions or tasks that support the primary functions. Notes, Tips, and Cautions augment the steps, presented in a separate column to not interrupt the flow of the steps. The introductions are minimal rather than narrative, and numerous illustrations and figures, many with callouts, support the steps.

QuickSteps books are organized by function and the tasks needed to perform that function. Each function is a chapter. Each task, or "How To," contains the steps needed for accomplishing the function along with the relevant Notes, Tips, Cautions, and screenshots. You can easily find the tasks you need through:

- The Table of Contents, which lists the functional areas (chapters) and tasks in the order they are presented

- A How To list of tasks on the opening page of each chapter

- The index, which provides an alphabetical list of the terms that are used to describe the functions and tasks

- Color-coded tabs for each chapter or functional area with an index to the tabs in the Contents at a Glance (just before the Table of Contents)

Conventions Used in this Book

Quicken 2007 Personal Finance Software QuickSteps uses several conventions designed to make the book easier for you to follow. Among these are

- A ⊙ or a ⊘ in the table of contents and in the How To list in each chapter references a QuickSteps or QuickFacts sidebar in a chapter.

- **Bold type** is used for words or objects on the screen that you are to do something with—for example, open the **[Apple]** menu and click **System Preferences**.

- *Italic type* is used for a word or phrase that is being defined or otherwise deserves special emphasis.

- Underlined type is used for text that you are to type from the keyboard.

- SMALL CAPITAL LETTERS are used for keys on the keyboard such as **ENTER** and **SHIFT**.

- When you are expected to enter a command, you are told to press the key(s). If you are to enter text or numbers, you are told to type them.

How to...

- Determine the Version for You
- Upgrading Quicken
- Install Quicken
- Viewing the Installation CD
- Complete the Installation
- Start Quicken
- Creating a Quick Launch Shortcut
- Register Quicken
- Use Quicken New User Setup
- Understand the Home Page
- Add Accounts Manually
- Using the Ticker Symbol Lookup
- Using the Address Book
- Find Help
- Updating Quicken
- Exit Quicken
- Recognize Quicken Terms
- Finding More Keyboard Shortcuts
- Use Windows Tools

Chapter 1
Stepping into Quicken

Welcome to Quicken 2007 Personal Finance Software! Quicken is more than a digital checkbook or a way of organizing your finances. It is a ready tool, an easy way to account for all of your income, expenses, loan payments, assets, and liabilities. Using Quicken can give you peace of mind and a way to control your money instead of letting your money control you. With Quicken, you can print checks; pay bills online with an Internet connection; reconcile your bank, credit card, and investment account statements; track your expenses; and plan your financial future.

This chapter introduces you to the various versions of Quicken, shows you how to install it on your computer, explains some terms used by Quicken, reviews some Windows concepts, walks you through the Quicken Setup Guide, and shows you how to close the program when you have finished using it. Even if you are an experienced user of Quicken, it might be good to review this chapter to see some of the new features of Quicken 2007.

UICKSTEPS

UPGRADING QUICKEN

If you purchase any version of Quicken 2007, except Quicken Home & Business, and later want to upgrade, you can do so easily with your Internet connection.

1. Click **Help** on the menu bar.

2. Depending on the Quicken version you have, you will see one or more of the following options for upgrading. Click the one that is correct for you:

   - **Which Quicken is best for you?** In either Quicken Basic or Deluxe editions, you can read about the other versions and decide if you want to upgrade.

   - **Add More Investing & Tax Tools.** In either Quicken Basic or Deluxe editions, you can read about Quicken Premier and decide if you want to upgrade.

   - **Add Business Tools.** In Quicken Basic, Deluxe, Aor Premier editions, you can read about Quicken Home & Business and decide if you want to upgrade.

3. The displayed window shows the features of the upgrades available to you. Select the upgrade you want, and then click **Order Online**. You will be prompted for your credit card information.

4. After your order has been accepted, Quicken will send you an e-mail to confirm your order with an *unlock code* to enter. The "unlock code" is the group of numbers or letters sent by Quicken to unlock the upgrade features in your Quicken version.

5. Click **Help** and then click **Unlock**.

6. You are prompted to either go online to unlock your file automatically or to enter the code from your confirmation e-mail.

Meet Quicken

Quicken 2007 helps you set up your checking, savings, investment, and credit card accounts; enter transactions into those accounts; balance or reconcile the accounts to the institution's records; print checks; create reports; design and print graphs; manage your debt; and see tips to help save your hard-earned dollars. If you are connected to the Internet, you can download information from your bank, investment house, and credit card company. Quicken also makes it quick and easy to transfer your data to TurboTax at year-end to make tax preparation less stressful.

Determine the Version for You

Quicken 2007 comes in four versions: Basic, Deluxe, Premier, and Home & Business. The version you select will depend on the tasks you want Quicken 2007 to perform:

- **Quicken 2007 Basic** is often the best choice for new users. It lets you track your bank accounts, credit cards, investment accounts, and loans. With an Internet connection, you can work online with any of your accounts. It gives you links to insurance and mortgage information, as well as some handy budgeting tools.

- **Quicken 2007 Deluxe** gives you more power to make future financial decisions. It includes all of the features in the Basic edition and offers planning tools for taxes, college, and other major financial events. It features free investment information, debt reduction tips, and a Home Inventory and Emergency Records Organizer.

- **Quicken 2007 Premier** adds investment reports, comparisons, analyses, and a report generator for income tax Schedules A, B, and D.

- **Quicken 2007 Home & Business**, in addition to everything in the Premier edition, helps you run your small business and supplies business estimates, invoices, vehicle mileage tracking, and a host of other features. It prints business financial statements in the proper forms, creates customer and vendor lists, and helps you track specific projects and jobs.

You can upgrade any of the first three versions directly from your computer with an Internet connection. See the "Upgrading Quicken" QuickSteps.

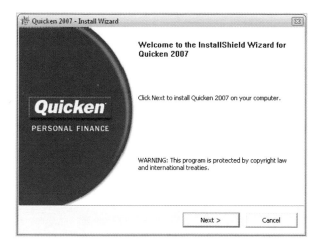

Install Quicken 2007

Quicken 2007 can be installed on your computer for the first time, or it can update an earlier version. Either way, you need only follow the directions in a series of simple windows and dialog boxes to complete the task.

Install Quicken

To install Quicken:

1. Put the Quicken 2007 CD in a CD drive. The installation dialog box appears. (If it doesn't appear, browse to the appropriate CD drive letter, and double-click the setup .exe file.) In Microsoft Windows Vista, you may be asked if you are sure you want to install this new software. Given that you do, take the necessary actions to proceed.

2. Click **Next** to begin the installation. The license agreement appears.

3. Use the vertical scrollbar (see "Use Windows Tools" later in this chapter) to read through the license agreement, and click **I Accept The Terms In The License Agreement** if you agree to its terms. If you do not accept the license agreement, the installation stops and Quicken 2007 will not be installed.

4. Click **Next**. If you want to install the program in its default location, click **Next** again. If you want to install the program in a location other than the default folder, click **Change**, and then:

   a. The Change Current Destination Folder dialog box appears. Click the **Look In** down arrow to see a list of the drives and folders on your computer.

   b. Click one of the existing drives and folders, or create a new folder by clicking a parent drive and folder, clicking the **New Folder** icon, and entering the folder name. Then click **OK**. Quicken shows your choice as the destination folder. Click **Change** again to change it, or click **Next** to continue.

5. In all cases, the Ready To Install The Program dialog box appears. If you have a previous version of Quicken installed on your computer, it will be uninstalled before Quicken 2007 is installed. Click **Install** to continue.

Depending on the speed of your computer, it should take between three and five minutes. Once the installation has finished, remove the CD from its drive and store it in a safe place. Should you ever need to reinstall the program, you will need the disk.

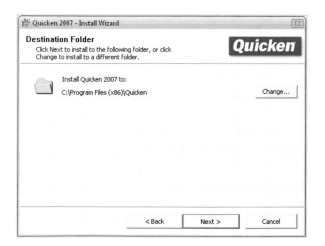

Quicken 2007 does not allow more than one version of Quicken on your computer. You may install Deluxe or Premier editions, 2006 or 2007 versions, but not more than one.

2
3
4
5
6
7
8
9
10

QUICKSTEPS

VIEWING THE INSTALLATION CD

The Installation CD has additional software, as well as troubleshooting help. You can try the Installation CD for a period of time for free. If you decide to keep using the additional software, you must purchase it after the free trial period is over.

1. Click **Related Software** to view additional available programs.

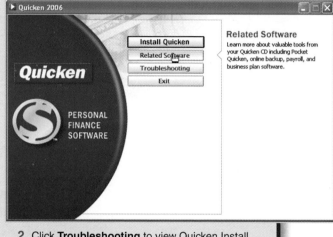

2. Click **Troubleshooting** to view Quicken Install Help. It can answer a number of your installation questions. If you have additional questions and have an Internet connection, click the link to the Quicken support page.

3. When you are ready, click **Exit** to exit the CD program.

Complete the Installation

Near the end of the installation process, you will see a dialog box asking if you want to go online for the latest Quicken updates. If you plan to download any financial transactions, it is best to update now.

1. Click **Get Update**. This requires a connection to the Internet. When the update is complete, you are given two choices. Click **Use Quicken Now** or click **Done** to exit the wizard without starting Quicken.

2. If you choose **Use Quicken Now**, you will see the Welcome To Quicken 2007 dialog box. If you are new to Quicken, leave "I am New to Quicken" selected and click **Next**. You are asked if you want to use the default file name of QData. It is recommended that you keep that file name. Click **Next**.

3. If you are already a Quicken user, select the **I am already a Quicken user** option in the Welcome To Quicken 2007 dialog box, and click **Next**. You are asked if you want to use an existing Quicken file, restore a file from a CD or disk (this could be on another computer on your network), or start a new data file. In either of the first two cases, a dialog box appears in which you can click the **Look In** down arrow to select the folder, click the file, and click **OK**. In the third case, a dialog box appears where you can select the folder in which the new file will be stored, enter a file name, and click **OK**.

4. If you are updating Quicken from a prior version, you will be told that Quicken will automatically convert your Quicken data to the Quicken 2007 format. Click **OK**.

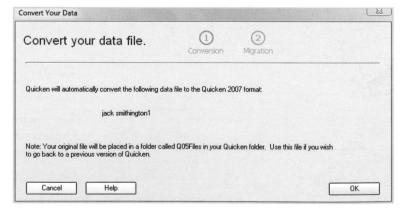

5. In each case the Quicken Home page will appear. If you chose to create a new Quicken file or are a new Quicken user, the Quicken New User Setup dialog box will appear.

Get Started with Quicken

As part of the installation, Quicken places a number of icons on your desktop. With them, you can order a free credit report and check your credit score, open new savings or checking accounts online, apply for a credit card through Quicken, and get one month bill paying for free. You also have a shortcut to start the program.

Start Quicken

You can start Quicken 2007 in several different ways:

- Double-click the **Quicken** icon on the Windows desktop.

- Click **Start** on the Windows taskbar, click **All Programs**, click **Quicken 2007**, and then click **Quicken 2007** again, as shown in Figure 1-1.

- Click the **Quicken 2007** icon on the Quick Launch toolbar on the Windows taskbar, as explained in the "Creating a Quick Launch Shortcut" QuickSteps.

Whatever method you use, whether you click an icon or use the Start menu, Quicken 2007 opens. Periodically, you will see the Update Quicken dialog box. See the "Updating Quicken" QuickSteps to handle updating.

NOTE

This book was written with the newest Windows operating system, Vista. If you are using Windows XP, there are some slight differences in what you see on your screen. However, the procedures and steps are very similar for both operating systems.

Figure 1-1: You should always be able to start Quicken through the All Programs option on the Start menu.

QUICKSTEPS

CREATING A QUICK LAUNCH SHORTCUT

The Quick Launch toolbar, located just to the right of the Start button on the Windows taskbar, is a handy place to store program shortcuts you use often so that you can open them with only one click. It allows you to cover your desktop with programs you are running and still quickly access your important programs. To create a shortcut on your Quick Launch toolbar:

1. Right-click a blank area of the Windows taskbar to display the taskbar menu.

2. Click **Toolbars**, and, if it is not already selected, click **Quick Launch** to activate the Quick Launch toolbar.

3. Ensure that **Lock The Taskbar** is unchecked. If the check mark appears, click **Lock The Taskbar** to turn it off.

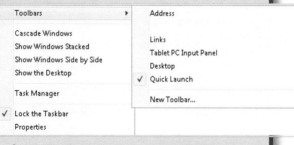

4. Drag the **Quicken** icon from the desktop to the Quick Launch toolbar. A small I-beam appears along with a shadow of the Quicken icon.

5. Drag the I-beam to where you want the Quicken icon, and then release the mouse button. Your icon appears on the Quick Launch toolbar.

Quicken icon on the Quick Launch toolbar

Register Quicken

At some point during your initial use of Quicken, the Product Registration dialog box will appear and prompt you to register Quicken and create a Quicken.com member name. This requires a connection to the Internet. You may also click **Help** on the Quicken menu and choose **Register Quicken** to connect to the Internet and register your program.

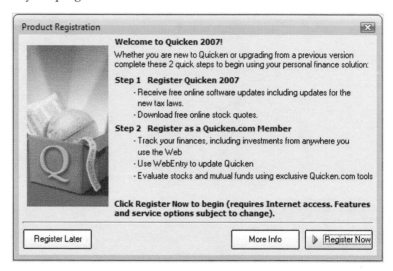

1. Click **More Info** to display a Help screen explaining how you get started with Quicken 2007 and what features are available online, such as Portfolio Export, Historical Quotes and Asset Classes, and Updated Investment Alerts. Click **Close** on the right of the title bar of the Help screen to return to the Product Registration dialog box.

2. Click **Register Now** to open the Quicken Registration dialog box. Enter the information in the required fields, scroll down, and click **Register** to submit the information.

3. Enter your existing Quicken.com member ID and password, and click **Sign In**. Or, click **Continue**; enter a new member ID, password, and other information; and click **Submit**.

4. When registration has been completed successfully and you are informed of that, click **Finished**.

You are returned to the Quicken Home page and ready to start using your Quicken file.

NOTE

The Quicken New User Setup is a one-time process to help you set up your accounts. You do not need to use it to set up new accounts. However, if you use Quicken New User Setup, you do not have to figure out what to enter; you need only type the information requested.

Use Quicken New User Setup

When you have completed the installation and have indicated that you are a new user, the Quicken New User Setup dialog box will appear. This walks you through a series of questions that will tailor the program to fit your needs.

1. Click **Next Step** to begin the process. The Customize Quicken For You dialog box asks for your personal information, including your marital status. Quicken uses this information, which is not required, in its planning area. Click **Next Step** to continue. Should you want to skip the process and enter your information manually, click **Skip Setup**.

2. The Set Up Checking Account dialog box asks for information about your primary bank account, including the name of the bank. Quicken uses this information to determine whether your bank offers online services.

3. Type the first few letters of your bank's name, and a drop-down list appears. If your bank is not listed in the drop-down list, look for another spelling or alternate name. For example, you might consider your bank's name to be Maintown Bank, while it is listed as Main Town Bank.

4. If your bank is not listed, type the name in the field, and then contact them for information as to how to download transactions into Quicken. If you do not provide a name, a warning dialog box will appear.

NOTE

If your bank is a large institution with many branches, you may see a warning dialog box indicating that Quicken needs to know the correct branch.

5. To go to the next dialog box, click **Next Step**.

6. The next dialog box offers you an opportunity to go online to download your information from your bank. If you have your user name and password from your bank, click **Yes**. Otherwise, click **No** and an account information screen will appear.

NOTE

Quicken protects your privacy by using secure Internet technology and encryption during any online transmission. For more information about Quicken's privacy policies, click **How does Quicken protect my privacy?**

TIP

If you and your spouse each have your own checking account, try calling the account "Brad's Checking" or "Sandra's Checking" for quick identification. You could also use the last four digits of the checking account number.

7. Type a name for your account in the **Name Your Account** field. You can use "Main Checking" or any other name that will mean something to you. This is a required field. If you leave it blank, a warning dialog box will appear when you press **ENTER**.

8. Click **Next Step** to continue.

9. If you choose not to download your information, or if your bank does not provide download services, enter the statement ending date for your last bank statement and the balance per the bank as of that date, as seen in Figure 1-2.

10. Click **Next Step** to continue.

ADD PAYCHECKS AND INCOME

The Add My Deposits And Other Income dialog box asks you for information about your income. This can be a paycheck, retirement income, or any other income. It doesn't need to be the same amount each time; you can enter a monthly average. Tracking income helps save time so that you do not have to enter the same information each pay day, and allows Quicken to help you with your tax planning. It also allows Quicken to track your disposable income at the end of each month. For more information, see "Add Paycheck Information" later in this chapter.

1. Type the name of the company from whom you receive your paycheck. The red asterisk shows that this field is required. If you do not receive a paycheck, enter "Social Security" or some other name that represents this income source.

2. Press **TAB** to move to the Category field. "Salary" is the default entry, but you can click the down arrow to choose Other Income.

3. Press **TAB** to move to the Take-Home Pay field. If you do not receive the same amount each time, enter an average.

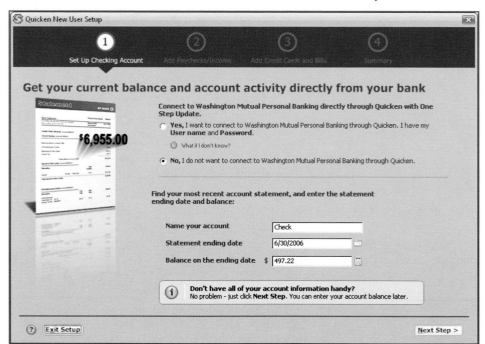

Figure 1-2: Enter the last statement date and the balance from that statement if you don't download it.

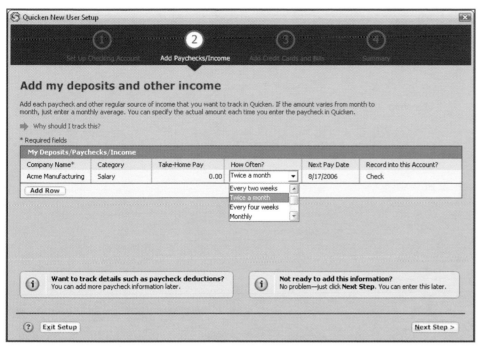

Figure 1-3: You tell Quicken how often to enter your income.

4. Press **TAB** to move to the How Often? field. This field also has a drop-down list from which you can make a selection. Click the down arrow to see the list, and use the vertical scrollbar to see more choices. Figure 1-3 shows some of the choices available.

5. Press **TAB** and enter the next date you will receive this income.

6. Press **TAB** to show the name of the account into which the income should be recorded. If you are not ready to enter any information, click **Next Step** to continue.

ADD CREDIT CARDS AND BILLS

The next dialog box asks for information about your regular monthly expenses. You can enter credit card information as well as your regular monthly expenses, such as utilities and gasoline.

1. The first field is for the name of a credit card. You do not have to identify the credit card company—just create a name that will identify the account for you.

2. Press **TAB** and enter the average payment for this credit card account.

3. Press **TAB** and enter the date the next payment is due on this credit card. The account from which this payment will be deducted appears in the Record Into This Account? field. If you choose to designate another account, press **TAB** to move to that field, and click the down arrow to choose from a list.

4. To add another credit card, click **Add Row** and enter the information as described previously.

5. Click **Name** in the My Bill Reminders section to enter a regular payment you make. This can be a payment for electricity or any other regular payment.

6. Press **TAB** to move to the Category field. A drop-down list appears. Click the down arrow to see your choices. If the category you want is not on the list, you can enter it later. Figure 1-4 shows an example.

TIP

Many banks and credit card companies now offer online transaction services. You can learn more about online transactions in Chapter 2.

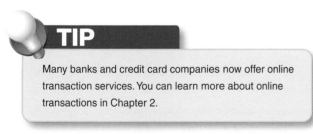

NOTE

If you don't have all of your information available at the time you are using Quicken New User Setup, you can enter the information later.

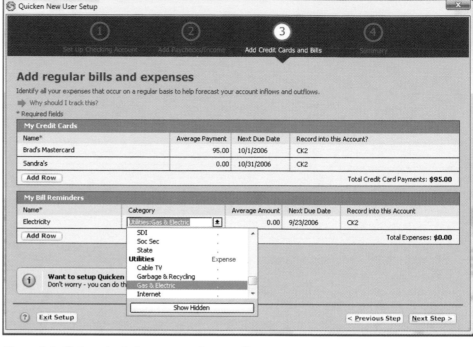

Figure 1-4: *Categories help you organize your finances.*

7. Press **TAB** and enter the average amount of this payment. Press **TAB** again and enter the next time a payment is due.

8. Press **TAB** and enter the name of the account from which you make this payment.

9. To add another bill, click **Add Row** and enter the information as described previously.

10. Click **Next Step** to continue. The Review Your Information dialog box appears showing each of the items you entered. By clicking the relevant **Add Row**, you can add more deposits, credit cards, and bills in this dialog box.

11. Click **Next Step**. The Congratulations window opens. You can click **Finish** or click **Show Me A Video On How To Pay Bills In Quicken**. This screen also shows an area on the Home page where you can add a new account and another area where you can learn to pay bills online.

12. When you click **Finish**, you will see the Quicken Home page, as shown in Figure 1-5.

Understand the Home Page

The Quicken Home page provides a summary of all the accounts you have entered into Quicken. Figure 1-5 shows one of the default displays of the Home page. You will see how to customize it in Chapter 2.

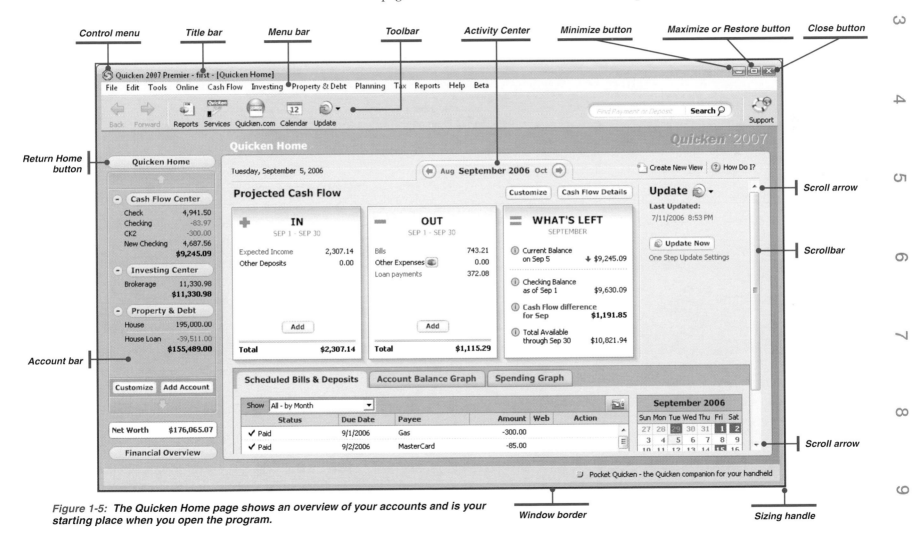

Control menu **Title bar** **Menu bar** **Toolbar** **Activity Center** **Minimize button** **Maximize or Restore button** **Close button**

Return Home button

Account bar

Scroll arrow

Scrollbar

Scroll arrow

Window border

Sizing handle

Figure 1-5: The Quicken Home page shows an overview of your accounts and is your starting place when you open the program.

The Quicken Home page has two major sections: the Account bar on the left that shows the summary of your accounts, and the Activity Center on the right that shows the principal object of the window, such as a register, a transaction list, an analysis, alerts, or a report. Around these panes are a number of objects that are common to other Windows programs and include:

- The **Control Menu icon**, which opens the Control or System menu and allows you to move, size, and close the window.

- The **title bar**, which contains the name of the program or folder in the window and is used to drag the window around the screen.

- The **menu bar**, which contains the menus that are available in the window. Click a menu to open it, and then click one of its options.

- The **toolbar**, which contains tools related to the contents of the window. Click a tool to use it.

- The **Minimize button**, which decreases the size of the window so that you see it only as a task on the taskbar.

- The **Maximize button**, which increases the size of the window so that it fills the screen. When the window is maximized, the Maximize button becomes a Restore button to return the window to the size it was before being maximized.

- The **Close button**, which closes the window and any program it contains.

- The **sizing handle**, which you can drag to size a window diagonally or to increase or decrease its height and width.

- The **window border**, which separates the window from the desktop and other windows, and can be used to size the window horizontally or vertically by dragging either the vertical or horizontal border.

- The **Return Home button**, which will redisplay the Quicken Home Activity Center when you are displaying a different Activity Center.

Add Accounts Manually

Quicken 2007 separates your accounts into three specific areas: Cash Flow, Investments, and Property & Debt. Each of these areas is part of a Center, as shown on the left side of the Home page in Figure 1-5. Each Center also appears on the menu bar at the top of the window. If you choose not to use the Quicken New User Setup, you can add new accounts manually.

1. Click **Add Account** on the Quicken Home page.

2. The New Account dialog box appears. The most common accounts are checking, savings, credit card, and cash accounts, and they appear in the Cash Flow Center.

3. Type the name of the bank where this account is held. If this account is not with a financial institution, click **This account is not held at a financial institution**. Click **Next** to continue.

4. If your bank offers download services, you are asked if you want to set up your bank accounts by downloading them at this time. You will need your password and PIN should you click **Yes**.

5. If you choose not to download your account information at this time, click **Next**.

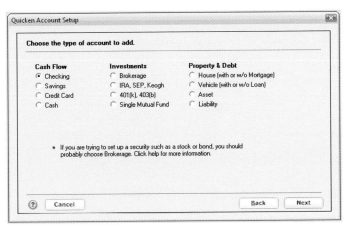

6. If you chose **This account is not held at a financial institution** in step 3, a dialog box appears asking that you choose the type of account you want to create. Click your choice and click **Next** to continue.

7. Enter a name for this account. The default name for any new account is the type of account you chose in step 6. Click **Next**.

8. Enter the date on the last statement you received. Quicken uses today's date by default.

9. Enter the ending balance shown on that statement. If you don't have the statement available, you can complete this information later.

10. Click **Done**. The Register For Your New Account page appears, and your new account is displayed on the Account bar.

ADD INVESTMENT ACCOUNTS

To enter an account in the Investment Center:

1. Click **Add Account**. Enter the name of the financial institution, or click **This account is not held at a financial institution**.

2. Click **Next** to choose the type of account. Depending on your version of Quicken, you can track several different types of investment accounts, including brokerage, IRA or Keogh, 401(k) or 403(b), and single mutual fund.

3. Click **Next** to name this investment account. You can read more about investment accounts in Chapter 8.

4. Click **Next**. Depending on the type of investment account you chose, you may be asked if this is a tax-deferred account.

TIP

You can use Quicken New User Setup to enter any type of account, but it is sometimes easier to use the Add Account dialog box.

QUICKSTEPS

USING THE TICKER SYMBOL LOOKUP

When setting up your investment accounts, you may not know the ticker symbol for a particular security. You can use Ticker Symbol Lookup if you have an Internet connection. From the What Securities Are In This Account? dialog box:

1. Click **Ticker Symbol Lookup**. You are connected to the Internet, and the Quicken Symbol Lookup window will open. `Ticker Symbol Lookup`

To paste the ticker symbol into Quicken:
- Highlight the symbol for your investment and press CTRL+C
- Go back to Quicken
- Click in the ticker symbol box and press CTRL+V

Quicken Symbol Lookup
1. Select a type:
○ Stock ○ Mutual Fund ○ Index ⦿ Any
2. Enter a full or partial name:
[   ] [Search]

2. Click **Stock**, **Mutual Fund**, **Index**, or **Any** to select the type of security for which you are looking.

3. Enter either the full name or part of the security name.

4. Click **Search**.

5. A list of choices will appear, with what Quicken considers to be the best match shown at the top of the list.

Quicken Symbol Lookup
1. Select a type:
⦿ Stock ○ Mutual Fund ○ Index ○ Any
2. Enter a full or partial name:
[Intu] [Search]

Best match:
Name	Symbol
INTUIT INC	INTU

All matches for "Intu" (Most likely matches first):
Name	Symbol
INTUIT INC	INTU
INTUITIVE SURGICAL INC	ISRG

Page 1 (Records 1 - 2 of 2)

Continued . . .

5. Click **Next** to enter the date of the last paper statement you received or the date the information was posted to the Web site, if you are entering from a brokerage Web site.

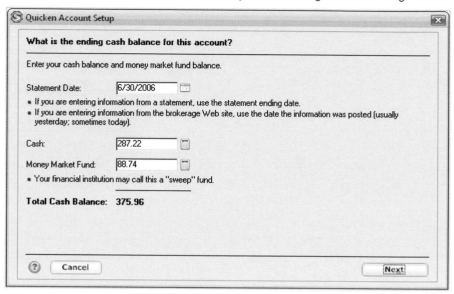

6. Click **Next** and enter the ticker symbol for securities (if any) in this account.

7. Click **Next** to enter your current holdings information.

8. Enter the number of shares you own of each security.

9. Choose whether the security is a stock or mutual fund. If it is neither, click **Other**. You will have a chance to enter your cost information later in the process.

10. Click **Next**. The information you entered is displayed in a Summary window.

11. Click **Done**. The account is displayed in the Investing Center and also shown on the Account bar.

ADD PROPERTY & DEBT ACCOUNTS

You use accounts in the Property & Debt Center to give Quicken information about your house, your car, or other major assets. (An asset is something you own that has significant value, like a rare painting or a stamp collection.)

1. Click **Add Account**. This type of account is typically not held at a financial institution, so click **This account is not held at a financial institution**. Then click **Next**.

USING THE TICKER SYMBOL LOOKUP *(Continued)*

6. Highlight the symbol for your security.

7. Press **CTRL+C** to copy the symbol. You can also right-click to display a menu. Click **Copy** from the menu.

8. Close the Quicken Symbol Lookup window.

9. Return to Quicken and click the **Ticker** field.

10. Right-click, click **Paste** (or press **CTRL+V**) to copy the information into the Ticker field.

2. Choose the type of account. Click **Next** and name the account.

3. Click **Next** to enter the starting point information. You can enter approximate values and change them later.

4. Click **Next**. Quicken asks if there is a loan against this asset. If so, it prompts you to set up the liability account and leads you through the steps. Chapter 6 has more detailed information about property and debt accounts.

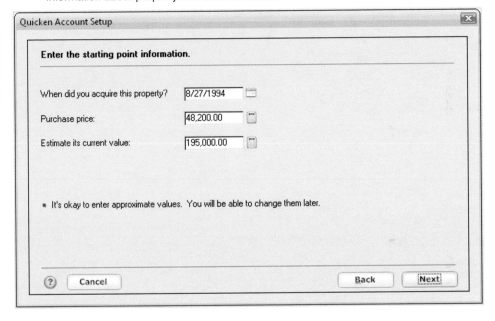

ADD PAYCHECK INFORMATION

By using information from your regular paycheck, Quicken can create tax reports, help you plan for taxes, and export information to TurboTax for year-end tax reporting. To set up a paycheck:

1. Click the **Set Up Paycheck** button on the Quicken Home Activity Center.

2. In some versions of Quicken, you can also access the Paycheck Setup dialog box from the menu bar. Click **Tax** on the menu bar, click **Tax Activities**, and click **Set Up Paycheck**.

3. If you didn't set up a paycheck during the Quicken New User Setup, the Welcome To Paycheck Setup dialog box will appear. If you already entered this information, skip to step 7.

4. Click **Next** to enter information about your paycheck. Quicken uses your paycheck information to help you with tax planning. Quicken can also enter your check automatically and keep track of your payroll deductions. This feature saves you time entering data and makes your information more complete. The Tell Quicken About This Paycheck window opens.

5. Choose whether this is your paycheck or that of your spouse. Fill in the **Company Name** field. Click **Next**.

6. Quicken asks how much of your paycheck information you want to track. Choose the **I Want To Track All Earnings, Taxes, And Deductions** option if you want to simplify your tax preparation and track your tax withholdings. Skip to step 8. If you only want to track your net check, click **I Want To Track Net Deposits Only**. Click **Next** and skip to step 9.

7. If you put the beginnings of a paycheck into Quicken during the initial setup, the Manage Paychecks dialog box will appear. If you want to enter deductions and further information about one or more checks, select the paycheck and click **Edit** to open the paycheck window. If only the summary information is shown and you want deduction information displayed, click **Track Deductions**.

8. If you chose to enter all of your earnings and deductions, the Set Up Paycheck dialog box appears, as shown in Figure 1-6. Click each item on your paycheck to enter your salary, taxes, and other deductions. Click **Done** to close the window.

9. If you chose to have Quicken track only your take-home, or net, paycheck, a dialog box asks the net amount of your check as well as the dates on which you receive it. Quicken will enter your paycheck information when you are paid in the account you designate. Click **Done** after you have entered the information. A dialog box will appear offering you the opportunity to enter all of your year-to-date information. Select the relevant option and complete that process, if you want. Click **Done** again, if needed, to close the Manage Paychecks dialog box.

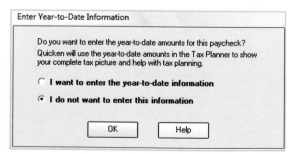

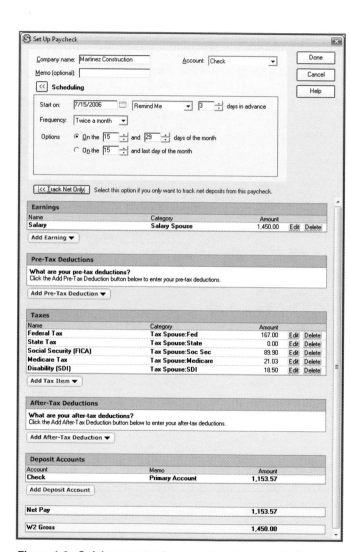

Figure 1-6: Quicken can track your salary, taxes, and other deductions when you enter your paycheck information.

ADD RECURRING BILLS

When you add a bill to Quicken, you are creating a reminder to yourself to pay that bill. There are three steps to handling your bills in Quicken. The first is actually entering the bill; the second is recording the bill payment; and the third is sending the payment to the payee.

1. Click **Quicken Home** to display the Home page. Click **Add Bill or Deposit** at the bottom of the Activity Center. The Add Scheduled Transaction dialog box will appear, as shown in Figure 1-7.

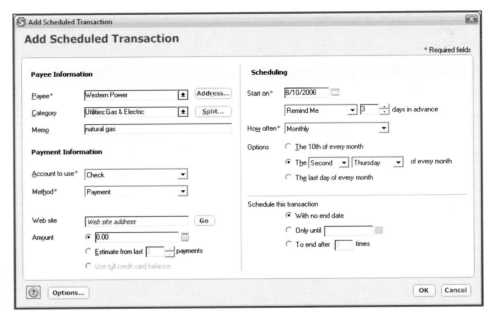

Figure 1-7: By scheduling your regular bills, you may never pay another late charge.

2. Enter the name of the company you pay in the **Payee** field.

3. Click **Address** to enter the payee's address and other information. The Edit Address Book Record dialog box will appear. Enter the address information, and click **OK**. For more information, see "Using the Address Book" QuickSteps.

4. Complete the information for this bill. Click **OK** to return to the Quicken Home page.

CAUTION

Don't forget about annual or semi-annual payments, such as property taxes and insurance.

TIP

If you pay most of your bills with a check, consider using checks you can print on your printer. You can order these checks directly from Quicken or from a number of other, and less expensive check printers you can easily find on the Internet.

USING THE ADDRESS BOOK

You can use the Quicken Address Book to keep track of addresses for your payees, contact information, secondary address information (such as physical addresses), personal information (including the name of the payee's spouse and/ or children), and up to three other types of miscellaneous information. To access the Address Book, click **Tools** on the menu bar, and then click **Address Book**.

1. Click **New**. The Edit Address Book Record will appear. You see this same dialog box when you click the Address button when entering a scheduled transaction. The following illustration shows the Edit Address Book dialog box.

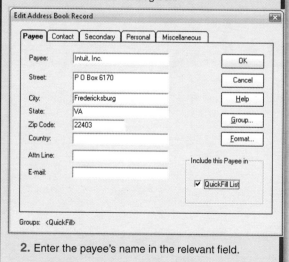

2. Enter the payee's name in the relevant field.

3. Click **TAB** to move to the Street field, enter the information, and continue through the fields using the **TAB** key.

4. Click the **Contact** tab to enter information about the person to contact, his or her work phone, work fax, Web site, and other contact information.

5. Click **OK** when you have entered all of the information you want to record.

Find Help

The Quicken Help window, shown in Figure 1-8, provides a ready reference to answer your questions about Quicken and show you how to accomplish tasks. At any point in the program, pressing the F1 key brings up the Help window with information about the current Quicken window; or you can click the **Help** menu, and click **Quicken Help** to open the Help window for a broad range of information about Quicken.

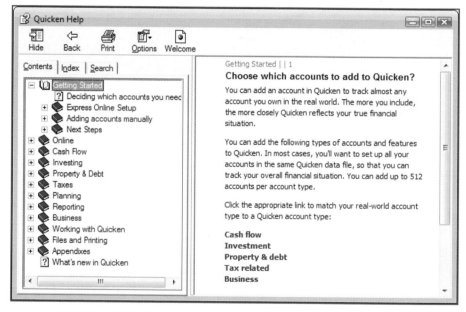

Figure 1-8: Quicken Help gives you answers to questions you ask.

USE HELP

The Help window gives you four ways to find information:

● The **Contents** tab in the left pane of the Help window allows you to open a topic by clicking the plus sign on its left, open sub-topics in the same way, and eventually click and view an article with the information you want.

● The **Index** tab provides an alphabetical list of all articles in Help. In the text box at the top of the list, you can type the topic to have it automatically found in the list; or you can scroll through the list using the scrollbar, and then click a topic.

2

3

4

5

6

7

8

9

10

- The **Search** tab allows you to enter a word or words in the text box at the top of the left pane and be given a list of articles, which you can click to display and read in the right pane.

- In the initial Help menu in the right pane, shown in Figure 1-8, you can select one of several topics to display the article requested.

USE OTHER HELP RESOURCES

The Help menu provides a number of other resources to assist you, which you can access by clicking one of the following options:

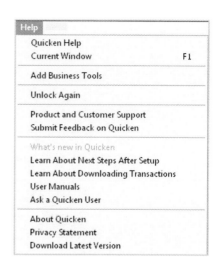

Help
Quicken Help
Current Window   F1
Add Business Tools
Unlock Again
Product and Customer Support
Submit Feedback on Quicken
What's new in Quicken
Learn About Next Steps After Setup
Learn About Downloading Transactions
User Manuals
Ask a Quicken User
About Quicken
Privacy Statement
Download Latest Version

- **Product And Customer Support** opens the Quicken Help options window, with troubleshooting tips, a link to frequently asked questions, and Quicken Technical Support on the Quicken.com Web site (you must have an Internet connection to view the site).

- **Submit Feedback On Quicken** allows you to give Intuit feedback on Quicken. This also requires an Internet connection. It is through feedback from users such as you that Quicken improves its products. Your input is important, and Quicken encourages you to contact them.

- **What Is New In Quicken** links to areas such as "Learn About Setting Up Quicken" and "Learn About Downloading Transactions," which provide foundational information that will help you get started using the product.

- **Learn About Next Steps After Setup** gives you suggestions for setting up Quicken to gain the most benefit from it.

- **Learn About Downloading Transactions** answers many questions about the actual process of downloading information from both banks and credit card companies.

- **User Manuals** provides documentation that you can print or view using Adobe Acrobat Reader. If you don't have Adobe Acrobat Reader, you can click the link in the Quicken User Manual window to download the program for free.

- **Ask A Quicken User** takes you, through the Internet, to a group of Quicken Personal Finance Forums for discussions and answers to questions from other Quicken users.

- **About Quicken** shows you which version of Quicken you are using, should you need to call Customer Support.

- **Privacy Statement** tells you how Quicken protects your personal information.

- **Register Quicken** appears on the Help menu if you did not register the Quicken program during the installation process. Click this link to register at any time. There are two parts to registration. The first registers your product with Intuit so that you can receive online updates and download stock quotes. The second part of registration helps you create a Quicken.com name. Quicken.com is full of helpful tips and other features to make managing your finances easier. The registration process requires an Internet connection.

QUICKSTEPS

UPDATING QUICKEN

Intuit provides online updates to Quicken that you can access when you install Quicken and periodically thereafter. When you start Quicken 2007, the Quicken Update dialog box appears. If you have an Internet connection, it is a good idea to use this update feature to ensure your program is completely current. Thereafter, you can update at any time by clicking either the **Update Now** button in the Quicken Home Activity Center or **One Step Update** from the Online menu on the menu bar.

1. Click **Update Now** to go online at once. The program opens the One Step Update Settings dialog box. After you choose what you want to update or download, click the **Update Now** button.

2. You may see the Missing Ticker Symbols dialog box. Click **Update Now** to continue.

3. When the download is complete, today's date (the last date you updated) displays on the Quicken Home page.

Exit Quicken

When you have completed a Quicken session, you should exit the program. You will usually be encouraged to back up your work before you close it. That is always a good idea. Hard drive crashes, power outages, and computer malfunctions happen to all of us at one time or another. Backing up your files is discussed in more detail in Chapter 2.

You can exit Quicken in several ways:

- Click the **Close** button on the right side of the title bar.
- Click **File** on the menu bar, and then click **Exit**.
- Click the **Quicken** icon (on the Control menu) on the left side of the title bar, and then click **Close**.
- You can also hold down the **ALT** key on your keyboard and press the **F4** key.

Quicken automatically saves everything you enter into the program, so there is no need to save your files on your hard drive as you enter the information. However, it is prudent to have a backup of your hard drive on external media in case of hardware failure.

Use Quicken and Windows Basics

If you are new to Quicken, take a few minutes to read this section. It discusses terms used with Quicken as well as some that are used with all Windows-based programs. The dialog boxes and windows make more sense when you understand their contents.

Recognize Quicken Terms

Quicken is meant to be intuitive. You do most tasks with one or two clicks, and the design of each window is intended to be easy to use and understand. The terms defined here are used throughout Quicken and this book:

- **Accounts** in Quicken represent the separate checking, savings, credit card, and brokerage accounts you have, as well as your mortgage and car loans, as you can see in Figure 1-9. Each is considered an account by Quicken. The information about all of

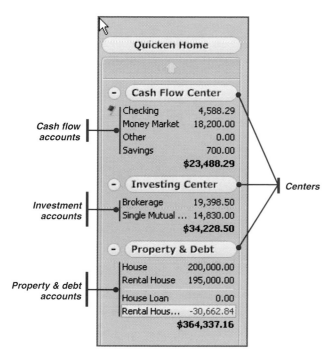

Figure 1-9: Quicken's information is organized into accounts within Centers.

the accounts of any type that relate to *you* is kept within one Quicken data file. There are standard accounts within each account type, such as Checking within Cash Flow.

- **Data files** (or just "files") are how Quicken stores the information about your financial records. Just as a word-processing document is stored as a document file in a folder on your hard disk, Quicken stores your data file in a folder on your hard disk. A data file contains information about all of your accounts, assets, liabilities, financial goals, and tax plans. Each family's or person's information is stored in a separate file. For example, if you are taking care of Aunt Harriet's financial matters, her information is stored in a file separate from your personal data file.

- **Folders** are similar to the manila folders you store in a filing cabinet. Data files for your documents, spreadsheets, and Quicken files are stored in folders. Compare your hard drive to the filing cabinet in which you store paper files in folders to see the relationship with digital files and folders.

- **Centers** are groupings of similar types of accounts. There are three main Centers: Cash Flow, Investment, and Property & Debt. If you run your small business using Quicken Premier for Home & Business edition, you have an additional Center just for the business accounts. Quicken combines the information from all of the Centers to calculate and display your net worth in the Financial Overview Center.

- **Registers** are similar to the paper check register used with a checking account, and show the checks you write and the deposits you make. Each non-investment account in Quicken has its own register. You open a register by clicking the account in the Summary pane. The menu items on the top of the register let you locate and delete transactions, write checks, and reconcile the account to a statement. The Overview tab shows the account attributes and status as well as a graphic display of activity for a period of time you designate.

Checking	Register	Overview					Quicken 2007

Delete Find Transfer Reconcile Write Checks Set Up Online   View ▾ Report ▾ Options ▾ ⑦ How Do I?

Date/ ▲	Num	Payee/Category/Memo	Payment	Clr	Deposit	Balance
7/25/2006	DEP	Good Company Net Salary			925 77	2,688 90
7/27/2006	Sched	George Ellison --Split--	525 00			2,163 90
8/1/2006	DEP	Retirement			925 00	3,088 90
8/1/2006	DEP	Retail Firm --Form--			1,160 19	4,249 09
8/19/2006	DEP				3,915 22	8,164 31
		Bonus	annual bonus net Enter Edit Split ☆ Rate 📎 Attach			
9/11/2006	Num	Payee	Payment		Deposit	
		Category	Memo			

☆ Rate your payees   **Current Balance:** 191.91   **Ending Balance:** 8,164.31

- **Transactions** are the checks you write, the payments you make, and all of the other individual financial events in your life. Quicken puts each event in either an account register or on an investment account transaction list.

- **Transaction lists** are used with investment accounts, such as a brokerage account or a 401(k) account, in place of a register. Quicken designed these lists to look like a brokerage statement, showing every transaction that has taken place.

- **Categories** are used to group similar transactions. Every time you enter a transaction into a Quicken register, you have the option of assigning it to a category.

- **Windows** are used to display related information on the screen. In addition to the basic Quicken window shown previously in Figure 1-5, there are several other types of windows used by Quicken to display various types of information:

  - The Internet window uses the built-in Quicken Web browser to display the Quicken .com Web page.

  - List windows display information about related items, such as classes or categories.

  - Report windows let you create customized reports from your accounts in a way you understand.

- **Menus** and the menu bar are the tools Quicken and many other Windows-based programs use to give you access to the commands and features within the program. Click a menu name in the menu bar to open the menu, and then click one of the *options* in the menu to select it. Some menu options have a right-pointing arrow on the right of the option. When you move the mouse pointer over that type of option, a submenu or *flyout* menu will open. When you right-click some objects within a window or dialog box, a *context* menu will open. Context menus show options specific to the item clicked.

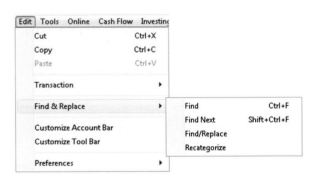

- **Toolbars** are rows of buttons, frequently directly below the menu bar. Click a button to perform its task, open a window, or display a dialog box. You can customize your Quicken toolbars—you will see how in Chapter 2.

- **Keyboard shortcuts** allow you to perform tasks from the keyboard rather than use the mouse and menus or toolbars. If the shortcut is **CTRL+P**, for example, you are to hold down the **CTRL** key while pressing the **P** key on the keyboard. Then let go of both keys.

NOTE

Some of the more familiar Windows keyboard shortcuts may use a different keyboard combination in some areas of Quicken.

FINDING MORE KEYBOARD SHORTCUTS

To see additional keyboard shortcuts:

1. Click the **Help** menu, and then click **Quicken Help**.

2. Click the **Search** tab, type keyboard shortcuts, and then press ENTER.

3. Double-click **Keyboard Shortcuts** in the Selected Topic list to see the upper part of the list of shortcuts, shown here:

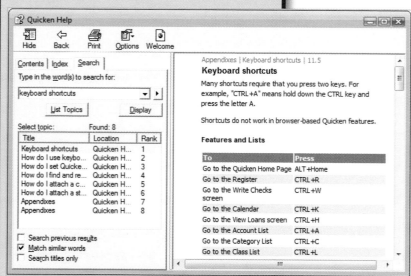

4. Click the scrollbar on the right side of the window to see the remainder of the shortcuts list.

5. When you are done, click **Close** in the title bar to close the Quicken Help window.

Use Windows Tools

Quicken 2007 has a familiar feel if you are used to working with other Windows-based programs. For example, the Minimize, Maximize, and Close buttons appear in the title bar on the upper-right of every window.

As with all Windows programs, if you have more than one window (or program) open at the same time, the *active window* is the one with the brightest title bar.

- **Windows** are areas of the screen in which you can see a program that is running and provide primary control of that program. When Quicken starts, it opens in its own window, as shown in Figure 1-5 earlier in the chapter. Windows generally have menus and can be sized.

- **Dialog boxes** are used by Quicken and other Windows programs to communicate with you, the user, and for you to communicate with the program. They can be message boxes that require no action other than clicking OK, or smaller areas of the screen with check boxes, options, drop-down lists, text boxes, and other controls that let you add information and control what is happening in a program, as you can see in Figure 1-10. The primary parts of dialog boxes are:

  - The **title bar** contains the name of the dialog box and is used to drag the box around the desktop.

  - A **drop-down list box** opens a list from which you can choose one item that will be displayed when the list is closed.

  - A **list box** (not shown) lets you select one or more items from a list; it may include a scrollbar.

  - A **check box** lets you turn features on or off.

  - A **text box** lets you enter and edit text.

  - **Command buttons** perform functions such as closing the dialog box and accepting the changes (the OK button), or closing the dialog box and ignoring the changes (the Cancel button).

  - **Tabs** let you select from among several pages in a dialog box.

  - **Option buttons**, also called *radio buttons,* let you select one among mutually exclusive options.

  - A **spinner** lets you select from a sequential series of numbers.

  - A **slider** lets you select from several values.

2

3

4

5

6

7

8

9

10

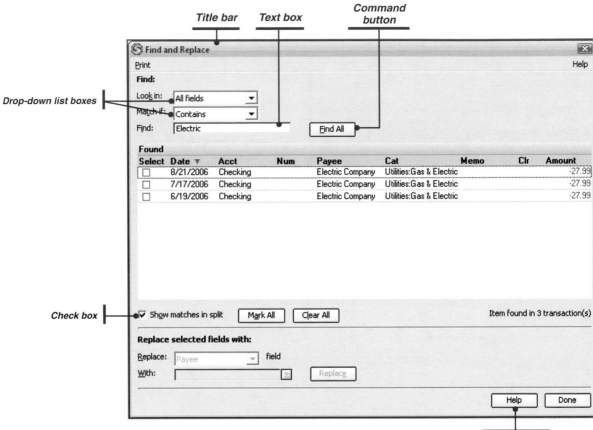

Title bar *Text box* *Command button*

Drop-down list boxes

Check box

Figure 1-10: Dialog boxes provide the primary means of controlling what is happening in a program.

Help button

Chapter 2
Making Quicken Yours

In Chapter 1 you saw how to install Quicken and how to use Quicken New User Setup to establish your initial accounts. When you were finished, however, the look and feel of Quicken is the default style built into the product. For many people, this is fine, and their whole experience with Quicken is with the default style. However, Quicken provides a number of ways that you can customize it—both in how it looks and how it operates—allowing you to tailor the program to meet your specific needs. Quicken most likely will become an important program that you use often. As a result, it should reflect what you want. In this chapter you will see how to customize the Home page so that it reflects you, how to add and change accounts, how to set up online banking, and how to add and delete categories so that they provide the level of organization you want for your finances.

Customize the Home Page

After you have completed Quicken's installation and setup, the default Quicken Home page is displayed, as shown in Figure 2-1. You can customize the Home page by customizing the toolbar, changing the Account bar, managing accounts, creating additional views, and setting your preferences for the way various elements on the page are used.

Customize the Toolbar

The Quicken toolbar, which appears just below the menu bar, can be customized to display any of the more than 70 command icons available. You can also include reports that you save and want to access quickly. To customize the toolbar:

1. Right-click anywhere on the toolbar to display the Customize Toolbar button. Click **Customize Toolbar** to display the Customize Toolbar dialog box, as shown in Figure 2-2.

2. To add a command icon to the toolbar, select the command in the **Add To Toolbar** list on the left, and then click **Add**.

3. To remove an icon from the toolbar, select the command in the **Current Toolbar Order** list on the right, and then click **Remove**.

4. To change the order in which icons are displayed on the toolbar, select the command in the **Current Toolbar Order** list on the right, and click either the **Move Up** or **Move Down** button. One click moves the icons up or down one place.

5. To assign a keyboard shortcut to a command icon or to change its label, click the command in the right column, and then click the **Edit Icons** button. The Edit Toolbar Button dialog box appears.

Figure 2-1: The Quicken Home page provides an overview of your financial information.

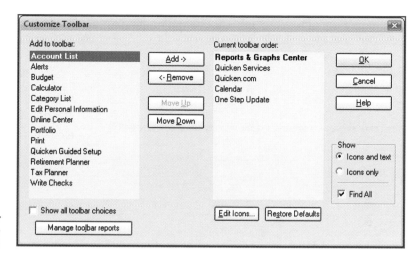

In the Customize Toolbar dialog box, click **Restore Defaults** to reset the toolbar settings to their original state.

Figure 2-2: The Customize Toolbar dialog box allows you to personalize your Quicken toolbar.

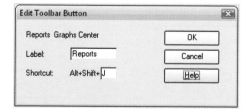

If you choose to turn off the global search field, clicking the Restore Defaults button does not turn it back on. You have to right-click the toolbar, click the **Find All** check box, and then click **OK** to restore it to the toolbar.

Ensure you right-click in the Account bar itself—below the up arrow and above the Customize and Add Accounts buttons; clicking in the up or down arrows does nothing.

6. To change the label of the icon, highlight the label name, and type the label you choose.

7. To assign a keyboard shortcut to a command icon in the Edit Toolbar Button dialog box, type a letter from the keyboard in the text box opposite **Alt+Shift+**.

8. Click **OK** to set the new label and/or shortcut and close the dialog box.

9. Choose whether to show both icons and text or only icons by clicking the relevant option.

10. Click the **Find All** check box, if it is not already selected, to have the global search field present on the toolbar.

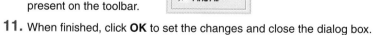

11. When finished, click **OK** to set the changes and close the dialog box.

CHANGE THE ACCOUNT BAR

The Account bar on the left side of the Home page shows your accounts in the various Activity Centers. At the top of this bar is the Quicken Home button. This button is normally in view; clicking it will bring you back to the Home page from any place in Quicken.

TIP

You can also access the Home page by clicking the **Tools** menu, and then clicking **Go to Quicken Home**.

Collapse all accounts
✔ Expand all accounts

✔ Show amounts
Hide amounts

✔ Show Current Balance in bar
Show Ending Balance in bar

✔ Show Account Bar on left
Show Account Bar on right
Hide Account Bar

Add new account
Add/remove accounts from bar
Rearrange accounts
Delete/hide accounts in Quicken

⊕ Cash Flow Center
$1,594.81

Quicken Home

NOTE

Your *net worth* is the value of everything you owe subtracted from everything you own.

The Account bar can be changed in the following ways:

- Right-click anywhere within the Account bar to view the Account Bar menu. With this menu you can:

  - Click **Collapse all accounts** to show only the totals in each Center.

  - Click **Expand all accounts** to show the amounts in each separate account in each Center.

  - Click **Show amounts** to show the balance in each account. Click **Hide amounts** to show the account name only.

  - Click **Show Current Balance in bar** to display the balance in each account as of today's date. Click **Show Ending Balance in bar** to display the balance after any future transactions have been entered.

  - Click **Show Account Bar on left** to display the Account bar on the left side of your Activity Center. Click **Show Account Bar on right** to display it on the right side. Click **Hide Account Bar** to hide it entirely.

  - Click **Add new account** to display the Quicken Account Setup dialog box.

  - Clicking **Add/remove accounts from bar**, **Rearrange accounts**, or **Delete/hide accounts in Quicken** will open the Account List dialog box.

- A plus sign to the left of each Activity Center name indicates that there are accounts within that Center. A minus sign indicates that there are no accounts set up in that Center or that all accounts are displayed. Click the plus sign (+) to display each account.

- Click the up or down arrows at the top or bottom to scroll through the Account bar if there are too many accounts to display at one time.

- Click **Customize** at the bottom of the Account bar to display the Account list. See "Manage Accounts" next in this chapter.

- Click **Add Account** to set up a new account as described in Chapter 1.

- Click **Financial Overview** to display your net worth graphs. More information about the Financial Overview Center is covered in Chapter 9.

Customize | Add Account

Net Worth $157,083.81

Financial Overview

Manage Accounts

You manage your accounts and determine how they are displayed using the Account List dialog box, which appears when you click **Customize** at the bottom of the Account bar. The Account List dialog box, shown in Figure 2-3, allows you to review and manage your accounts in more detail using the View Accounts and Manage Accounts tabs:

- Click **View Accounts** to see a list of all accounts in all Activity Centers with their current and ending balances. Normally, these amounts are the same. However, if you have a scheduled transaction that will occur after today but within the current accounting period (normally a month), the ending balance may be higher or lower than the current balance by the amount of the future transaction. This tab also shows whether the account is hidden in Quicken, whether it uses online services, the number of transactions that have been posted against it, and the account description. In the Status column of the View Accounts tab, the check mark icon (a red check mark on top of a gray check) means that there are checks to print in this account. At the bottom of this window is the total of all of your accounts.

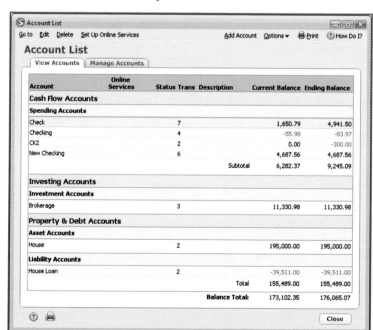

Figure 2-3: The View Accounts tab in the Account List dialog box shows your current account balances.

CAUTION

Be careful when changing an account from one Activity Center to another. Some accounts should not be moved, such as a checking account linked to a *liability*. (A liability is something that you owe.)

- Click **Manage Accounts** to determine how accounts are displayed and figure into the totals, as shown in Figure 2-4:

  - Rearrange the order in which your accounts are displayed by clicking an account, and then clicking **Move Up** or **Move Down** to change the account's position.

  - **Change Group** allows you to move a selected account from one Center (or group) to another if you have Quicken Deluxe, Premier, or Home & Business versions.

  - **Hide In Quicken** removes the account and its balance from the Account bar, the View Accounts tab, and the Activity Center totals. The account only appears in the Manage Accounts tab. (If you don't see this at the top of the Manage Accounts tab, widen the window or scroll it to the right.)

  - **Don't Include In Totals** shows the account in its normal location but does not include its balance in the total for that Center.

    - **Hide In Navigation** hides the name of the account from the Account bar and View Accounts tab but includes its balance under the name "Other Accounts"; it is also included in the Center total.

  - Click **Close** to close the Account List dialog box.

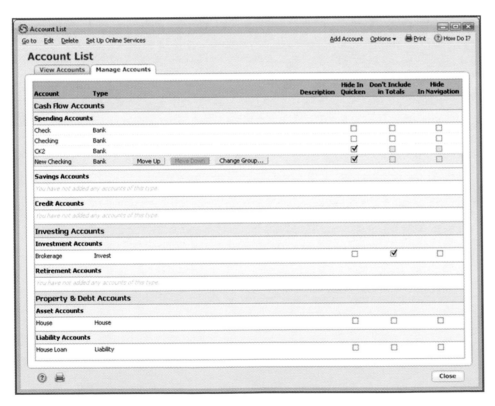

Figure 2-4: The Manage Accounts tab in the Account List dialog box lets you determine whether an account is displayed and included in the totals.

UICKSTEPS

EDITING AN ACCOUNT

You can edit information about each account from the Account List dialog box. Click **Edit** on the menu bar to display the Account Details dialog box, as seen in Figure 2-5.

1. Click **Account Name** to change the name of the account.

2. Click in the fields you want to change, and type the information you want there.

3. Click the **Delete Account** button to delete the account.

4. Click **Tax Schedule Info** to display any tax schedules for transfers in or out of this account. Click the relevant down arrow to display a drop-down list of tax schedules from which you can choose.

NOTE

If your balance today is more than it was on the first of the month, a small green upward arrow appears to the left of the current balance. If the balance is less today than it was on the first of the month, the arrow is red and points downwards.

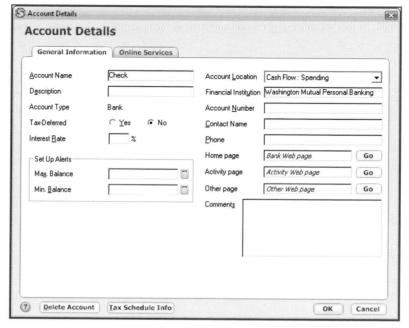

Figure 2-5: *The Account Details dialog box gives you a chance to edit, delete, and add information about an account.*

Work with the Default Quicken Home Page

The default Quicken Home page consists of several sections, as seen in Figure 2-6.

- The **Projected Cash Flow** section displays the income and expenditures expected for the month, based on your earlier entries, the current balance, the balance at the first of the current month, the differnce between the first of the month and today, and how much will be available in your cash flow accounts through the end of the current month. This In/Out/What's Left snapshot is explained further in the "Understanding the In/Out/What's Left Snapshot" QuickSteps later in this chapter.

In/Out/What's Left snapshot

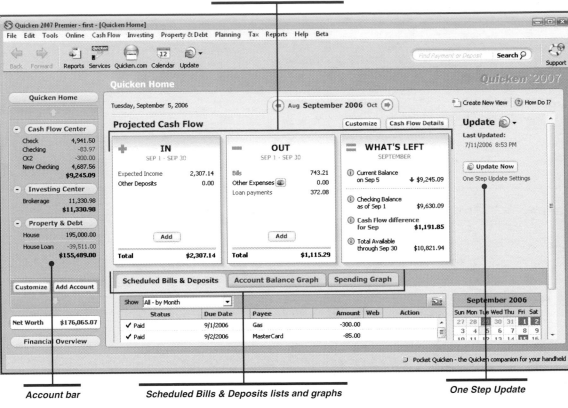

Figure 2-6: The default Quicken Home page displays your current financial position.

Account bar

Scheduled Bills & Deposits lists and graphs

One Step Update

● The **Scheduled Bills & Deposits** area shows any scheduled transactions for the current month. You can change the displayed information in several ways by clicking the down arrow:

  a. **All – By Month** displays the transactions you've previously scheduled for the current month, as well as any items from previous months you have not paid. Use this view to check that all bills have been paid.

  b. **All – By Bills And Deposits** displays all of your scheduled transactions sorted by the date they are due, first displaying all the bills, then Deposits And Other Scheduled Transactions, and finally by Schedule These. Use this view to verify the next date a specific bill is due, even if it is not in this month.

  c. **Current – By Status** displays a list of your upcoming transactions sorted by Due Today, Due Soon, Overdue, Paid, Reconciled, and so on.

  d. **Current – By Bills And Deposits** displays your upcoming transactions sorted first by Bills, then by Deposits And Other Scheduled Transactions, and then Schedule These.

QUICKSTEPS

CHANGING THE DATES FOR SCHEDULED TRANSACTION LISTS AND GRAPHS

The default setting for the information displayed in the Scheduled Bills & Deposits area of the Quicken Home page is the current month. To change the date of these reports and graphs:

1. Click the **Show Full Calendar** button. The Calendar window will open, as seen in Figure 2-7.

   > **Show Full Calendar**

2. Click the left arrow in the middle of the page to display previous months. Click the right arrow to display future months.

   > (◄) Aug **September 2006** Oct (►)

3. The Scheduled Bills & Deposits, Account Balance Graph, or Spending Graph is displayed below the calendar.

4. Transactions on each day of the month are color-coded per the legend on the bottom of the calendar.

5. Close the calendar to return to the Quicken Home page and the current month's information.

NOTE

On the Quicken Home page, you can display the full calendar by double-clicking the calendar to the right of the graphs.

- The **Account Balance Graph** displays your current balances in graphic format. You may display the information for one or multiple accounts:

  a. Click the down arrow to display the drop-down list to display the accounts from which you can choose.

  b. Click **Multiple Accounts** to display the Scheduled Transactions & Bills Accounts dialog box.

  c. Click **Mark All** to select all of your accounts or click the name of the accounts you want included in the graph.

  d. Click **OK** to close the dialog box.

- A color-coded legend appears to the right of the Account Balance Graph indicating which bar is for which account.

- If you are displaying only one account, today's date is represented by a green bar.

- The shortest bar represents the lowest balance projected for this account for the current month.

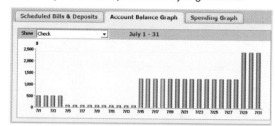

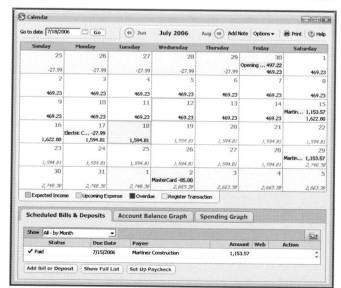

Figure 2-7: The full calendar gives you a visual picture of when during a month you will receive income and have to pay bills.

UNDERSTANDING THE IN/OUT/ WHAT'S LEFT SNAPSHOT

A new feature in Quicken 2007 is the In/Out/What's Left Snapshot on the default Quicken Home page. This feature compiles the information you have entered previously about your income and anticipated expenses, and displays how much you will have left at the end of the month:

- The In section displays the scheduled income payments you entered previously. Click **Expected Income** to see a breakdown of each item. Click **Close** to close the Expected Income window.

- The Out section displays scheduled bills, other expenses, scheduled transfers, and loan payments. Click any of these items to display more information. Click **Close** to close the window.

- The What's Left section shows your current balance, balance at the first of the month, the difference in cash flow for this month, and how much will be available at month-end. Click **Cash Flow Difference** to see the details for this month.

- In any of the sections, you can click any item displayed in blue to see more information about it.

- You can also use the In and Out sections to add transactions. Click the **Add** button in either section to see the Add Transaction dialog box, as shown in Figure 2-8.

Design a New Home Page View

Other than the modifications described in the previous sections of this chapter, the default Quicken Home page cannot be changed. You can, however, create a new, alternate view of the Home page that will appear as a tab on the title bar of the Activity Center for the Quicken Home page. To create a new view of the Home page:

1. Click **Create New View** in the upper-right corner of the Activity Center. The Customize View dialog box appears. From here, you can add items to your view from the Available Items list on the left, and remove items from the Chosen Items list on the right.

2. Click an item on the Available Items list, and click **Add**. The item appears in the Chosen Items list.

3. Click an item on the Chosen Items list, and click **Remove**. The item disappears from the Chosen Items list but does not disappear from the Available Items list.

4. Click an item on the Chosen Items list, and then click **Move Up** or **Move Down** to change the position of the item on the list.

5. Repeating steps 2–4, create one or more views that meet your needs. When finished, click **OK**. Your new view(s) will appear in the Activity Center.

Set Preferences

Preferences are the ways in which you make Quicken behave the way you want. For example, when you start Quicken, instead of displaying the Home page, you can display the Cash Flow Center. This is a startup preference. Other types of preferences in Quicken include backup preferences, register preferences, and report preferences. This section will discuss startup and setup preferences. The remaining preferences will be discussed elsewhere in this book. To change the startup and setup preferences:

1. Click the **Edit** menu, click **Preferences**, and then click **Quicken Program**. The Quicken Preferences dialog box appears with the startup preferences displayed, as shown in Figure 2-9.

2. Click the **On Startup Open To** down arrow, and choose the Center or account that you want to appear when you start Quicken.

3. Click **Setup** in the left column. The setup preferences are displayed.

Add Transaction

Add Transaction

*Required fields

Would you like to schedule this transaction? ⑦ Tell Me More

(● YES) I would like to schedule this transaction.

(● NO) I would like to record it.

Payee Information

Payee* | Telephone Company | ± | Address...

Category | Utilities:Telephone | ± | Split...

Memo | |

Payment Information

Account to use* | Check | ▼

Method* | Deposit | ▼

Amount | 39.54 |

Date* | 8/10/2006 |

Number: | | ±

⑦ | OK | Cancel

Figure 2-8: You can schedule or enter a transaction into any Cash Flow Center account directly from the Quicken Home page by using the Add Transaction dialog box.

NOTE

The reason most people keep the Windows standard for the **CTRL+C**, **CTRL+V**, **CTRL+X**, and **CTRL+Z** shortcut keys is that the Windows commands are heavily used in many Windows programs, while the Quicken commands are infrequently used.

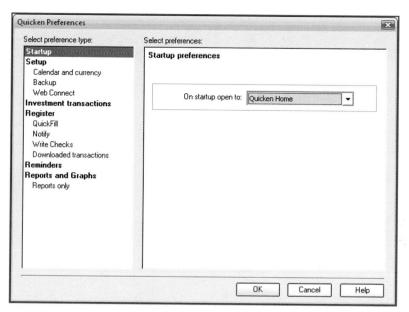

Figure 2-9: You can control many of the nuances of Quicken through the Quicken Preferences dialog box.

4. Choose whether to display the Account bar on the left or right side of the window or not at all.

5. Choose whether to map keyboard shortcuts to Quicken or Windows standards. See Table 2-1 for what these shortcuts do in each case. The Windows standard is the default (see Chapter 1 for more information).

6. Choose whether to turn off the Quicken sounds—for example, the "ka-chung" sound that plays every time you enter a transaction—by clicking that option to deselect it.

7. Choose whether to automatically minimize pop-up windows by clicking that option.

8. Click **OK** to close the dialog box when you are finished.

SHORTCUT KEYS	WINDOWS	QUICKEN
CTRL+C	Copy	Open the Category List
CTRL+V	Paste	Void a transaction
CTRL+X	Cut	Show the matching entry, for example, in a liability register
CTRL+Z	Undo	Display more detail about a report amount

Table 2-1: Alternative Mappings of Shortcut Keys in Windows and Quicken

Add and Change Accounts

Accounts are central to Quicken's operation, whether they are checking, investment, or property and debt accounts. In Chapter 1 you saw how to get started setting up accounts with Quicken New User Setup. As you use Quicken, it is likely that you will want to add additional accounts and modify the accounts you already have. This section will look at adding and modifying cash flow accounts. In later chapters you'll see how to add and modify accounts in other Centers.

Add Cash Flow Accounts

If you did not use Quicken New User Setup to create the checking, savings, and credit card accounts you want, you can do it here:

1. Right-click the **Cash Flow Center** button in the Account bar, and click **Add New Account** in the context menu that opens.

   –Or–

   Click **Add Account** at the bottom of the Account bar.

   –Or–

   Click the **Cash Flow Center** button in the Account bar to open it in the Activity Center, and then click the **Add Account** button at the bottom of the applicable section: Spending & Saving Accounts or Credit Card Accounts.

   –Or–

   Click the **Cash Flow** menu, click **Cash Flow Accounts**, and then click **Add Account**.

   All methods open the Quicken Account Setup dialog box.

2. Type the name of your financial institution. Often, you can begin typing the first few letters of the name of your institution to display a list, and then click yours. To set up an account without online banking services, click **This Account Is Not Held At A Financial Institution**. You can set up online banking later if you want. Click **Next** to continue.

3. Click **Yes** to connect to your bank through Quicken using your Internet connection. The download availability for this bank displays in the dialog box. Click **Next**.

4. You are prompted to enter your customer ID and PIN provided by your bank. If you do not have them and wish to use your bank's online services, click the relevant options on the right of the dialog box.

TIP

For the account name, you can use any combination of letters, numbers, and spaces, except the following characters: right and left brackets ([ ]), the forward slash (/), colon (:), caret (^), and vertical bar (|). If you do not type a name, Quicken uses the type of account as the default name.

NOTE

If you do not have a bank statement handy, you can enter the statement date and ending balance later.

TIP

Many Quicken users find that using the 10-key pad on their computer keyboard is the easiest way to enter numbers.

CAUTION

You can enter dates into Quicken 2007 in any format except formats that use dashes, such as 10-8-06.

UICKSTEPS

ADDING A CASH ACCOUNT

Cash accounts are useful for tracking where your money goes. You can set up cash accounts for each member of the family. To set up a cash account:

1. Click the **Cash Flow** menu, click **Cash Flow Accounts**, and click **Add Account**.

2. Click **This Account Is Not Held At A Financial Institution**, and then click **Next**.

3. For the type of account, click **Cash**. Click **Next**, type a name, such as Nick's Allowance, and click **Next**.

4. If you want to start keeping track of your cash spending as of today, leave the default of today's date. If you want to use another date, enter the one you want.

5. Press TAB, enter the amount of cash you are starting with, and click **Done**. If you want to go back to earlier dialog boxes, click **Back**. If you decide you do not want to enter this account, click **Cancel**.

Tracking your spending with cash accounts allows each member of the family to see exactly where his or her money goes. It can be a valuable tool for anyone, but especially for young people as they learn to handle money. When you use a cash account, make sure you include ATM withdrawals and deposits to and from your cash account. You could even set up a cash account just for ATM withdrawals.

5. If you already have your customer ID and PIN, enter them and you are connected to your bank's download page. You then need to locate on the bank's Web site a command to download the current transactions (in most cases, this is a Download button). Click it and follow your bank's instructions to download your account information.

6. When the download is complete, sign out and exit the bank's Web site.

7. If you are adding the account from the Cash Flow Center and chose to not download your transactions, you are prompted to choose from a checking, savings, credit card, or cash account. Choose one and click **Next**.

8. Type a name for the account, and click **Next**.

9. Enter the last statement date and the ending balance, and then click **Done**.

MODIFY CASH FLOW ACCOUNTS

Once you have set up an account, you will likely need to make some changes to, or even delete, an account. To change or delete an account:

1. In the Account bar on the left, click the account you want to change. The account is shown in the Activity Center with the register displayed.

2. Click the **Overview** tab to view the account attributes and current status, as shown in Figure 2-10.

3. To delete an account, click **Delete Account** in the Activity Center's menu bar. Type yes to confirm the deletion, click **OK** to carry out the deletion, and then click **OK** again in response to the message that the account was deleted. If you change your mind before clicking **OK**, click **Cancel** and then click **OK** in response to the message that the account was not deleted.

4. To modify the account, click **Edit Account Details** at the bottom of the Account Attributes area. The Account Details dialog box appears.

5. In the **General Information** tab, you can change the account name, description, location, financial institution, and other information, as described in the "Editing an Account" QuickSteps and shown in Figure 2-5, both earlier in this chapter.

6. In the **Online Services** tab, you can activate or deactivate online transaction downloading and Quicken bill paying, as described in "Use Quicken Online," next.

7. When finished, click **OK**.

TIP

Recording each credit card charge helps you prevent errors and credit card fraud. If a charge appears that you have not made, you can notify your credit card company at once. If your credit card company offers a Quicken download service, you can download the information directly into your Quicken register.

TIP

You can also open the Account Details dialog box by right-clicking an account in the Account bar, and clicking **Edit Account** in the context menu that opens.

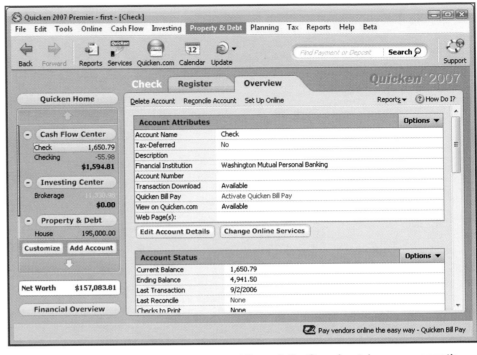

Figure 2-10: *You can edit or delete an account through the Overview tab on an account's register.*

Use Quicken Online

Most banks and credit unions, as well as brokerages, mortgage lenders, and insurance companies, give you the option of connecting to them online and potentially interfacing with Quicken. With banks and credit unions, at least two services are usually offered: online account access and online bill paying. With the online account access service, you use an Internet connection to connect to your financial institution's computer to see what checks have cleared, what deposits have been posted, and what service charges or other *automatically recurring* transactions have been posted to your account. (Automatically recurring transactions are transactions that you have agreed to be automatically deducted from or added to your account on a regular basis, such as property tax, car loan payments, or Social Security checks.) Online banking also allows you to transfer between accounts—from checking to savings, for example, or from your savings account to your credit card account to pay your credit card bill.

The online bill-paying service lets you pay bills electronically rather than by writing a check. You tell the bank the name of the payee, the address, and the amount to pay, and the bank facilitates the payment, either electronically or by writing the check. You can usually set up regularly scheduled payments, such as insurance or mortgage payments, so that those payments are never late.

Quicken also offers bill-paying services through Quicken Bill Pay. Available for any U.S. checking account, the service stores payee information for you, so whenever you make a new payment, account numbers and payee information appear automatically. You just fill in the correct amount to pay. As with many banks, but not all, there is a charge for this service.

Understand Online Services

Today, most financial institutions offer some type of online financial service. This saves them money and offers consumers a valuable tool. All such online services require an Internet connection. Some institutions charge a fee for these services, although many do not. Over time, your costs may be less than working with paper statements, paying bills by check, mailing payments, and buying stamps. Check with your institution to determine its costs for the services they provide. Go to Quicken Help for additional information about online services.

Working online can save you time and money, but as more financial institutions are going online, their security procedures are becoming more stringent. Many institutions discuss these procedures on their Web sites, and others provide brochures about maintaining security online. You can help by ensuring you keep your password and PIN in a secure place, by keeping your antivirus program up to date, and by using a good firewall. When using any online service, remember that with any benefit comes some risk.

UNDERSTAND INTERNET SECURITY

As the Internet has gained popularity, so have the risks in using it. Viruses, worms, spyware, and adware have become part of our vocabulary. As you start

TIP

Quicken provides a virtual "vault" where you can store your PIN from many different organizations. Click **Online** from the menu bar, click **Password Vault**, and then click **Set Up**.

1   3   4   5   6   7   8   9   10

QUICKFACTS

DECIDING TO USE ONLINE BANKING SERVICES

In making the decision whether to use online banking services, consider the following points:

- While electronic banking is becoming more common, not all financial institutions make it available through Quicken—or even offer it at all. Ensure your bank or credit union has the service available.

- You need an Internet connection to use these services.

- To ensure security, carefully protect the identification number and PIN provided by your financial institution. Most financial institutions transmit with *encrypted* data. That means anyone intercepting the transmission would see only gibberish. Quicken uses the same method to send information to your financial institution.

- Your records should be up to date and your last paper statement reconciled before you start the services.

- You should understand how to use Quicken to record a check, create a deposit, reconcile your accounts, and transfer between accounts before you use the electronic services.

- Most financial institutions charge a fee for these services. Compute the cost of doing it yourself (postage, gas to go to the post office, envelopes, and so on). Compare those costs to the fees charged by Quicken or your financial institution.

to work online, take a moment to understand what each problem is and how to guard your computer and data, as described in Table 2-2.

Before you start your online financial transactions, understand the online security issues and take steps to protect your computer. Your financial institution is working to protect your information on its end, but you need to do your part as well.

Set Up Online Banking

Before you can use online banking services, you must have a working Internet connection. You get such a connection through an *Internet service provider*, or

PROBLEM	DEFINITION	SOLUTION
Virus	A program that attaches itself to other files on your computer. There are many forms of viruses, each performing different, usually malevolent, functions on your computer.	Install an antivirus program with a subscription for automatic updates, and make sure it is continually running.
Worm	A type of virus that replicates itself repeatedly through a computer network or security breach in your computer. Because it keeps copying itself, a worm can fill up a hard drive and cause your network to malfunction.	
Trojan horse	A computer program that claims to do one thing, such as play a game, but has hidden parts that can erase files or even your entire hard drive.	
Adware	The banners and pop-up ads that come with programs you download from the Internet. Often these programs are free, and to support them, the program owner sells space for ads to display on your computer every time you use the program.	Install an anti-adware program.
Spyware	A computer program that downloads with another program from the Internet. Spyware can monitor what you do, keep track of your keystrokes, discern credit card and other personally identifying numbers, and pass that information back to its author.	Install an antispyware program.

Table 2-2: Security Issues Associated with the Internet and How to Control Them

ISP. Check your phone book or call your local telephone company or cable TV company to find an ISP in your area. The ISP will give you the information you need to get an Internet connection and set it up in Windows. To set up your Internet connection in Quicken:

1. Click the **Edit** menu, click **Preferences**, and then click **Internet Connection Setup**. The Internet Connection Setup dialog box appears.

2. Choose one of the following three options:

   a. Click **Use The Following Connection** to use a listed connection that is different from what your computer normally uses. For example, if your ISP or financial institution requires that you run a program before connecting, or if you are unsure of or unable to use your Windows Internet connection, select this method.

   b. Click **Use My Computer's Internet Connection Settings To Establish A Connection When This Application Accesses The Internet**, which is the default, whereby Quicken can detect an Internet connection in Windows.

   c. Click **I Do Not Have A Way To Connect To The Internet. Please Give Me More Information On Setting Up An Internet Account** for information that may help you connect to the Internet.

3. Click **Next**. The Connection Settings dialog box appears and confirms the way you are to connect to the Internet. Click **Done** if you're satisfied with this connection. Otherwise, click **Back** to return to the previous dialog box and make another selection.

Once you have established your Internet connection, you are prepared to contact your bank to sign up for their online services. Many financial institutions allow you to sign up on their Web site, while others require that you call your local branch. Either way, most institutions need you to fill out an application, send a voided check or complete other paperwork, and agree to their fees. Then, you may need to wait a few days to get your identification number, password, or PIN sent to you by regular mail.

CONNECTION METHODS

There are several methods by which Quicken can update your transactions and balances. Depending on your financial institution, Quicken chooses the best method. Table 2-3 explains the differences.

CAUTION

Unless you are an expert with Internet settings, do not make a change through the Advanced Connection Settings dialog box. Any change you make in that Windows system dialog box may affect how other programs connect to the Internet.

TIP

While you are waiting for the bank to send you your information to use online banking, ensure that all your transactions are entered into Quicken and your latest paper statement has been reconciled.

FEATURE	DIRECT CONNECT	EXPRESS WEB CONNECT	WEB CONNECT	AUTO-1 WAY CONNECT
You must set up this service in Quicken even if you already log on to your financial institution's Web site.	X	X		X
Quicken can remember your logon information for you. This can include customer ID, password, and, in some cases, supplemental information.	X	X		X
Two-way communication with your financial institution is possible. You can access account information, transfer money from one account to another, pay bills, and so forth.	X			
All services are available from within Quicken. You don't need to log on to your financial institution's Web site.	X	X		X
You can use One Step Update to update multiple accounts during one session on the Internet.	X	X		
You can usually specify a date range for transactions you want to download.			X	
Downloaded transactions are automatically matched with existing transactions, and new transactions are entered into your register.	X	X	X	X
Your financial institution may require a monthly fee for this service.	X	X		X

Table 2-3: Methods by Which Quicken Updates Account Information from Your Financial Institution

TIP

If you don't see Set Up Online in the register menu bar, it means that the account has already been set up.

IMPLEMENT ONLINE BANKING

Once you have received the information from the bank, you have several ways to implement the online service.

1. For an existing account, open its register by clicking the account name in the Cash Flow Center. When the register appears, click **Set Up Online** on the register menu bar. The Quicken Account Setup dialog box appears.

2. If you have previously entered the name of your financial institution and the institution provides Direct Connect services, the dialog box asks for your customer ID number or account number and PIN number or password.

   If Quicken is unable to determine the name of your institution, the dialog box displays a list of possible institutions from which to choose. This dialog box may also provide a link to the complete list of financial institutions that work with Quicken to provide online services.

3. If you want to update several accounts, you can activate One Step Update. See "Activate One Step Update" next.

4. Click **Next**. Some institutions may display a dialog box that asks for more information. Fill in the information as needed, and then click **Next**. A dialog box appears notifying you that you have successfully set up the account.

5. Click **Next** to download your first set of transactions. When you are notified that you have successfully completed the download, click **Done**.

Activate One Step Update

You can update all of your transactions and balances at once with One Step Update.

1. Click **Update** on the Quicken toolbar. The Quicken Online Services dialog box appears. Click **Continue**.

2. If you have already registered Quicken, the One Step Update dialog box will appear.

3. If you have not yet registered Quicken, the Welcome to Quicken Registration dialog box appears. Ensure you have a working Internet connection, and complete the registration information. When you are done, click **Finish**. You are returned to the One Step Update dialog box.

4. If you haven't already, set up your financial institutions for One Step Update, if that is what you want, by clicking **Activate For One Step Update** for each institution.

5. Choose the information you want to download, and click **Update Now**. Your balances will be updated and transactions downloaded for the accounts you chose.

   a. While the information is being downloaded, you can continue to work in other parts of Quicken.

   b. If your Quicken Home page is open, you will see the status of the download displayed.

   c. Should you need to cancel the update, click **Cancel Update**.

6. If you want to change how Quicken manages your passwords, click Manage My Passwords. For further information, see the "Managing Your Passwords" QuickSteps.

7. When the update is completed, you are returned to the Quicken Home page or to the page from which you started the update.

Use Quicken Bill Pay

If your financial institution does not supply online bill-paying services, or if you choose not to use them, Quicken offers a similar service. Quicken Bill Pay

QUICKSTEPS

MANAGING YOUR PASSWORDS

Most financial institutions require passwords to access your information. There are two methods of managing your passwords. The first is the least convenient—entering each password individually. The most secure and convenient method is to store your passwords in the Quicken Password Vault. To do so:

1. Click **Manage My Passwords** from the One Step Update dialog box.

   Manage My Passwords...

2. Select the financial institution for which you want to store a password.

3. If you have more than one account for this financial institution, select the relevant customer ID for the password you want to store.

4. Enter the password you use for this account.

5. Enter the password again for confirmation.

6. If you are finished storing passwords, click **No**.

7. Enter a master password. The master password protects your Password Vault. It should contain at least six characters, preferably both numbers and letters.

8. Enter the master password again to confirm it.

It is a good idea to change your master password every six months or so. To change it:

1. Click **Online** from the Quicken menu bar.

2. From the menu, click **Password Vault** and then click **Edit**.

3. Enter your current master password (Password Vault password), and click **OK**.

4. Create a new password that is easy for you to remember.

5. Enter the new password again to confirm it.

6. Click **Change** to complete the process.

Continued . . .

is available for all U.S. customers with an Internet connection, who can use it to pay bills to any United States vendor from anywhere in the world.

1. Click **Online** on the Quicken menu bar, and then click **Quicken Bill Pay** to display the Quicken Bill Pay menu.

2. Click **Learn About Quicken Bill Pay** to read a complete description of this service. The Overview tab in the Quicken Bill Pay window provides information on the service, while the other tabs give you more detailed information.

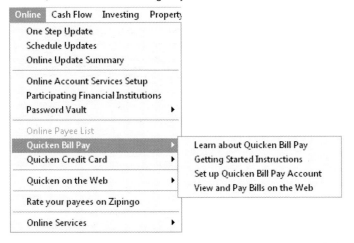

This service is especially useful if you have a small business or travel extensively. The service allows you to choose the account from which to pay, how much to pay, when to pay, and to schedule recurring payments. The cost for this online service may be offset by postage, time in check preparation, and ease in handling this task.

Understand Categories

A *category* is a description or label for an expense or a source of income. For example, payments to your telephone company might use the Telephone category. You can create subcategories for each category. For example, your trash pickup service might be a subcategory of Utilities. There are two types of categories: Income and Expense. As you set up your accounts and prepare to enter transactions, it is a good idea to set up categories at the same time.

To completely reset the Password Vault, delete the existing Password Vault and set it up again. To delete the current Password Vault:

1. Click **Online** from the Quicken menu bar.

2. Click **Password Vault**.

3. Choose **Delete** from the menu.

4. Click **OK**.

CAUTION

Deleting the Password Vault removes all stored passwords and erases the current Password Vault master password.

TIP

When you create a password, make it a strong password. A strong password is at least eight characters long and contains *all* of the following: both uppercase and lowercase letters, numbers, and one or two special characters, like !, @, #, $, %, ^, &, or *. A *strong* password should not be recognizable as any kind of name, an address, a date, a telephone number, or a word in any language. Also, it is important to change passwords at least two to four times a year.

TIP

You can also open the Category List by pressing **CTRL+SHIFT+C**.

Quicken supplies a number of preset categories for you to use. It also remembers the category you assign for each payee. Quicken customizes your list of categories in response to your answers in Quicken New User Setup. You can add new categories and delete any of the preset categories that do not apply to you.

Work with Categories

To view the preset Category List and add and remove categories:

1. Click the **Tools** menu, and then click **Category List**. Your Category List is displayed. The list shows all of the Income and Expense categories in alphabetical order.

2. Click **Options** on the right side of the menu bar to choose whether to display the category description, group, and type, and to assign groups to categories:

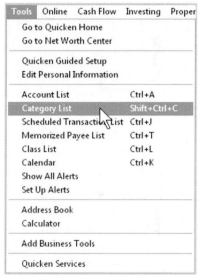

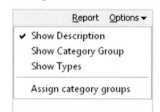

   a. Click **Assign Category Groups**. The Assign Category Groups dialog box appears.

   b. Click a category from the Category Name List.

   c. Click a category group from the Category Group List.

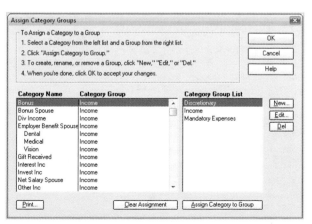

TIP

Assigning tax-line items to categories makes it easier to create tax reports and plan for tax time.

QUICK**FACTS**

USING TAX-LINE ASSIGNMENTS

While Quicken does not require that you include tax information in categories, entering this information can save a lot of time when preparing your taxes. By using them, Quicken can:

- Display up-to-date tax information in the Tax Center window. By knowing your tax position, you can talk to your tax professional about options well before year-end.

- Prepare tax reports by tax schedule or form. These reports will assist your tax professional and perhaps save you money in tax-preparation fees.

- Create reports that describe taxable and nontaxable dividends, interest, and other items separately.

- Help you use the Tax Planner within Quicken (see Chapter 10).

- Export your data directly into Intuit's TurboTax to help you prepare your income tax return.

The few minutes you spend assigning tax-line items to your categories can save a lot of time and money at the end of the year.

TIP

Do not combine alimony payments you receive with child support payments you receive. Instead, create a separate category for each item. Check with your tax professional for further information.

d. Click the **Assign Category To Group** button.

e. Click **OK**. Repeat the process for all the assignments you want to make. When you are done, close the dialog box.

3. Click the **Display Tax Information** check box. An additional pane opens displaying the income tax line and form assigned to a category. If the Display Tax Information check box is not selected, the list of transactions used in this category appears on the right side of the dialog box. If tax information is being displayed, this list appears below the Tax Information pane.

Add a Category

To add a new category:

1. Click the **Tools** menu, click **Category List**, and click **New** in the bottom-left corner of the list. The Set Up Category dialog box appears.

2. Type a name for your new category. Press **TAB** or click in the **Description** field.

3. Type any description necessary, such as <u>Part-time job</u> or <u>Annual homeowner dues</u>.

4. Press **TAB** or click in the **Group** field. You have the option to assign this category to a group. Quicken predefines three groups: Discretionary, Income, and Mandatory Expenses. You can add new groups or choose not to use groups.

5. Click either **Income** or **Expense** to properly designate this category.

6. If this category is tax-related, click **Tax-Related**. Then choose the tax-line item to which it applies:

a. Click the **Tax Line Item** down arrow to display a list of possible tax lines from which to choose.

b. Click the relevant line, or you may choose to leave this field blank. A small explanation appears in the box below when a tax-line item is chosen.

7. Click **OK** to finish adding the category and close the dialog box.

RENAMING A CATEGORY

You can rename a category to make it more meaningful.

1. In the Category List window, right-click the name of the category, and click **Edit**.

–Or–

In the Category List window, click the name of the category, and then click **Edit** at the bottom of the list.

2. In either case, the Edit Category dialog box appears.

3. Click in the **Name** field to select it, and type a new name.

4. If this category is tax-related, review the tax-line item to ensure it is still correct.

5. Click **OK** to close the Edit Category dialog box.

TIP

When selecting categories in the Add Categories dialog box, you can select multiple contiguous categories (categories that are next to each other) by holding down the **SHIFT** key while clicking the first and last categories.

ENTER MULTIPLE CATEGORIES AT ONCE

Quicken includes several preset lists of categories: Standard, Married, Homeowner, Business, Children, Investment, and Rentals & Royalties. The one you automatically start out with when you install and begin using Quicken, and the one we have been talking about in previous sections, is the Standard Category List. If you want to include another preset list, you can add all the categories in that list to your Category List at the same time.

1. Click the **Tools** menu, and click **Category List**.

2. Click **Add From List** at the bottom of the dialog box. The Add Categories dialog box appears.

3. Click the **Available Categories** down arrow to display the lists of preset categories.

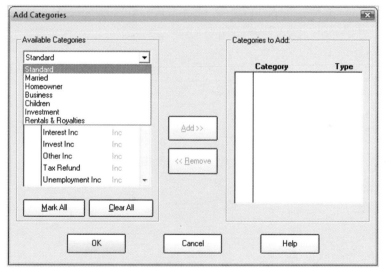

4. Click the preset list you want to add to the Standard list. The categories included in the list display in the Available Categories list.

5. Click the categories you want to use, or click **Mark All** to select all of them.

6. Click **Add** to move the categories into the Categories To Add list on the right side of the dialog box.

7. If you want to remove one or more of the new categories from the Categories To Add list, click the category and click **Remove**.

8. Click **OK** to add the categories and close the dialog box.

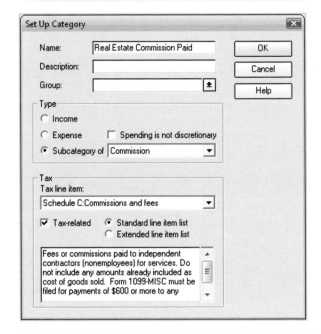

INSERT AN EXPENSE CATEGORY WITH SUBCATEGORIES

Expense categories are the best way to find out just where you are spending your money. You can use any of the predefined categories or add your own. You can also create subcategories to show more detail. When you categorize each item, you can create reports and graphs that show spending patterns and habits. You can even create budgets for categories or groups of categories.

1. Follow the instructions in "Add A Category" earlier in this chapter to add a category to which you want to add subcategories.

2. To add a subcategory to your new category, click the parent category in the Category List, and click **New** at the bottom of the Category List. The Set Up Category dialog box appears.

3. Type the name of your subcategory. Press **TAB** to move to the Description field, and type a description if you want.

4. Leave the **Group** field blank, or click the **Group** down arrow, and make a selection from the drop-down list.

5. Click the **Subcategory Of** option. Type the name of the parent category, or choose it from the drop-down list.

6. If this expense has tax implications, click **Tax-Related** and choose the tax-line item from the drop-down list. Otherwise, leave the **Tax** field empty.

7. Click **OK** to close the dialog box.

You will see the new category as a subcategory on the Category List. The Category List displays the categories in alphabetical order. Subcategories are displayed in alphabetical order indented underneath the parent category.

Protect Your Quicken Data

Computers have been a great asset to many of us. However, like any machine, they are prone to failures of many kinds. Once you have started using Quicken regularly, it becomes important to protect your information and store it in another location should your hard drive fail or something else happen to your computer.

QUICKSTEPS

DELETING CATEGORIES

As you are working with your Category List, you may see some items that you will not use and want to delete.

1. Click the **Tools** menu. and click **Category List**, or press **CTRL+SHIFT+C**, to display the Category List.

2. Click the category you want to delete, and click **Delete** in the bottom-right corner of the dialog box.

   –Or–

   Right-click the category you want to delete to display a context menu. Click **Delete**.

3. A warning message appears, notifying you that this account is about to be deleted. Click **OK** if you want to delete the account, or click **Cancel** if this was an error.

4. If you click **OK**, the category disappears from the Category List.

5. Click **OK** to close the Category List.

Quicken offers an easy solution to this problem called Quicken Backup. *Backup* (or back up—the verb form) is a computer term that means storing a copy of your information in a location other than on your computer.

You can back up your information to a floppy disk, a CD, another drive that is connected to your computer (such as a flash or thumb drive), or to a hard drive on another computer. You may want to perform backups to a couple of these items, and a couple of times a year, back up your data to a CD and put it in your bank safety deposit box. Your Quicken data might help you track down a tax question, and can be valuable to you just from the amount of work you put in it.

Back Up Your Data to External Media

To create a backup data file to a disk on your computer:

1. Click **File** on the Quicken menu bar, and then click **Backup** to display the Quicken Backup dialog box.

   –Or–

   Press **CTRL+B**.

2. Choose **On my computer [e.g. CD or floppy disk]**.

3. Select the drive letter for the disk to which you want to back up. "A:\" is displayed by default; click the **Browse** button to choose another drive.

4. Click the **Add Date To File Name** check box if you want to add the date to your backup file name.

5. Click **OK**.

6. When the backup is complete, a message box appears telling you that your data file has been successfully backed up.

7. Click **OK** to close the message box.

BACK UP YOUR DATA ONLINE

New in the 2007 version, Quicken has formed a partnership with @Backup, and you can now back up your Quicken data files directly to the Web using this service. This is a subscription service and prices vary, depending on the amount of data you want to back up. As part of your new Quicken 2007 program, you may have a free month of backup service available.

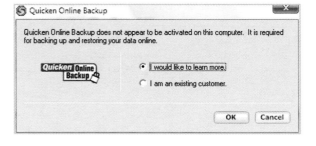

1. Click **File** on the Quicken menu bar, and then click **Backup** to display the Quicken Backup dialog box.

   –Or–

   Press **CTRL+B**.

2. Choose **Online**. If you have not already activated Quicken Online Backup, a message box appears asking if you would like to learn more or if you are an existing customer:

   a. If you click **I Would Like To Learn More**, you are directed to the Quicken Online Backup sign-up site.

   b. If you click **I Am An Existing Customer**, you are prompted for your account ID and password.

3. If you are an existing customer and have entered your account ID and password, click **OK** to start the backup.

4. A message box will display when the backup is complete. Click **OK** to close the dialog box.

Chapter 3

Setting Up the Other Centers

In the first two chapters, the focus was on setting up the Cash Flow Center for checking, savings, and credit card accounts. In this chapter you'll look at the Investing Center and the Property & Debt Center, learn how to set up their accounts, and examine some of the Quicken tools that are available in those areas. Both Centers are optional, depending on how much detail you want to maintain in Quicken.

Understand Financial Terminology

Before you begin working with the Investing and Property & Debt Centers, review the terms that are used in these areas, as explained in Table 3-1.

TERM	DEFINITION
Asset	Something you own that you expect to increase in value.
Brokerage	A company that buys and sells stocks and bonds for a fee on behalf of their clients.
Default	A setting or other value used by a computer program. Quicken names an account "Asset" by default if you do not choose another name.
Depreciation	A decrease or loss in value due to age, wear, or market conditions.
Equity	The market value of an asset, less any debt owed on that asset.
Interest	Rent on borrowed money.
Interest rate	The percentage of a debt charged for borrowing money.
Investment	Something you expect to increase in value or to generate income.
Market value	The amount for which an asset can be sold today.
Mutual fund	An investment company that invests in the securities of other companies and sells shares of those investments.
Performance	How a specific investment behaves over time—for example, how much money it earns.
Portfolio	The total of your investments.
Principal	The original amount of a debt or investment on which interest is calculated.
Real property	Assets that consist of land and/or buildings.
Securities	Documents that show ownership, such as a stock certificate or a bond.
Stock	Capital raised by selling portions (*shares*) of the ownership of a corporation. Stockholders receive a share of profits called *dividends* based on the number of shares they own.

Table 3-1: Definitions Pertaining to the Investing and Property & Debt Centers in Quicken

Use the Investing Center

The Investing Center can contain four types of investment accounts:

- **Standard brokerage accounts** allow you to track stocks, bonds, mutual funds, and annuities. You can download information directly from your brokerage company or enter items manually to keep track of your capital gains or losses, cash balances, market values, performance, and shares for one or more securities.

- **IRA or Keogh accounts** track your retirement plans.

- **401(k) and 403(b) accounts** track your pre-tax contribution investment accounts for your retirement. It is important to set up a separate account for each plan.

- **Single mutual fund accounts** track capital gains or losses, income, market value, share balance, and performance of a single mutual fund. This type of account does not track cash balances, interest, or miscellaneous expenses or income.

INVESTMENT	USE THIS ACCOUNT TYPE
401(k) and 403(b)	401(k) or 403(b)
Annuities	Standard brokerage account
Brokerage account	Standard brokerage account
CD or money market account	Standard brokerage account (Note: You can also set these up as standard savings accounts in the Cash Flow Center.)
Dividend reinvestment program	Standard brokerage account
Employee stock options or employee stock purchase plans (ESPP)	Standard brokerage account
IRA (any type)	IRA or Keogh account
Real estate investment trusts (REIT)	Standard brokerage account
Real property	Asset account
Single mutual fund (no cash balance)	Single mutual fund account
Stocks and bonds (certificates that you hold, including U.S. savings bonds)	Standard brokerage account
Treasury bills	Standard brokerage account

Table 3-2: Types of Quicken Investment Accounts to Use with Various Investments

TIP

If you hold bonds or stock certificates in a safe deposit box or other secure location, you can still track your information in a standard brokerage account.

NOTE

Log on to http://preferencecenter.intuit.com/optin/quicken/ to subscribe to a free newsletter about personal finance sent directly to your e-mail address.

TIP

Review your portfolio each year at the same time you receive your Personal Earnings and Benefit Estimate Statement from the Social Security Administration.

Table 3-2 describes which type of account to use for a particular type of investment.

Track Investments

Using Quicken to track your investments allows you to consolidate all of your investment information so that you can easily see the value of your total portfolio at any time. Understanding the performance history of several different types of investments and being able to calculate capital gains quickly can be extremely helpful throughout the year, as well as at year-end for tax purposes.

You open the Investing Center by clicking **Investing** on the menu bar or by clicking **Investing Center** in the Account bar of the Quicken Home page. Figure 3-1 shows the Investing Center.

Get real-time information
with today's data

Use the Performance tab to compare
your portfolio with the market

Update all of your financial
transactions in one easy step

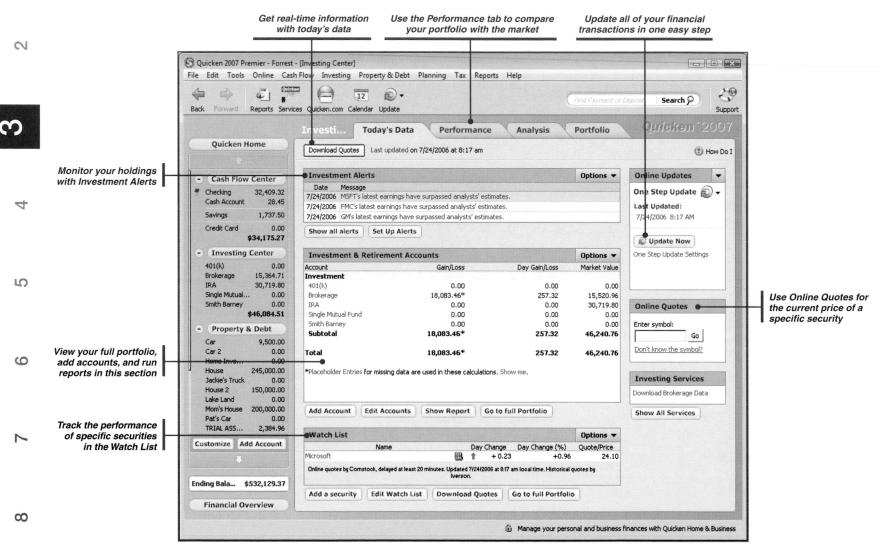

Monitor your holdings
with Investment Alerts

View your full portfolio,
add accounts, and run
reports in this section

Track the performance
of specific securities
in the Watch List

Use Online Quotes for
the current price of a
specific security

Figure 3-1: The Investing Center allows you to see your investment accounts, track the performance of specific
stocks or funds, and quickly update your portfolio using an Internet connection.

Set Up a Standard Brokerage or IRA Account

Setting up an account in the Investing Center is similar to setting up an account
in the Cash Flow Center.

1. Click **Investing Center** on the Account bar to open the Investing Center in the Activity Center, and then click **Add Account** at the bottom of the Investment & Retirement Accounts window.

   –Or–

   Click the **Investing** menu, click **Investing Accounts**, and click **Add Account**.

2. Either way, the Quicken Account Setup dialog box appears. If your financial institution (which includes most brokerages, mutual funds, and other investment companies) offers automated data entry, type the name of the institution, and click **Next**.

   If your brokerage firm or other institution supports online setup, you'll see a dialog box that asks if you want to connect to your financial institution now or later. The dialog box also displays what type of download method is supported by your institution. Follow the instructions you receive for the automated setup.

3. If you do not choose online setup, or if your institution does not support online setup, the next dialog box asks what type of investment account you want to add. Refer to Table 3-2 for some suggestions as to which Quicken investment account you should use for each of your investments.

NOTE

Most financial institutions require that you sign up for their download service prior to using the Quicken download. Most institutions require an account number or ID and a password or PIN that they assign.

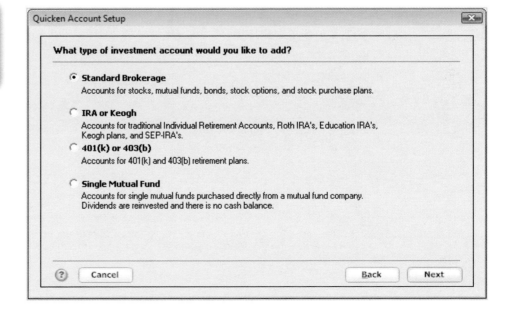

QUICK**FACTS**

UNDERSTANDING PLACEHOLDERS IN INVESTMENT ACCOUNTS

You may see a note in an investment account that says "Placeholder entries for missing data are used in these calculations." Quicken uses these entries when you have not entered either the purchase date or purchase price of a security. Placeholder entries simply record the name and number of shares in an investment account transaction. When you enter all of the information about a security, including purchase date and price, Quicken can track the performance of these securities.

If you want to let Quicken correctly reflect the data, either download the information from your financial institution, if it is available, or enter the information directly from the original purchase information statement. As you enter each transaction, Quicken subtracts what you enter from the placeholder entry until all of the current shares have been entered.

NOTE

If you use Quicken Deluxe, Premier, or Premier Home and Business versions, you can also add a 401(k) or 403(b) retirement account.

TIP

Some firms call the cash amounts not invested on a given date a *sweep account*.

---

4. Click the type of account you want to set up, and then click **Next**.

5. Type a name for this account. You can type any name that identifies the account for you. You might consider using the name of the brokerage firm or other institution. If this account is an IRA or Keogh account, you are asked if this is for you or your spouse. You are also asked to choose the type of IRA from a drop-down list. Choose one and click **Next** to continue.

6. Using either your last statement or your account on the firm's Web site, enter the last statement date (or the "as of" date), the ending cash balance in the account, and any money-market fund balances in the account, and then click **Next**.

7. Enter the securities that are in the account. If you want Quicken to download current information about each security, type its symbol. If you do not have an Internet connection, you can just type the name of the security. You can add more information later. Click **Next** to continue.

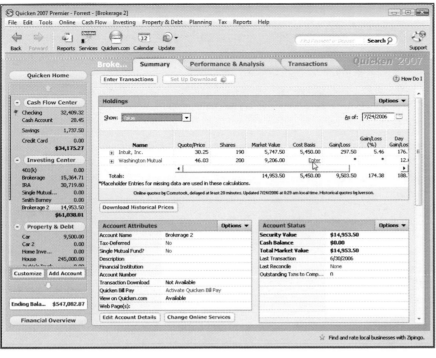

Figure 3-2: Quicken automatically updates the current price of your securities if you're online, and it can calculate your gain or loss if you enter the cost.

8. In the **Quicken Account Setup Current Holdings** dialog box, enter the number of shares you hold for each security and whether it is a stock, a mutual fund, or something else. Click **Next** to see a summary of the securities in the account. Click **Done** to complete the account setup.

Your new account information appears in the Investing Center, as shown in Figure 3-2. Quicken cannot calculate your gain or loss on each investment without knowing what you paid for your securities. This amount is your cost basis. Quicken displays an asterisk in the Gain/Loss columns, called a *placeholder entry*, until you complete the information. You may enter this information now or later. To enter the cost for your security:

1. Click **Enter** under the Cost Basis column. The Enter Missing Transactions dialog box appears.

Enter Missing Transactions

Enter Missing Transactions for Disney Entertainment

This security is missing all or part of its transaction history. When you downloaded or manually entered transactions, the total number of shares in those transactions did not equal the total number of shares you own. Quicken has added a Placeholder Entry to account for missing transactions.

To get complete performance reporting and tax calculations, enter the missing transactions now.

Disney Entertainment Transactions as of 9/30/2006

Date	Transaction	Description
		Enter Missing Transactions to complete cost basis

Holdings as of 9/30/2006	Shares	Cost
Total shares you own:	103	*
Shares from transactions (above)	0	0.00
Shares in Placeholder Entry	**103**	**Unknown**

[Enter Missing Transaction...]   [Estimate Average Cost...]

[Help]   [Finish Later]

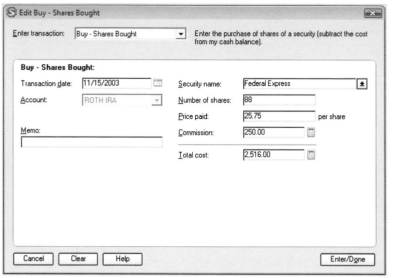

2. Click **Enter Missing Transaction**. The Edit Buy - Shares Bought dialog box appears:

   ● Enter the transaction date, number of shares, the price per share that you paid on that date, and the commission you paid. Quicken will calculate a total cost. Click **Enter/Done** when finished.

   –Or–

   ● If you purchased the shares over a period of time, click **Estimate Average Cost**. Enter values in either the **Total Cost** or the **Share Price** fields, and click **OK**. This option is not as accurate as entering each batch of shares you purchased, but it is quicker and may be enough if you don't need all the detail. You can come back and enter the individual transactions at a later date.

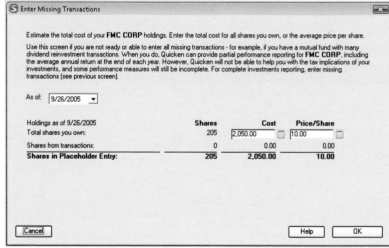

3. Repeat steps 1 and 2 for each security you own.

Set Up One Step Update

Quicken 2007 allows you to update all of your financial information in one step. You can download transactions from your bank, credit union, brokerage firm, or credit card company. This single-access feature allows you to schedule downloads at your convenience or whenever you use Quicken. To set up One Step Update:

1. Click **Update** on the Quicken toolbar to display the One Step Update Settings dialog box. Click **Quotes** to open the Customize Online Updates dialog box. You can also

access this dialog box from the Quicken menu. Click **Edit**, click **Preferences**, and then click **Customize Online Updates**.

2. Depending on how you have managed the passwords for each of your financial institutions, you may be prompted for individual passwords or for your Quicken 2007 Password Vault password.

3. Click **Download Quotes, Asset Classes, Headlines And Alerts** to obtain information about the holdings you have entered. Click **Select Quotes** to choose the holdings.

USE THE QUOTES TAB

1. Click the **Quotes** tab, and click **Mark All** to mark all securities for which you want current quotes. Click **Clear All** if you want to choose only a few.

2. To exclude any one item, click the check mark in front of the security name to clear it. To add a new security, click **New Security** and enter the security's ticker symbol. Click **Next**.

3. Depending on your Internet connection, you may see a dialog box stating that Quicken will include this security in its update, or the Internet Connection dialog box may appear. If you see the Internet Connection dialog box, click **Connect Now For Easier Security Setup** or click **Don't Connect** if you want to add the security manually or do not have a current Internet connection available.

4. In either case, click **Done** or **Next**, depending on the dialog box with which you are working.

USE THE PORTFOLIO TAB

The Portfolio tab lets you set up accounts on Quicken.com so that you can track your investment accounts and Watch List from any Internet connection throughout the world. If you have created your Quicken.com account during registration, you can access it by going to http://www.quicken.com/investments and signing in.

WORK WITH THE ACCOUNTS TAB

The Accounts tab allows you to select accounts to view with Quicken.com anywhere you have access to the Internet. After you have synchronized your accounts with Quicken.com for the first time, the Resend All Items check box becomes available.

UNDERSTAND THE CONNECTION TAB

The Connection tab has several options, each of which helps you customize what will be sent via the Internet when you establish a connection.

TIP

Keep the Resend All Items check box cleared for faster use of One Step Update.

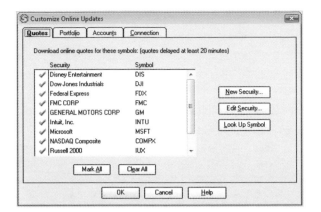

When you have selected the accounts to update and chosen your other settings, click **OK** to close the Customize Online Updates dialog box. You are returned to the One Step Update Settings dialog box. From here, you can click **Quicken.com** to update your information that you have previously selected. You can also manage your passwords with the Quicken Password Vault. If you want to schedule updates, click **Schedule Updates** to establish what you want updated and how often.

Click **Update Now** to run the update or click **Cancel** to close the One Step Update Settings dialog box.

Add a 401(k) or 403(b) Account

Entering a 401(k) or 403(b) account is similar to setting up an investment account, as described in "Set Up a Standard Brokerage or IRA Account" earlier in this chapter. Use steps 1 through 6 in that section, choosing **401(k)** or **403(b)** as the type of account. Then, in the **Tell Us About This Account** dialog box:

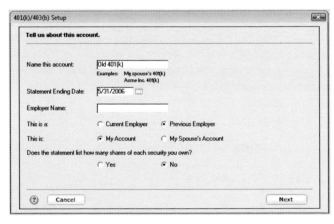

1. Enter the date of your last paper statement (optional), enter your employer's name, select whether this account is from your current employer or a previous employer, and designate whether this account is your account or that of your spouse.

2. If your statement shows how many shares you own, click **Yes**. If not, click **No**. Click **Next** to continue.

3. When asked if there are any outstanding loans against this account, click **No** if there are no loans. If there are loans against this account, click **Yes** and enter the number of loans. Click **Next** to continue.

4. If you clicked **Yes** in step 3, you are asked for a description of this loan and its current balance. Click **Set Up An Account To Track The Remaining Balance Of This Loan**, type the original loan amount, and click **Next**.

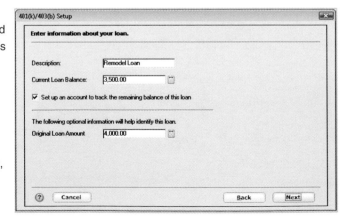

CAUTION

While some 401(k) plans allow you to take loans against the funds in the plan, it may not be a good idea. The interest payments on these loans are not tax-deductible, and you lose the growth you would have gotten on the amount of the loan. See your tax professional for more information.

QUICKSTEPS

CREATING A SINGLE MUTUAL FUND ACCOUNT

When you first buy, or if you already own, a single mutual fund from a mutual fund company, you can use a single mutual fund account to track it. Typically, these funds pay no dividends and there is no cash balance. To add this type of account, follow the first six steps in setting up an investment account as described in "Set Up a Standard Brokerage or IRA Account" earlier in this chapter. Then:

1. Choose **Single Mutual Fund** as the type of account, type a name for this account, choose whether this account is tax-deferred, and click **Next**.

2. Enter the date of your last paper statement, and click **Next**.

3. If you want to download the security details, type the ticker symbol for the security in this account. If you are not connected to the Internet or want to add information later, simply type the name in the Security Name field, and click **Next**.

4. If you do not enter the name, you will see a warning message that since this is a single mutual fund account, you must provide the name.

Quicken 2007	
⚠ Since this is a Single Mutual Fund Account, you must enter a security before continuing.	
[OK]	

5. Type the number of shares you own, and click **Next**. The Summary dialog box appears. Review your account and, when you are ready, click **Done** to complete the setup.

---

5. You are asked abut the securities in this account. Type the ticker symbol if you know it, or type the name of the security. You can enter all the details later if you want. Click **Next** to continue.

6. Enter the total shares you own and, if Quicken hasn't entered it for you, the market value shown on your last statement. Click **Next**.

7. Review the summary of what you have entered. If you have chosen to enter the information from your paper statement, the summary should match the total shown on that statement. Click **Done** to finish setting up this account.

Use the Property & Debt Center

The Property & Debt Center provides a way to integrate all your other financial information into Quicken so that you can see your total financial position at any given moment. Property & Debt Center accounts include:

- **House** accounts are used for your main residence, vacation home, rental properties, or other real estate. You can create a liability account for each property at the same time you create the asset account.

- **Vehicle** accounts are used for all types of vehicles, including cars, trucks, motorcycles, boats, motor homes, and campers. You can create liability accounts for the loans on each vehicle at the same time you create the asset accounts.

- **Asset** accounts are used for assets other than real property, vehicles, or investments. Examples include sterling silver, antiques, baseball card collections, first-edition and rare books, and business equipment.

- **Liability** accounts are used for personal debts other than credit cards, which use the Cash Flow Center. Examples include personal loans and promissory notes you owe banks, loan companies, and individuals, as well as student loans. You can also link a liability with an asset, such as a home equity loan or line of credit. For more information on linking asset and liability accounts, see Chapter 6.

Work with the Property & Debt Center

You use the Property & Debt Center to:

- Record your major assets and debts to better understand your overall financial standing.
- Allow Quicken to calculate the amount due on your mortgage and other obligations.
- Track the amount of interest you are paying on any specific debt and in total.

Not all Quicken users need to enter information in the Property & Debt Center, but if you have a mortgage, make car payments, or have other assets and liabilities, you might want to consider adding the information to Quicken so that you can see your true financial picture.

Set Up a House Account with a Mortgage

For most people, their biggest asset is their home. To enter this asset and any associated liability:

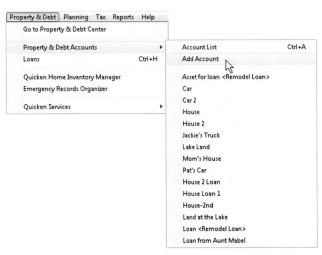

1. Click the **Property & Debt** menu, click **Property & Debt Accounts**, and click **Add Account**.

    –Or–

    Click **Property & Debt** in the Account bar, and then click **Add Account** at the bottom of the Property & Debt Accounts list in the Activity Center.

    In both cases, the Quicken Account Setup dialog box appears with several choices.

2. Click **House** (**With Or Without Mortgage**), and click Next.

3. Type a name for the account. Quicken uses "House" as the default. If you have more than one house account, Quicken uses "House 2," "House 3," and so forth, unless you type another name. Click **Next**.

4. Enter or select the date you acquired the property. You can use the small calendar icon to the right of the date of acquisition field to select the date. Press **TAB** to move to the next field.

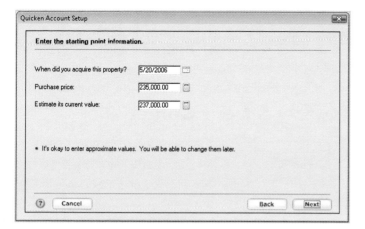

5. Enter the purchase price, and again press TAB. Estimate the value of your home today. Quicken requires that you enter an amount, so use your best guess. You can change the value later. Click **Next**.

6. Choose if and how you want the liability account set up for the house:

- Click **Yes, Create A Liability Account For Me** if you have not already created a liability account for the mortgage.

- Click **There Is A Mortgage And I'm Already Tracking It In Quicken** if you have entered the liability account. Choose which account is associated with this asset in the **Account** drop-down box.

- Click **The House Is Paid For, So I Don't Need A Liability Account** if you have no mortgage or do not want to track your mortgage through Quicken.

7. Click **Done** to create the asset account. A new dialog box appears asking for the loan information. It shows the opening date of the loan as being the acquisition date of the property.

8. Enter the original balance and length of the loan, how it is compounded, and how often you make payments, pressing TAB to move from field to field. Use the small calculator icon to the right of the **Original Balance** field if you want. Click **Next** to continue.

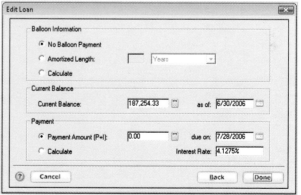

9. If you are unsure of the payment amount, enter the interest rate, and click **Calculate**. Quicken will compute the amount of principal and interest for each payment. Click **Done**. A message appears advising you that Quicken has calculated the next loan payment. You are instructed to click **OK** to return to the View Loans dialog box. You see the estimate of the next payment amount and the date on which it is due. You can change this later if you want.

10. Click **Done**. The Edit Loan Payment dialog box appears. If you want, change the interest rate and/or adjust the principal and interest payment.

TIP

Try using the 10-key pad on your keyboard to enter numbers (make sure the NUMLOCK light on the keyboard is lit; press the NUMLOCK key if it isn't). The 10-key pad will give you an experience similar to that when using a calculator.

TIP

The compounding period reflects how your lending institution computes the interest charged on the loan. The more often the institution calculates the interest, the more interest you pay. Most institutions compound interest daily.

If you want to remove an account from view in Quicken, you can *delete* it, which means the account and all its related transactions are permanently removed from Quicken; or you can *hide* it so that it is not seen in the Account bar and not included in the totals. If you hide an account, you still have access to all of its related transactions.

DELETE AN ACCOUNT

1. Click the **Tools** menu, and click **Account List**, or press **CTRL+A**, to display the Account List.

   –Or–

   Right-click the account in the Account bar, and click **Delete/Hide Accounts** In Quicken.

2. Click the account you want to delete, and click **Delete** on the Account List menu bar. A dialog box appears, prompting you to confirm that you want to delete this account. Type **yes** to verify that you want to delete the account (it does not matter if you use uppercase or lowercase letters).

3. Click **OK** to delete this account.

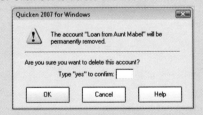

HIDE AN ACCOUNT

1. Click the **Tools** menu, and click **Account List**, or press **CTRL+A**, to display the Account List.

   –Or–

   Right-click the account in the Account bar, and click **Delete/Hide Accounts In Quicken**.

Continued . . .

11. Click **Edit** to include other amounts you pay with your mortgage payment, such as real estate taxes and homeowners' insurance. In the **Split Transaction** dialog box, enter the category for each portion and the amount for each category, and then click **OK**.

12. Click in the **Payee** field to enter the name of your mortgage lender. Adjust the next payment date, and, if desired, change the interest category. By default, Quicken uses "Mortgage Int:Bank" as the category.

13. After you have completed editing the loan, click **OK** to return to the Property & Debt Center. Depending on how you set up your payment, you may see a message stating that Quicken automatically set up the payment transaction. If you see such a message, click **OK**.

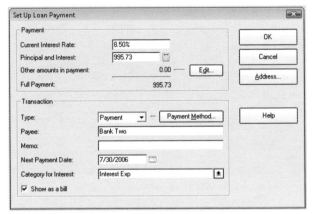

Some variable-rate or adjustable-rate loans change the interest rate with the next payment that is due. Others change the interest rate for all future payments.

Your new asset account and its related liability account appear in both the Activity Center and the Quicken Account bar. Information about each loan appears at the bottom, in the Loan Accounts Summary section.

Add Other Property and Debt Accounts

You can create other accounts within the Property & Debt Center. As you work with the dialog boxes, you will see similarities between the various accounts. To add a vehicle, for example:

1. Click **Add Account** from the Account List or Property & Debt Activity Center, click **Vehicle**, and click **Next**.

2. Enter the name of the vehicle, and identify its make, model, and year, pressing **TAB** to move from field to field. Click **Next** to continue.

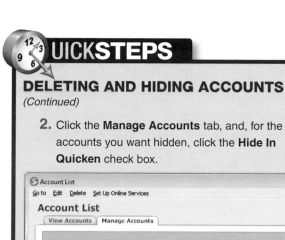

DELETING AND HIDING ACCOUNTS
(Continued)

2. Click the **Manage Accounts** tab, and, for the accounts you want hidden, click the **Hide In Quicken** check box.

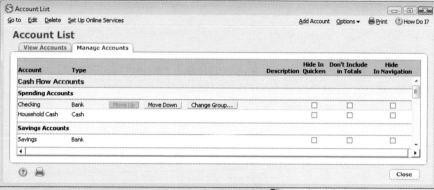

3. Enter the date you acquired the vehicle, its purchase price, and its estimated current value, and then click **Next**.

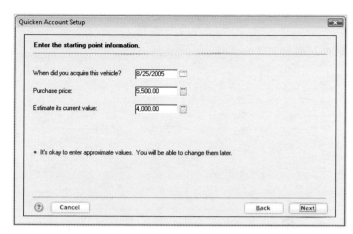

4. Choose whether to create a liability account for this vehicle, identify an existing loan account, or indicate that there is no loan on it. In all instances, click **Done** to create the account.

5. If you indicated that you wanted to create a loan, the Edit Loan dialog box appears. Enter the opening date, original balance, term, and the compounding period. When finished, click **Next**.

6. Indicate whether the loan has a balloon payment, the current balance, and payment information, and click **Done**. (A balloon payment is usually larger than regular payments and is often the last payment.)

7. If you asked Quicken to calculate the payment, click **OK** and then click **Done** again to accept Quicken's calculation.

8. Review the loan payment information; enter the payee and any additional information you want, such as the payee's address; and click **OK**.

Add Other Liability Accounts

Another liability account is used for loans other than for your house or vehicle. These types of loan can be promissory notes, student loans, loans against insurance policies, loans for medical expenses, or any other liability.

1. Click **Add Account** in the Property & Debt Center Activity Center or Account List.

2. Click **Liability** and click **Next**. Type a name for the liability, and click **Next**.

NOTE

If one of your vehicles is a motor home, consult your tax professional to see if you should consider this your primary home or a second home.

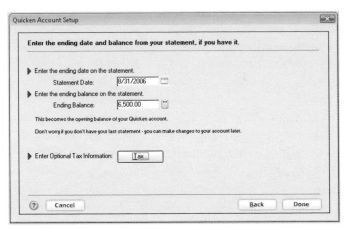

3. Enter the starting date of the loan or the date on which you want to start keeping track of this loan. Then enter the value of the loan—that is, what you owed on that date.

4. If the liability has tax implications, click **Tax**. Consult your tax professional for information on tax implications, and, if needed, enter the recommended information. Click **Done**.

5. A dialog box appears asking if you want to set up an amortized loan to be associated with this account. This provides a payment schedule. If so, click **Yes**, and the EasyStep Loan Wizard will start (see "Use EasyStep Loan Setup"). If not, click **Done**.

Use EasyStep Loan Setup

Quicken provides EasyStep Loan Setup to help you set up an amortized loan. This feature can be opened automatically, as described in the previous section, or you can open it directly.

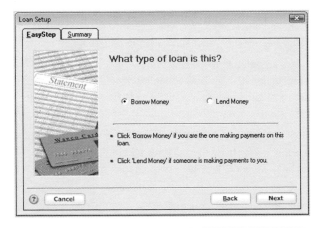

1. Click **Property & Debt** from the Quicken menu, and then click **Loans**; or press **CTRL+H**. Either way, the View Loans dialog box appears.

2. Click **New** in the menu bar of the View Loans dialog box. The EasyStep Loan Setup dialog box appears. You can also click **Add Loan** from the Property & Debt Center to open this dialog box. Click **Next** to continue.

3. Choose between borrowing money and loaning money. Borrowing is the default. Click **Next**.

4. Enter the name of a new account, or link this loan to an existing account, and click **Next**.

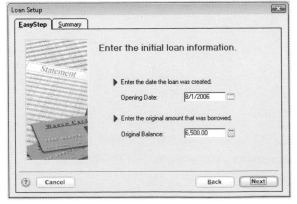

5. If you have made payments on this loan, click **Yes**; otherwise, click **No**. Then click **Next**. You are asked for the initial loan information.

6. If this is a new account, you are required to provide the opening date and original balance of the loan. If this is an existing account, Quicken provides the information for you. Click **Next** to continue.

NOTE

By default, the EasyStep Loan Setup compounds interest monthly, but many lending institutions compound it daily.

TIP

If you pay additional principal payments on your home mortgage or on another loan, you can reduce the total amount of interest you have to pay.

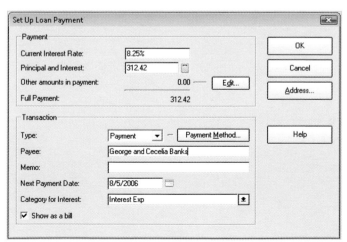

7. If there is a balloon payment, click **Yes**; otherwise, click **No** and then click **Next**. Enter the original length of the loan, and click **Next**. Select how you pay the loan (the default is monthly), and click **Next** again. Enter how often interest is compounded, and click **Next**.

8. If you said you made a payment amount in step 5, you are asked if you know the current balance. If you haven't made a payment, skip to step 11. If you know the current balance, click **Yes**, click **Next**, enter the date and amount of the current balance, and click **Next** again. Otherwise, click **No** to have Quicken calculate the amount for you.

9. Click **Next**. Enter the date on which the next payment is due, and click **Next**. If you know the amount of the next payment, click **Yes** and click **Next**. Enter the payment and click **Next** again. If not, click **No** to have Quicken calculate it for you. Click **Next** to continue.

10. Enter the date on which the next payment is due, and click **Next**. If you know the amount of the next payment, click **Yes**, enter the payment, and click **Next** again. If not, click **No** to have Quicken calculate it for you. Click **Next** to continue. Skip to step 12.

11. Enter the date of the first payment, and click **Next**. If you know the amount of the first payment, click **Yes**, click **Next**, enter the amount of the payment, and click **Next** again. Otherwise, click **No** and click **Next**.

12. In any case, enter the interest rate, and click **Next**. Two summary screens appear. Click **Next** after each. If you didn't know the payment, a third summary screen would appear showing you the basis upon which Quicken will calculate the amount for you. Click **Done**.

13. You are told that Quicken has calculated the next loan payment. Click **OK** and, if all is in order, click **Done** again.

14. Review the loan payment information, and enter the name of the payee. The default is the standard Interest Exp category, but you can change it to another category or create a new category. At the bottom-left corner of the dialog box is the **Show As A Bill** check box, which Quicken selects by default. Click the check mark to deselect the check box if you want. If all appears to be correct, click **OK**.

PRINTING AN AMORTIZATION SCHEDULE

As you continue to work with loans in Quicken, you may want to print a payment schedule. To print this payment schedule (often called an *amortization schedule*):

1. Click **Property & Debt** on the Quicken menu bar, and click **Loans** to display the View Loans dialog box. Click **Choose Loan** to see a drop-down list of all your loans, and click the loan for which you want to print the schedule.

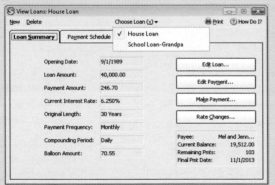

2. Click **Payment Schedule** and click **Print** on the menu bar.

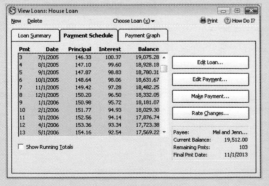

3. Close the View Loans dialog box.

15. If there is an associated asset with this loan and you want to enter the asset, click **Yes** to create the asset account; enter the asset name, acquisition date, and current value; and then click **Done**. Otherwise, click **No** to finish creating the liability account and return to either the Property & Debt Activity Center or the View Loans dialog box, depending on which way you accessed the Loan Setup Wizard.

Chapter 4
Using Quicken Every Day

In earlier chapters you learned how to install Quicken and set up your Quicken accounts. In this chapter you will learn how to use Quicken every day to record your checks, deposits, and other transactions. You'll learn to use the check register and credit card registers, with both manual and online transactions. But first, you'll be introduced to some definitions that are used throughout this chapter.

Understand Basic Transactions

A *transaction* in Quicken is something that affects the balance in an account. You enter a transaction into the *register* of the account. A register looks like a checkbook register, where you enter the activity, or transactions, regarding your accounts. Table 4-1 explains some of the terms used when talking about transactions. When using these terms, it is important to distinguish between:

- **Checking or savings accounts** in which you deposit your money and write checks or make withdrawals against your own funds. In essence, the bank owes you your money.

- **Credit card accounts** in which the bank extends you a line of credit, you make charges against that line, and then make payments to it. In essence, you owe the bank their money.

TERM	DEFINITION
Charge or debit	A transaction that increases the balance in a credit card account or decreases the balance in a checking account. A charge can also be something you purchased with a credit card or a fee from a financial institution.
Credit	A transaction that decreases the balance in a credit card, like a payment, or increases the balance in a checking account, like a deposit.
Deposit	A transaction that increases the balance in a checking or savings account.
Field	An area where you can make an entry, such as the date *field* or the amount *field*.
Payee	The company or person to whom you make a payment; for a deposit, it is the person from whom you get money you are depositing.
Payment	A transaction that lowers the balance in a credit card account.
Reconcile	To make what you have entered into a Quicken account agree with the statement you receive from your financial institution.
Transaction	An action that changes the balance in an account.
Transfer	To move funds from one account to another.

Table 4-1: Terms Used with Quicken Transactions

You create a transaction when you write a check, make a deposit, enter a credit card charge, or make a payment on your credit card. To keep your account register up to date, you need to enter the transaction into the account register, either manually or by downloading the information from the financial institution. You also need to reconcile your accounts on a regular basis against your financial institution's records. Quicken offers an Automatic Reconciliation feature. Chapter 7 discusses that and other methods of reconciling your accounts in more detail.

Establish Preferences for Your Registers

Before you use a register for the first time, you may want to set your preferences. Preferences are the ways in which you tell Quicken how to display and process your information.

Set Register Preferences

To set your preferences for an account:

CAUTION

The settings used for investment accounts are slightly different because they use transaction lists rather than registers.

1. Click the **Edit** menu, click **Preferences**, and then click **Quicken Program**.

2. Click **Register**. The Quicken Preferences dialog box appears, as shown in Figure 4-1. Select the order in which you want the register fields displayed:

   - **Show Date In First Column**, which is selected by default, can be deselected to show the check number as the first field and the date as the second field.

   - **Show Memo Before Category**, which is not selected by default, can be selected to display the Memo field first, instead of showing the Category field on the left.

3. In the Data Entry area, click the relevant check boxes:

   - **Automatically Enter Split Data** changes the way you enter a split transaction (see "Create a Split Transaction" later in this chapter). This check box is not selected by default.

   - **Use Automatic Categorization** lets Quicken choose the category for a transaction based on an internal database or on the category you used before for this payee. This check box is selected by default.

   - **Automatically Place Decimal Point** sets the decimal point to two places. By default, Quicken enters zero cents when you enter a number. For example, if you type the number 23 in the Amount field, Quicken displays it as $23.00. If you choose to set the decimal point automatically, the number 23 becomes .23, or 23 cents. This check box is not selected by default.

4. In the Register Appearance area, select how you want the register to look:

   - **Show Transaction Toolbar** allows you to display the transaction toolbar on the right side of your transaction entry field. It has Enter, Edit, Split, Rate, and Attach buttons displayed by default:

     - Click **Show Rate Button For Payee** to clear the check box if you do not want to see the Rate button. This button allows you to rate your payees.

     - Click **Show Attach Button** to clear the check box if you do not want to see the Attach button. The Attach button allows you to add notes, images, or flags to a transaction.

Figure 4-1: Quicken gives you a number of ways to customize the register to meet your needs.

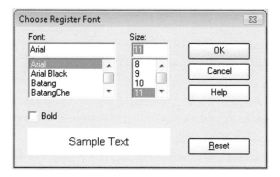

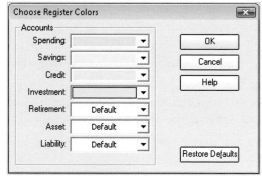

- **Gray Reconciled Transactions**, which is selected by default, displays all reconciled transactions in gray rather than in black. This feature allows you to quickly scan your register and find transactions that have not yet cleared the bank.

- **Maximize My Register View** fills your screen with the register. Use the small arrow in the upper-left corner to restore the Account bar.

- **Show Rate Payee Link** displays a small link in the lower-left corner of your register. See "Rate Your Payees" later in this chapter for more information.

5. Click the **Fonts** button to see a menu of available fonts for the register. You can choose from several different fonts and sizes. Click the font and size to see in the preview box how characters in the register would look using this font. When finished, click **OK**.

   If you choose too large a font, Quicken displays a warning message. Click **OK** to close the dialog box.

6. Click the **Colors** button to display the available colors for each register. Click the down arrow to the right of each account name to see the available choices. You can choose from seven different colors, including the default color. Click **OK** to close the dialog box.

7. Click the **Remove Memorized Payees Not Used In Last __ Months** check box to limit the list of memorized transactions displayed. By default, Quicken retains the first 2,000 transactions that you enter and then does not memorize any more. When you click this check box and type a number in the field, for example, 5, Quicken saves only the transactions you've entered over the last five months. See Chapter 5 for more information on memorized transactions.

8. Click the **Keep Register Filters After Quicken Closes** check box, which is not selected by default, to use the filter utility to quickly find specific types of transactions, such as all unreconciled transactions or all payments made within a certain period.

9. Click **OK** to close the dialog box when you have selected your register preferences.

Determine QuickFill Preferences

Quicken saves you time during data entry with what Intuit calls *QuickFill* features. For example, Quicken provides drop-down lists from which you can choose categories and payees. You can choose to complete a field after typing only a few letters using Quicken's memorization of payees, transactions, and categories. You can determine how these features work in the QuickFill Preferences dialog box, shown in Figure 4-2.

NOTE

Some fonts display better than others. Look at how your choice appears in the register. If you can't read it easily, choose another font and/or size.

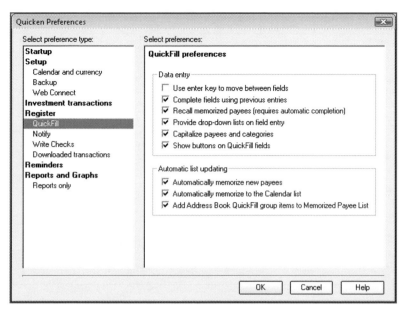

Figure 4-2: Use QuickFill preferences to
configure your registers according to the
way you want to enter and view your data.

1. Click the **Edit** menu, click **Preferences**, click **Quicken Program**, and then click **QuickFill**. The QuickFill Preferences dialog box appears.

2. Choose whether to use the **ENTER** key in addition to the **TAB** key to move between fields in your registers. By default, the **ENTER** key is used only to complete a transaction.

3. Choose whether to automatically complete each field using the entry previously made for this payee. If you choose this option, which is selected by default, you can also choose whether to have Quicken recall your memorized payees.

4. Choose whether to have Quicken display a drop-down list for the number, payee, and category fields (this is selected by default).

Cable Company			
Deluxe Expresso	-6.24	Entertai...	Susan
Dependable Cleaners	-37.55	Clothing	
Downtown Associa...		<Addre...	
Dynamic Repair Se...	-59.27	Auto:Se...	
Electric Company	-84.37	Utilities:...	
Electric Company	-84.37	Utilities:...	

Show Memorized Payee List

5. Choose whether you want payee and category names capitalized and whether to display the drop-down list arrow every time you click in a number, payee, or category field (both of these check boxes are selected by default).

6. Choose whether you want Quicken to memorize new payees, memorize transactions to the Calendar List, and add Address Book items to the Memorized Payee List.

7. Click **OK** when finished.

Set Notify Preferences

Notify preferences tell Quicken the circumstances in which you want to receive warning messages. By default, all warnings are activated.

1. Click the **Edit** menu, click **Preferences**, click **Quicken Program**, and then click **Notify**. The Notify Preferences dialog box appears.

2. Choose whether to get a warning message when:

- Entering transactions that are not in the current year
- Changing an existing transaction

Notify preferences

Notify
- ☑ When entering out-of-date transactions
- ☑ Before changing existing transactions
- ☑ When entering uncategorized transactions
- ☑ To run a reconcile report after reconcile
- ☑ Warn if a check number is re-used

NOTE

If you choose a two-digit year, the on-screen image still shows four digits, but when you print the check, only the rightmost two digits are printed.

- Entering a transaction without a category
- Not running a reconciliation report after you complete a reconciliation
- Using a check number more than once

3. Click **OK** when finished.

Set Preferences for Writing Checks

Quicken gives you six options from which to choose when using the program to write checks, as shown in Figure 4-3. To set those options:

1. Click the **Edit** menu, click **Preferences**, click **Quicken Program**, and then click **Write Checks**. The Write Checks Preferences dialog box appears.

2. Choose whether you want a four-digit year, such as 4/5/2007, or a two-digit year, such as 4/5/07, to be printed on your checks.

3. Click the **Spell Currency Units** check box to have Quicken print the currency amount on your check with the currency unit displayed, for example, "Twenty Dollars and 37 cents" rather than "Twenty and 37/100."

4. Click the **Allow Entry Of Extra Message On Check** check box if you want to include information for the payee's records, such as your account number or the invoice number you are paying with this check.

5. Click the **Print Categories On Voucher Checks** check box if you want to include that information. A voucher check has a perforated portion that can include additional information. This setting allows Quicken to include up to 16 lines of category information on this voucher.

6. Click the **Change Date Of Checks To Date When Printed** check box if you enter data over time and print all your checks at once.

7. Click **OK** to close the dialog box.

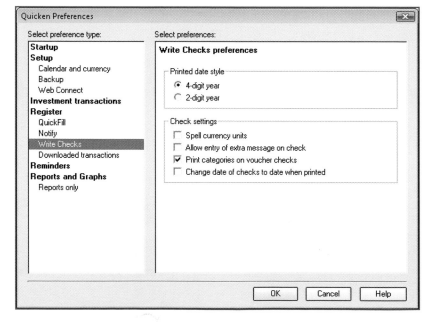

Figure 4-3: Quicken's check-writing options allow you to format checks the way you want.

You can set preferences for transactions you download from financial institutions:

Downloaded transactions preferences

☑ Apply renaming rules to downloaded transactions
   ☑ Automatically create rules when manually renaming
   ☐ Don't display a message when renaming
   [Renaming Rules...]

☑ Capitalize first letter only in downloaded payee names

1. Choose whether to apply renaming rules to downloaded transactions. Renaming rules change the name of a payee on a downloaded transaction, for example, "Grocery 198775" becomes "Corner Grocery" in your register. Renaming rules are discussed further in Chapter 5.

   - Click **Automatically Create Rules When Manually Renaming** to clear the check box. This option will create a renaming rule when you manually change the name of a payee.

   - Click **Don't Display A Message When Renaming** to turn off the automatic message that appears when renaming a downloaded transaction's payee.

   - Click **Renaming Rules** to see any existing rules, add, change, or delete renaming rules.

2. Choose whether to capitalize only the first letters in the payee names you are downloading.

3. Click **OK** to close the dialog box.

![Pushpin icon] **NOTE**

When you click in the Date field, the month is selected, which you can change by typing a new number. To move to the day, press the **RIGHT ARROW** key, and press it again to move to the year. Change the day and year again by typing.

Work with the Register

The register in Quicken looks a lot like the paper check register you may have used in the past. It displays in the color choices you selected in your preferences setup. You can open a register in two ways:

- Click the **Tools** menu, and then click **Account List**. Double-click the name of the account whose register you want to open.

–Or–

- Click the name of the register's account on the Account bar on the left of your Quicken Home page.

Either way, the register opens. Figure 4-4 displays a register window for a checking account.

Enter a Check

To enter a check into the register:

1. If it is not already selected, click in the empty line at the bottom of the **Date** column. By default, this is highlighted a light orange. This activates the transaction line.

2. Accept today's date, type a date using either the numeric keys at the top of the keyboard or the 10-key pad on the right of the keyboard (with **NUMLOCK** activated), or click the small calendar to the right of the field. In the calendar, click the date you want using the arrows in the upper-left and upper-right corners to select a different month.

≪	September – 2006	≫				
Su	Mo	Tu	We	Th	Fr	Sa
					1	2
3	4	5	6	7	8	9
10	11	12	13	14	15	16
17	18	19	20	21	22	23
24	25	26	27	28	29	30

3. Press **TAB** to move to the Num field, or click in the **Num** field. By default, a drop-down list of potential entries will display. Type the check number, if you haven't entered one before, or use the drop-down list by pressing the following keys on your keyboard:

   - Press **N** to move to the next check number if you have been using the check register.

   - Press **A** if you want "ATM" to appear in the Num field.

   - Press **D** if you want "DEP" (for "Deposit") to appear in the Num field.

   - Press **P** if you plan to print this check later and want "Print" to appear in the Num field.

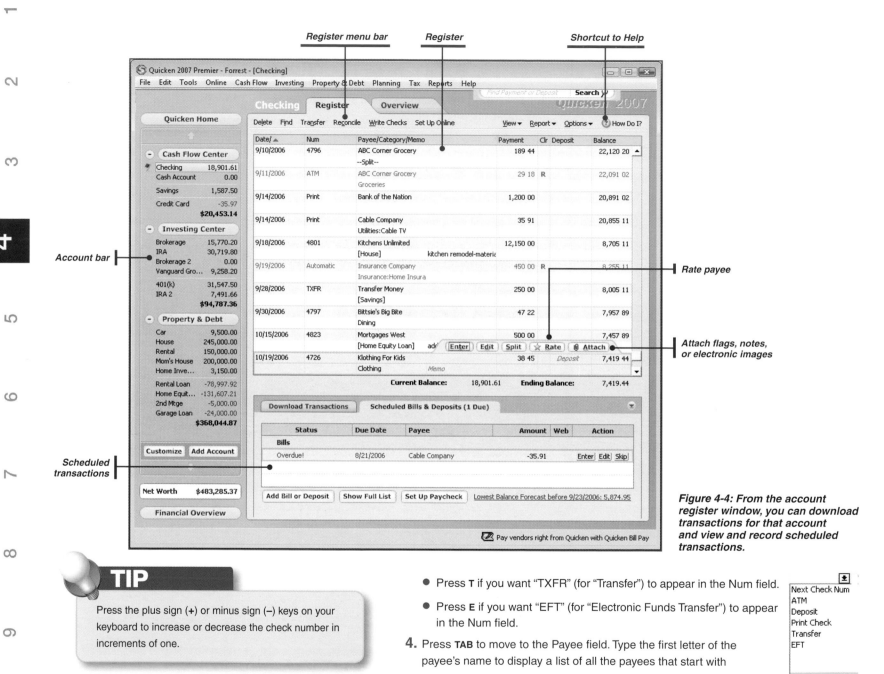

Register menu bar **Register** **Shortcut to Help**

Account bar

Rate payee

Attach flags, notes, or electronic images

Scheduled transactions

Figure 4-4: From the account register window, you can download transactions for that account and view and record scheduled transactions.

● Press **T** if you want "TXFR" (for "Transfer") to appear in the Num field.

● Press **E** if you want "EFT" (for "Electronic Funds Transfer") to appear in the Num field.

4. Press **TAB** to move to the Payee field. Type the first letter of the payee's name to display a list of all the payees that start with

Next Check Num
ATM
Deposit
Print Check
Transfer
EFT

Edit List

that letter. Choose the name you want, or type a new payee name.

5. Press **TAB** to move to the Payment field. Type the amount of the check. You can use either the 10-key pad with **NUMLOCK** activated or the numbers at the top of the keyboard. If you have paid this payee before and have set your preferences to automatically enter it, the amount of the most recent transaction for this payee appears.

Dependable Cleaners	-37.55	Clothing
Downtown Associa...		<Addre...
Dynamic Repair Se...	-59.27	Auto:Se...
Electric Company	-84.37	Utilities:...
Garage Contractor	-25,000.00	[House] new garage
Gas Company	-17.22	Utilities:...

Show Memorized Payee List

6. Press **TAB** to move to the Category field. Type the first letter of the category you want to use. By default, the category you used the last time you paid this payee appears in the Category field. If you want to change the category, click the name in the drop-down list. If the transaction is for more than one category, you can create a split transaction. See "Create a Split Transaction" later in this chapter.

7. Press **TAB** to move to the Memo field. Type any special information, such as an invoice number or what you purchased.

8. Press **ENTER** or click the **Enter** button to complete and save the transaction.

Print Checks with Quicken

Quicken will print checks for you if you have special paper checks for your printer. You can order these checks through your bank, through Quicken, or through third-party companies (do an Internet search on "Quicken checks"). Printing your checks makes them easier to read and potentially saves you time in that you can enter information directly into a check form or print checks already entered into the register. Before you start, you need to load the special paper checks into your printer.

PRINT CHECKS IN THE REGISTER

If you have transactions to print in your register with "Print" in the Num field, you can directly print them instead of entering them into the check form to be printed. When you use the form, however, the information is automatically entered into the register.

1. Click the **File** menu, and then click **Print Checks**. If you do not have transactions in your register with "Print" in the Num field, you will see a message stating that you do

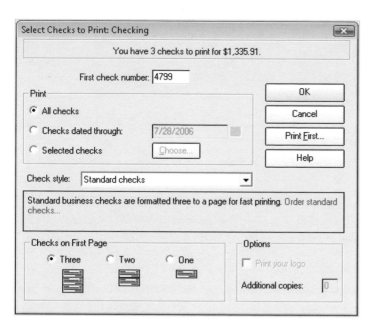

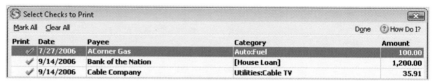

not have any checks to print. If you do have transactions with "Print" in the Num field, the Select Checks To Print dialog box will appear.

2. Enter the number of the first paper check in the printer.

3. Choose which checks to print:

- **All Checks** prints any checks that have not yet been printed. This includes any postdated checks you may have entered.

- **Checks Dated Through** allows you to print unprinted checks through a date you enter or select.

- **Selected Checks** allows you to choose which checks to print. Click **Choose** and clear the check marks for any checks you don't want to print at this time:

Print	Date	Payee	Category	Amount
✓	7/27/2006	ACorner Gas	Auto:Fuel	100.00
✓	9/14/2006	Bank of the Nation	[House Loan]	1,200.00
✓	9/14/2006	Cable Company	Utilities:Cable TV	35.91

- Click **Mark All** to print all of the checks.

- Click **Clear All** to clear all of the listed checks, and then click in the **Print** column just the checks you want to print.

- Click **Done** to close the dialog box and print the checks.

4. Click the **Check Style** down arrow, and choose a style. Depending on the style you are using, click the number of checks on the first page with your style.

5. Click **Print First** to print the first check and see how it looks. Click **OK** if your check printed correctly. Otherwise, enter the check number of the check, and Quicken will reprint it. Make any necessary corrections to how checks are printed.

6. Click **OK** to print all the checks you selected. When the printing is completed, click **OK** if all checks printed correctly. Otherwise, enter the check number of the check on which there was a problem so that Quicken can reprint it.

NOTE

Standard-style checks are normally thought of as business checks, and are 8½ x 3½ inches. Wallet-style checks are normally thought of as personal checks, and are 6 x 2¾ inches.

NOTE

Legislation enacted in 2004, often referred to as "Check 21," means that financial institutions no longer have to retain paper copies of your checks. For more information about Check 21 and how it may affect you, go to http://www.federalreserve.gov/paymentsystems/truncation/faqs.htm.

NOTE

If you create payments in the register with "Print" in the Num field and then click **Write Checks** at the top of the register, the payments you created will appear in the list of checks to print in the Write Checks dialog box.

PRINT CHECKS FROM THE CHECK FORM

If you would like to see a representation of the check you will be sending, Quicken provides a form into which you can enter the information you want on the final printed check, as shown in Figure 4-5. To use the check form:

1. Click **Write Checks** from your register pane. The Write Checks dialog box appears with a blank check displayed that you can fill in.

2. Click in the **Pay To The Order Of** line, or click the down arrow at the end of the line, to display a drop-down list of previous payees.

3. Type as much of the payee's name as needed to select the payee you want, or click the payee you want in the drop-down list.

4. Press **TAB** to move to the Amount field. If you have sent checks to this payee previously, the most recent amount you paid will be filled in. Press **TAB** again to accept the previous amount and move to the Address field. Otherwise, enter the new amount, and then press **TAB**.

Figure 4-5: The Write Checks dialog box gives you a way to visualize the checks you are writing.

5. Type the address, if one is not already attached to the payee. If you want to edit the address, click **Address** to open the Address Book. Make any changes or additions to the address, and click **OK**.

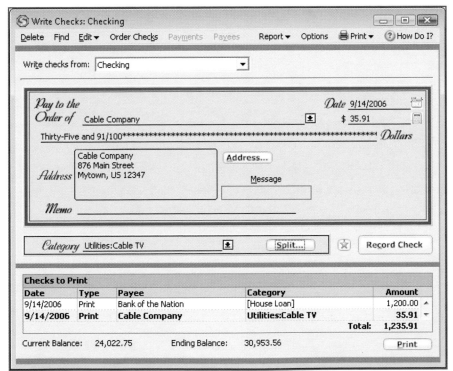

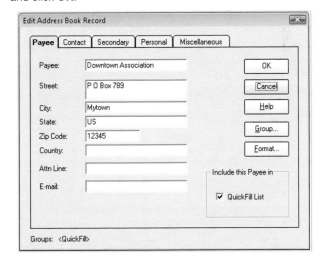

NOTE

If you selected the "Allow Entry Of Extra Message On Check" check box in the Write Check Preferences dialog box, a Message field appears on the check. Because the Memo field can be visible when you use window envelopes, confidential information, such as your account number, can be entered into the Message field rather than the Memo field.

QUICKSTEPS

ENTERING A DEPOSIT

Entering a deposit is like entering a check, except that you enter the amount in the Deposit field rather than the Payment field. To enter a deposit:

1. If it is not already selected, click in the empty line at the bottom of the **Date** column.

2. If you want to change the date, use one of the techniques described in "Enter a Check."

3. Press **TAB** to move to the Num field, and press **D** to have "DEP" placed in the field.

4. Press **TAB** and enter the name of the payer, or select it from the drop-down list that is displayed.

5. Press **TAB** to move to the Deposit field, and enter an amount.

6. Press **TAB** to move to the Category field. Type a category or choose one from the drop-down list.

7. Click **Enter** to complete the transaction.

6. Press **TAB** to move to the Memo field. Type a memo entry, if you want, and press **TAB** again to move to the Category field.

7. Begin to type the category. If there is an existing category starting with the letters you've typed, it will be filled in. Alternatively, you can click the down arrow at the end of the **Category** line, and click the category you want to use.

8. If you want to have portions of the money you are paying go to different categories, click **Split** and follow the instructions in the section "Create a Split Transaction" later in this chapter. Press **TAB** to move to the Rate This Payee field (the small blue star).

9. Click the **Rate This Payee** button (the small blue star) if you want to rate this payee. See "Rate Your Payees" later in this chapter.

10. If you don't want to use the default of today's date, click in the **Date** field, and enter a new date using any of Quicken's date-entering features described in "Enter a Check" earlier in this chapter.

11. When the check looks the way you want it, click **Record Check**. The new check appears on a list of checks to be printed at the bottom of the window, and the check form is once more blank.

12. When you have entered all the checks you want to print, click **Print**. The Select Checks To Print dialog box appears. To continue, see "Print Checks in the Register," and complete the steps in that section (starting with step 2).

Create a New Transaction Category

When you enter a check or a deposit, you can easily create a new category if there isn't one in the Category List that you want to use.

1. Press **TAB** to move to the Category field and automatically open the list of existing categories, or click the **Category** down arrow to open the list.

QUICKSTEPS

CHANGING, VOIDING, OR DELETING A TRANSACTION

From time to time, you may need to edit, or change, a transaction in your check register.

CHANGE A TRANSACTION

1. With the register containing the transaction you want to change displayed, click in any field of the transaction.

2. Type or select from drop-down lists the new or revised information.

3. Click **Enter** or press **ENTER** to save the changes.

VOID A TRANSACTION

You can void any transaction in an account register. Quicken keeps the check number, removes the dollar amount, and inserts ***VOID*** in front of the payee name. If you make a mistake, you can restore the transaction to the way it was originally.

8/9/2006	TXFR	**VOID**Transfer Money		Payment	c	Deposit	27,958 33
		[Savings]					

Enter   Edit   Split   ☆ Rate   📎 Attach

1. With the register containing the transaction you want to void displayed, click the transaction.

2. Click the **Edit** menu on the Quicken menu bar, and click **Transaction**; or click **Edit** in the

Continued . . .

2. Click **Add Cat**. The Set Up Category dialog box appears.

3. Type the name and description of the new category, and select the group you want it in. Press **TAB** to move from field to field.

4. Click **Income** or **Expense** to tell Quicken what type of category this is.

5. Enter the tax-line item if this category has tax implications.

6. Click **OK** to close the dialog box.

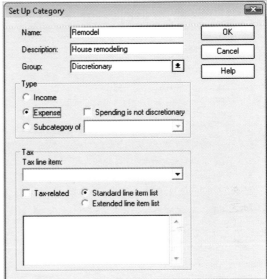

Perform Activities with Check Registers

Not all transactions in your register are as straightforward as a check or a deposit with one category. Some transactions require you to split categories or transfer funds from one account to another. Quicken makes all of these transactions easy to enter. Other activities you may want to perform are locating, sorting, or filtering transactions; attaching check copies or other images to your transactions; rating your payees; and printing your check register.

Create a Split Transaction

A *split* transaction is one that has more than one assigned category. For example, a check you write to the insurance company might be for both homeowners' and automobile insurance, or a deposit might be for both the principal amount of a loan and interest. You can assign up to 30 categories for any single transaction. To enter a split transaction:

1. Click the empty line at the bottom of your register.

CHANGING, VOIDING, OR DELETING A TRANSACTION

(Continued)

transaction toolbar. After either step, click Void Transaction(s). The transaction is voided.

3. If you have not yet pressed **ENTER** or clicked **Enter** and the transaction is still selected, you can restore it by clicking the **Edit** menu on the Quicken menu bar and clicking **Transaction**. Or, you can click **Edit** on the transaction toolbar. After using either of these methods, click **Restore Transaction**.

4. Press **ENTER** or click **Enter** to complete the procedures.

DELETE A TRANSACTION

When you delete a transaction, Quicken recalculates all balances and permanently removes that transaction from the register.

1. With the register containing the transaction you want to delete displayed, click the transaction.

2. Press **CTRL+D** and click **Yes** to delete the transaction.

–Or–

Click the **Edit** menu, click **Transaction**, and click **Delete**.

–Or–

Click **Delete** on the register menu bar.

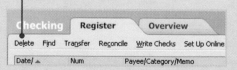

3. The transaction is completely deleted, and your balance is recomputed.

2. Enter the date, check number, payee, and the total amount of the check, as described in "Enter a Check" earlier in this chapter.

3. Click **Split** in the transaction toolbar.

–Or–

Click the Category field drop-down arrow to open the Category list. Click **Split** at the bottom of the list.

In either case, the Split Transaction dialog box appears, as shown in Figure 4-6.

4. The **Category** field on the first line should already be selected. Choose a category from the drop-down list, or type a category. Press **TAB**, type any additional information or notes in the **Memo** field, and again press **TAB**.

5. The total amount of the transaction appears under **Amount** on the first line. Over that amount, type the amount for the first category. Click **Next**.

6. Quicken computes the remainder and shows it in the Amount field of the second line. Enter or select the next category, press **TAB**, enter any information you want in the Memo field, press **TAB** again, and either accept the computed amount or type a new one. Click **Next**.

7. Repeat step 6 until you have all the categories you want. Then click **Next** once more. If you need to adjust any of the entries, click the amount that needs to be adjusted.

8. If the entries are correct and you have a difference, either positive or negative, from the original check amount, click **Adjust** to make the total for the transaction the sum of the split categories.

9. Click **OK** to close the Split Transaction dialog box. Instead of a single category appearing in the Category field, Quicken displays "--Split--" to remind you that there are multiple categories for this transaction.

9/10/2006	4796	ABC Corner Grocery	189 44		31,204 47
		--Split--			

10. Hover your mouse pointer over "--Split--" in the Category field to see the amounts in each split category.

ABC Corner		Groceries	-45.88
--Split--		Auto:Fuel	-39.75
Payee		Repairs	-39.00
--Split--		Personal Care	-29.74
Bank of the		Pet Supplies	-35.07

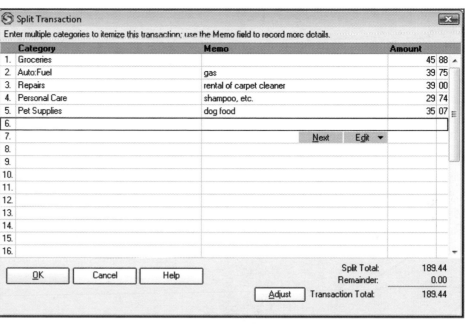

Figure 4-6: Splitting a transaction among multiple categories allows you to refine your accounting and get better control of where your money goes.

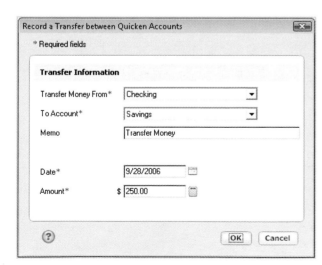

11. Click the transaction and three buttons appear next to "--Split--":

a. Click ✓ to open the Split Transaction dialog box, where you can edit the split.

b. Click ✗ to clear all of the split categories and amounts so that you can replace them with a single new category.

c. Click ▯ to open the Activity dialog box, where you can see the sum of the amounts in the categories used in this transaction.

Transfer Funds from One Account to Another

You can easily record the transfer of funds from one account to another in Quicken. The quickest way is to open the register of the account the money is from. Then:

1. Click **Transfer** on the register's menu bar.

2. Click the **To Account** down arrow, and select the account into which you are transferring the funds.

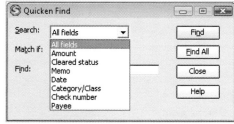

3. Press **TAB** if you want a different description other than the default: "Transfer Money." If so, type that description or edit the current text—for example, <u>To vacation savings</u>.

4. Press **TAB** and enter the date of the transfer if it is different from today's date.

5. Press **TAB** and type the amount.

6. Click **OK** to make the transfer and close the dialog box.

Locate Transactions

There are several ways to find a transaction within Quicken.

1. Click **Find** on the register's menu bar.

    –Or–

Click **Edit** on the transaction toolbar, and then click **Find**.

    –Or–

Press **CTRL+F**.

    –Or–

Click the **Edit** menu on the Quicken menu bar, click **Find & Replace**, and then click **Find**.

In all cases, the Quicken Find dialog box appears.

2. Click the **Search** down arrow to open a list of fields on which to search. Click the field you want to search on.

3. Click the **Match If** down arrow to open a list of expressions to use in the search. Click the expression you want to use.

4. Click in the **Find** text box, and type what you want to find.

5. Click **Find** to select the most recent transaction that matches your criteria. You may see a dialog box asking if you want to continue your search from the end of the register. If so, click **Yes**.

    –Or–

Click **Find All** to open the Search Results dialog box showing all the transactions that match your criteria. Figure 4-7 shows all the transactions containing the word "Bank" in any field.

UICKSTEPS

SORTING TRANSACTIONS

You can sort your transactions by any of the columns in your register except the Balance column. Depending on your choices in Preferences, Quicken can keep the sort column as you have set it or go back to its default of sorting by date.

- Click the column heading to sort by that column. A small triangle appears by the name **Date/ ▲** to indicate that it is the sort column.

- Click **Date** to sort first by date and then by check number. The oldest date is displayed at the top.

- Click **Num** to sort by check number. This places the words, such as "ATM" or "Deposit," first and then sorts the checks numerically, with the smallest check number at the top.

- Click **Payee/Category/Memo** to show payees displayed alphabetically, with "a" at the top.

- Click **Payment** to list payments, with the smallest payment amount at the bottom of the list.

- Click **Clr** to show all reconciled transactions first, and then any unreconciled transactions.

- Click **Deposit** to show the deposits in descending order, with the largest deposits at the top.

- Click **View** on the register menu bar to see additional sort options.

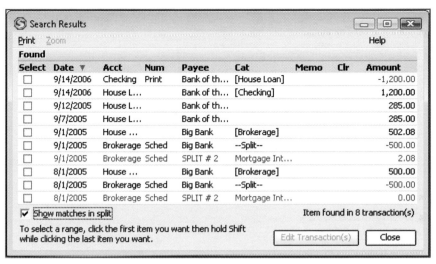

Figure 4-7: Quicken's ability to search transactions allows you to find, for example, all the transactions to a given payee or all transactions over a certain amount.

Filter Transactions for More Information

Quicken can filter the transactions displayed in a register so that only the ones you are interested in are shown. This can help you quickly locate specific information.

1. Click the **View** menu on the register menu bar, and then click **Filter Register View**.
The filter options appear at the top of the register.

2. Click the **View** down arrow to see a list of available filters. **View: All Transactions ▼**

3. Click the **Date** down arrow to narrow your choices to specific periods, like the current month or last quarter, or click **Custom** to enter or select a specific date range.

4. Click the **Close Filter** button to close the Filter toolbar.

NOTE

The manner in which the sort options and direction of sorting is described by Intuit for the Payment and Deposit fields is confusing. When you hover the mouse pointer over the Payment column heading, you get the message "Sort By Amount (Smallest First)." Yet when you do the sort, you get a downward-pointing arrow and the largest payments (leading to the smallest amount in your bank account possibly) are at the top of the register. In the View menu, there is the option "Sort By Amount (Largest First)," which sorts the Deposit field with the largest numbers at the top (leading to the largest amount in your bank account possibly).

NOTE

Filtering just selects the transactions to be viewed and does not sort them. You must do the sorting separately.

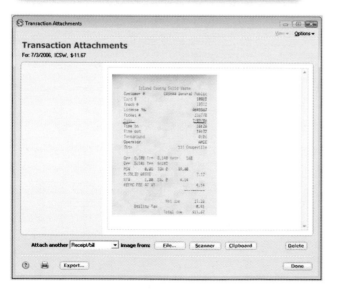

Attach Digital Images to a Transaction

If you use Quicken 2007 Deluxe, Premier, or Home & Business editions, Quicken works with your scanner, Windows Explorer, and the Clipboard in Windows so that you can attach digital images to each transaction in your register. You can attach any type of file that can be viewed in Microsoft Internet Explorer, such as .jpg, .gif, .txt, .html, .pdf, and .png. These attachments are then stored in the same file as your Quicken data. A digital attachment can be a picture of your new snowboard, a receipt for a donation, or any other item you may want to scan or download and keep with your transaction for tax or warranty purposes. You must first bring these items into Quicken and then attach them to a transaction.

ATTACH IMAGES TO TRANSACTIONS

1. Click the **Attach** menu on the transaction toolbar.
2. Click **Attach Electronic Image**.
3. Click the **Check**, **Receipt/Bill**, **Invoice**, **Warranty**, or **Other File** option, depending on the type of attachment you want to use.
4. Click in the **Attach New** field at the bottom of the window to choose the item you want to attach from the drop-down list.
5. Depending on how you intend to acquire the attachment, select one of the following:
   a. Click **File** to attach an image already in your computer.
      i. The Select Attachment File dialog box appears. Locate your file and click **Open**.
      ii. Your image appears on the screen with its default name, such as "Receipt/Bill" or "Invoice."
   b. Click **Scanner** to see the Select Source dialog box. Select the scanner you wish to use to scan the item. Follow the directions for your scanner. The image will appear in the Transaction Attachments window.
   c. Click **Clipboard** to attach an item you have copied to your Clipboard. The item appears in the Transaction Attachments window. For more information on using the Clipboard in Windows, see "Using the Clipboard in Windows" QuickSteps in this chapter.
6. Click **Done** when you have finished attaching documents.
7. A small attachment icon appears beneath the transaction's date.

QUICKSTEPS

USING THE CLIPBOARD IN WINDOWS

Microsoft Windows XP and other Windows operating systems have some handy keyboard shortcuts to capture on-screen images. An example of an on-screen image might be a scanned deposit slip from your bank's Web site. To capture this image directly from your screen:

1. Press the **PRINT SCREEN** button, usually located on the upper-right area of your keyboard, to capture the entire screen as shown on your monitor.

2. Hold down the **ALT** button, usually located on either side of the **SPACEBAR**, and press the **PRINT SCREEN** button to capture a copy of the active window.

3. Either action will put the image on the Clipboard in Windows.

4. Use the **Clipboard** button in the Transaction Attachment view to attach your captured image to a transaction.

ADD A FOLLOW-UP FLAG OR NOTE TO A TRANSACTION

1. Click the **Attach** menu on the transaction toolbar.

2. Click **Add Follow-Up Flag** or **Add Note**. Choosing either will cause the Transaction Notes And Flags dialog box to appear:

   a. Type any notes you want as part of this transaction. Press **TAB** after you have completed typing your notes.

   b. Click **Flag This Transaction** if you need to mark the transaction. Choose the color of the flag from the drop-down list.

   c. Click the **Alert For Follow-Up On** option, and enter a date to have this transaction appear on your Alert List in the selected day on the Quicken Home page.

3. Click **OK** to close the dialog box. A small flag appears beneath the date of the transaction.

Rate Your Payees

Did you ever want to tell the world about a really great deal or wonderful service at a local store? Quicken now has a service, called Zipingo, that allows you to do just that, anonymously and quickly. The Zipingo service allows all Quicken users in the United States to rate their experiences at any business by clicking the blue star ⭐ Rate in the lower-right area of a transaction or in the Write Checks dialog box and answering some questions. To use this service:

1. Click in or enter a transaction you wish to rate, and click the **Rate This Payee** blue star icon.

   –Or–

   With the transaction selected, click the **Edit** menu, and click **Rate This Payee**.

   In either case, the first time you try rating a payee, you will see a message about Zipingo and how it works. Click Try It! The Rate It! dialog box will appear.

2. Click in the **Payee Name** field, and type the name, if it does not appear. Press **TAB** and type either the ZIP code or the city and state of the company you are rating.

3. Click the number of stars you are awarding—one for poor and five for excellent.

4. Press **TAB** and type any comments about the transaction you want others to know.

5. Click the verification that you or anyone in your family do not work for nor compete with this business.

6. Click **Preview My Rating** to ensure that you have completed each required field, review the rating, and make any necessary changes.

7. Click **Don't Display Payment Range** if you don't want that information to be displayed on your rating.

8. Click **Continue** or click **Change My Comments** to change the comments you have written.

9. The Check Address dialog box appears. If your payee is included on the list, click its option button. Otherwise, click **None Of These**. Your review will still appear on the Web site. Click **OK** to continue.

10. The Sign In dialog box appears. You are prompted to either create a Zipingo name or sign in with one you have already created. Create a name if you don't already have one, and press **TAB**.

11. Enter your e-mail address and ZIP code as required.

12. Press **Continue** to open the next dialog box.

13. Your review screen appears as it will be published on the Zipingo Web site. Click **Add New Comments** if you want to change what you have written, or click **Close Browser** to return to Quicken.

Set Up Your Printer and Print a Register

As you continue to work with Quicken, you may want to print a register. Before you do, you may need to set up your printer to print reports or graphs.

SET UP YOUR PRINTER

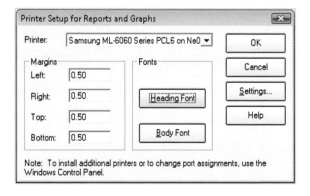

1. Click the **File** menu, click **Printer Setup**, and click **For Reports/Graphs**. The Printer Setup For Reports And Graphs dialog box appears.

2. Click the **Printer** down arrow to show a list of your printers, and click the one you want to set up.

3. Click in each of the margin text boxes you want to change, and type the new margin.

4. Click **Heading Font** to change the font, font style, and size. Click the name of the font, the style, and the size from their respective lists, and then click **OK**.

5. Click **Body Font** and repeat step 4. The choices you make will be used with all of the reports or graphs you print on this printer.

6. Click **OK** to close the Printer Setup dialog box.

Print Register dialog box

Print Register

Title: Check Register Aug-Sept 2006

Print Transactions From: 8/1/2006
To: 9/30/2006

Options

☑ Print Split Transactions

[Print...] [Cancel] [Help]

PRINT A REGISTER

1. With the register you want to print open, click the **File** menu, and click **Print Register**.

   –Or–

   Press **CTRL+P**.

2. Type a title for the report. The name of the account appears on the report by default.

3. Select a time period for which you want to display the transactions.

4. Clear the **Print Split Transactions** option if you do not want the multiple categories in your split transaction to be included on the report (it is cleared by default).

5. Click **Print** to print the report. In the Print dialog box that appears, make any needed changes, and click **OK**.

Use Other Cash Flow Center Registers

When you first open the register for a credit card account, its appearance is much like a check register. However, there are a few differences that you should recognize, as described in Table 4-2.

ENTER A CREDIT CARD CHARGE, FINANCE CHARGE, OR CREDIT

If you are familiar with entering checks into your checking account register, the process is similar in your credit card register.

> **NOTE**
>
> Only you can decide whether or not you need a printed copy of your check register. If you back up your information on a regular basis, you may never need one. You might consider printing one at year-end and filing it with your tax information.

CHECK REGISTERS	CREDIT CARD REGISTERS
Date: The date of the transaction.	**Date**: The date of the transaction.
Num: The check number or an alphabetic description of the transaction. There is a drop-down list to assist you in choosing.	**Ref**: The type of transaction, such as charge, payment, or finance charge. There is no drop-down list.
Payee/Category/Memo: The person or organization paid and its category. Drop-down lists are available for payees and categories.	**Payee/Category/Memo**: The person or organization paid and its category. Drop-down lists are available for payees and categories.
Payment: The amount of the check, charge, or deposit. There is a calculator available if you need it.	**Charge**: The amount of the charge, payment, or fee. There is a calculator available if you need it.
Clr: Whether a transaction has appeared on a statement from your financial institution and has been cleared.	**Clr**: Whether a transaction has appeared on a statement from your financial institution and has been cleared.
Deposit: The amount that has been deposited into this account. A calculator is available if you need it.	**Payment**: The amount you have paid on this credit card. A calculator is available if you need it.
Balance: The amount of money you have in this account after entering all of your deposits and checks.	**Balance**: The amount of money you owe on this credit card after entering all of your charges and payments.

Table 4-2: Differences Between Checking and Credit Card Registers

1. Click the credit card account in the Account bar to open that card's register. The empty transaction line at the bottom of the register should be selected.

2. If it isn't already selected and you want to change the date, click in the **Date** column, and used the date-picking techniques described in step 2 of "Enter a Check" earlier in this chapter.

3. Press **TAB** to move to the **Ref** column, and type a description of the transaction.

4. Press **TAB** or click **Payee**, and enter the name of the business.

5. Press **TAB** or click **Charge**, and enter the amount of the charge.

6. Press **TAB** or click **Category**, and select from the drop-down list or type the category.

7. Press **TAB** or click **Memo**, and enter any identifying information, such as <u>Dinner with Meg and Jack</u> or <u>School clothes for Sally</u>.

8. Click **Enter** or press **ENTER** to complete the transaction.

WORK WITH A CASH ACCOUNT REGISTER

Creating an account to track your cash spending can be useful. It is a great learning tool for young people to track where they spend their money. You can enter data each time money is spent or add information in bulk at the end of each week or month. Many people who use this type of account enter only whole-dollar amounts. Use the same procedures described earlier in "Enter a Check."

1. Create a cash account, as described in Chapter 2. Open that account's register, and, if it isn't already selected, click in the empty transaction line.

2. If needed, change the date, press **TAB**, type a description in the **Ref** column, and select or type a payee to identify the transaction.

3. Enter the amount spent in the **Spend** column or the amount received in the **Receive** column.

4. Click **Enter** or press **ENTER** to complete the transaction.

TIP

A credit card payment is easily made in one of your checking account registers. Simply identify the credit card you want paid in the Category field of the check using one of the "Transfer To/From" categories. When you go back into the credit card register, the amount of the payment and the checking account from which it was paid appear on the next transaction line.

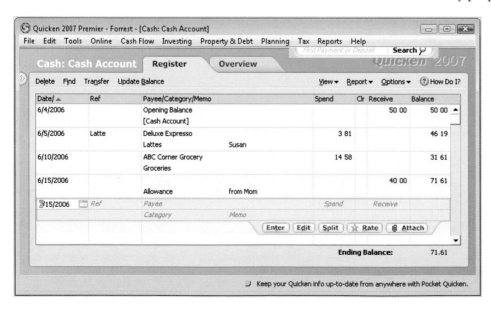

Chapter 5
Taking Control with Quicken

After using Quicken to enter your day-to-day transactions, you may want to step up to the next level and start using more of the features Quicken provides to help you save time as you manage your finances. Quicken can even alert you to recurring bills you forgot to pay! In this chapter you will learn how to automate Quicken, memorize payees, schedule transactions, use the Calendar, automate transactions or schedule your bills online, create reports, and produce useful graphs from accounts in your Cash Flow Center.

Memorize Your Entries

When you set your preferences (see Chapter 4), you told Quicken how to use QuickFill to make data entry faster and whether to automatically update new payees. You might recall that one choice was to automatically memorize new payees and then recall them when you next entered them. Whether or not you chose to have Quicken do this, you can also memorize transactions and payees manually.

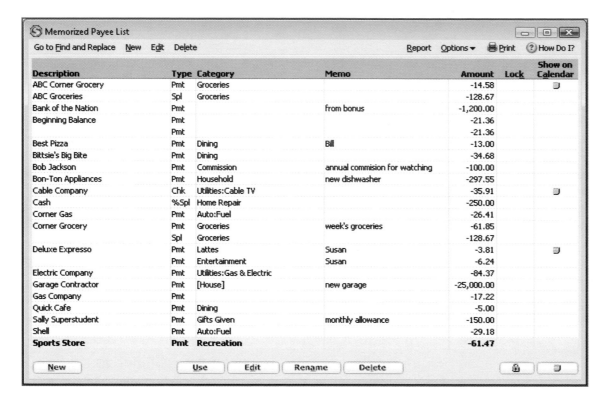

Description	Type	Category	Memo	Amount	Lock	Show on Calendar
ABC Corner Grocery	Pmt	Groceries		-14.58		▣
ABC Groceries	Spl	Groceries		-128.67		
Bank of the Nation	Pmt		from bonus	-1,200.00		
Beginning Balance	Pmt			-21.36		
	Pmt			-21.36		
Best Pizza	Pmt	Dining	Bill	-13.00		
Bittsie's Big Bite	Pmt	Dining		-34.68		
Bob Jackson	Pmt	Commission	annual commision for watching	-100.00		
Bon-Ton Appliances	Pmt	Household	new dishwasher	-297.55		
Cable Company	Chk	Utilities:Cable TV		-35.91		▣
Cash	%Spl	Home Repair		-250.00		
Corner Gas	Pmt	Auto:Fuel		-26.41		
Corner Grocery	Pmt	Groceries	week's groceries	-61.85		
	Spl	Groceries		-128.67		
Deluxe Expresso	Pmt	Lattes	Susan	-3.81		▣
	Pmt	Entertainment	Susan	-6.24		
Electric Company	Pmt	Utilities:Gas & Electric		-84.37		
Garage Contractor	Pmt	[House]	new garage	-25,000.00		
Gas Company	Pmt			-17.22		
Quick Cafe	Pmt	Dining		-5.00		
Sally Superstudent	Pmt	Gifts Given	monthly allowance	-150.00		
Shell	Pmt	Auto:Fuel		-29.18		
Sports Store	**Pmt**	**Recreation**		**-61.47**		

Figure 5-1: The Memorized Payee List lets you create, edit, use, rename, and delete your memorized payees.

Create a Memorized Payee

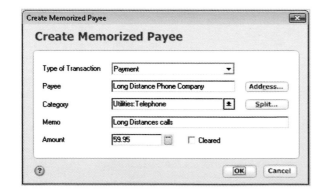

Memorizing saves you valuable data-entry time. Use the Memorized Payee List, shown in Figure 5-1, to create a memorization.

1. Click the **Cash Flow** menu, and click **Memorized Payee List** to display the list.

    –Or–

    Press **CTRL+T**.

2. Click **New** on the menu bar. The Create Memorized Payee dialog box appears.

NOTE

The Address button in the Create Memorized Transaction dialog box opens the Edit Address Book Record only when you select Print Check as the transaction type.

CAUTION

When a payee and amount are memorized by Quicken, the amount is automatically "locked" on the Memorized Payee List. If the amount of your payment varies each time you pay it, you can "unlock" the item. (See the "Locking a Memorized Payee" QuickSteps elsewhere in this chapter.)

NOTE

You can delete any transaction from a register by selecting it and pressing **CTRL+D**.

TIP

You can use your keyboard to access any menu item. Use the ALT key plus the underlined letter in the item to open the menu item.

---

3. Click the **Type Of Transaction** down arrow to choose the transaction type.

4. Press TAB and type the name of the payee in the Payee field.

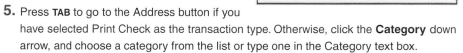

5. Press TAB to go to the Address button if you have selected Print Check as the transaction type. Otherwise, click the **Category** down arrow, and choose a category from the list or type one in the Category text box.

6. Press TAB to open the Split dialog box if this is a transaction with several categories. Otherwise, enter any memo item you want to appear on the payment.

7. Press TAB to move to the next field, and type an amount if you pay the same amount each time.

Change Memorized Payees

You can work with the Memorized Payee List in several ways. As you look at the list shown in Figure 5-1, you see the menu bar at the top of the list, as well as the buttons on the bottom of the list. Some of the things you can do with the Memorized Payee List include:

- If your Memorized Payee List isn't already displayed, press **CTRL+T**. Then click **New** on either the menu bar or using the buttons at the bottom to create a new memorized transaction.

- Click **Go To Find And Replace** on the menu bar to find an existing transaction and replace any of its information.

- Choose any payee on the list, and click **Edit** on either the menu bar or at the bottom of the screen to make changes to existing information.

- Select any payee and click **Delete** on either the menu bar or using the button at the bottom of the screen, to delete that payee. A dialog box appears prompting you to confirm this action. Click **OK**.

- Click the **Use** button at the bottom of the page to use the memorized payee as the next transaction in your current Cash Flow Account register.

Use Renaming Rules for Downloaded Transactions

When banks assign a payee name to a transaction, they may not use the name you want in your check register. Quicken allows you to establish renaming rules so that these transactions can be matched. You can add renaming rules from the Memorized Payee List or from the Quicken Preferences dialog box.

ADD RENAMING RULES FROM THE MEMORIZED PAYEE LIST

1. Click the **Cash Flow** menu, and click **Memorized Payee List**.

   –Or–

   Click **CTRL+T**.

   In either case, the Memorized Payee List appears.

2. Click the name of one or more payees that you want to rename. To choose multiple names and rename them with the same name, hold down the **CTRL** key while clicking them. This method allows you to fix several entries to the same payee with different spellings. For example, you may have entered J. Jameson and John Jameson for the same payee. You can create one payee—John L. Jameson—with this method.

3. Click **Rename** at the bottom of the window. Type the name in the New Name field. If you want to create a renaming rule for a downloaded transaction using this name, click that option and click **OK**. The Edit Renaming Rule dialog box appears.

4. Make any changes to the rule, and, if needed, click **Add New Item** to add additional names that should be renamed using this renaming rule. Click **OK** to close the Edit Renaming Rule dialog box and close the Memorized Payee List.

ADD RENAMING RULES FROM QUICKEN PREFERENCES

Quicken Preferences allow you to add a renaming rule when you don't have a current memorized name to work with.

1. Click the **Edit** menu, click **Preferences**, and click **Quicken Program**.

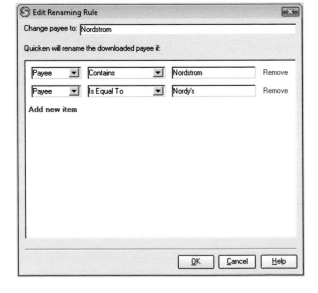

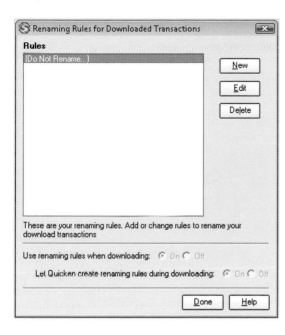

These are your renaming rules. Add or change rules to rename your download transactions

2. Click **Downloaded Transactions** and then click **Renaming Rules**. The Renaming Rules For Downloaded Transactions dialog box appears.

3. Click **New**. The Create Renaming Rule dialog box appears. Enter the new payee name and the name or names that should be renamed to that name. Then click **OK** to return to the Renaming Rules For Downloaded Transactions dialog box.

4. If you do not want Quicken to use these rules when downloading, click **Off** when prompted. The default is On.

5. If you do not want Quicken to create renaming rules when downloading, click the **Off** option by that direction as well.

6. Click **Done** to close the Renaming Rules For Downloaded Transactions dialog box, and then click **OK** to close Quicken Preferences.

Create and Memorize a Split Transaction Using Percentages

When you create a split transaction, there may be times when you want to use a percentage and have Quicken calculate an amount rather than entering the specific dollar amount for each category. To create such a memorized transaction:

1. Open the Cash Flow Account register that will contain the transaction, and enter the date, number or reference, payee, and total amount as you normally would.

2. Click **Split** on the Transaction toolbar.

   –Or–

   Click in the **Category** field, and click **Split**.

   In either case, the Split Transaction dialog box appears, as shown in Figure 5-2.

3. Click the **Category** down arrow, and select a category. Press **TAB**, enter a memo or description if you choose, and press **TAB** again.

4. In the **Amount** field, which contains the total amount, replace the existing amount by typing a percentage as a number followed by the percent (%) sign. Quicken automatically calculates the dollar amount for the category by multiplying the total amount of the transaction times the percentage and then displays the balance on the next line. For example, if the check is for $200.00 and you type 75% on the first line, the amount displayed on the first line will be $150.00 and $50.00 will be displayed on the second line.

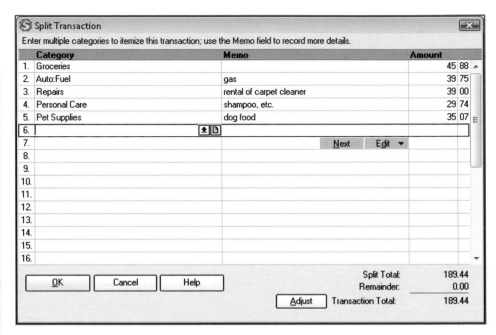

LOCKING A MEMORIZED PAYEE

If you choose to automatically memorize new payees in Quicken Preferences, each time you use a memorized payee, the transaction amount associated with that payee is updated. You can lock a memorized payee transaction so that the transaction amount won't change if you enter a transaction with a different amount for that payee. For example, let's say you send your daughter in college, Sally Superstudent, an allowance of $150 per month for spending money and have locked that transaction. If you send her a birthday check for $250, the locked transaction will not change. If you do not lock it, the new memorized payee amount will be $250. To lock a transaction that is already in the Memorized Payee List:

1. Click the **Cash Flow** menu, and click **Memorized Payee List**.

2. Click in the **Lock** column of the relevant transaction to lock the amount. The small lock icon is displayed.

   –Or–

   Select the transaction you want to lock, and click the **Lock** button at the bottom of the Memorized Payee List.

Sally Superstudent	Pmt	Gifts Given	monthly allowance	-150.00	🔒

3. Click **Close** to close the list.

You can unlock a transaction in the same way. When a transaction is unlocked and your preferences are set to automatically memorize new payees, the next time you enter a transaction for this payee, the new amount is memorized.

Figure 5-2: *The Split Transaction dialog box allows you to assign multiple categories to one transaction by either dollar amount or percentages.*

5. Press **TAB** to move to the next line, and repeat steps 3 and 4.

6. Click **OK** to apply the split and close the window.

7. Click **Edit** and then click **Memorize Payee** (or press **CTRL+M**) to memorize the transaction. A dialog box asks if you want to memorize the split payees as a percentage. If so, click **Yes**. Then click **OK** to complete the memorization.

Create a Schedule

Most of us have bills we pay every month. Your list may seem endless, with utility bills, rent or mortgage payments, property tax payments, and so on. Quicken's Scheduled Transaction feature helps you automate the process. You can select and schedule all recurring transactions so that you don't accidentally overlook a regular payment. Quicken can even enter them automatically. You can set up reminders or record transactions several days earlier than they are actually due to remind yourself to put money in the bank to cover them. You can set up your paycheck using Quicken Paycheck Setup to keep track of your gross wages and deductions to help with tax planning. (See Chapters 9 and 10 for information on taxes and budgeting.)

Understand Scheduled Transactions

Quicken has two types of scheduled transactions: recurring transactions, such as insurance or mortgage payments, and one-time transactions, such as the balance due on the new deck you're having built. You can also create a scheduled transaction to be paid later online. Other scheduled transactions can include:

- Income
  - Paychecks
  - Alimony or child-support payments
  - Social Security or retirement checks
- Payments
  - Mortgage or rent payments
  - Car payments
  - Health and other insurance payments
  - Taxes
  - Membership dues

Find Recurring Transactions

Quicken helps you find transactions you pay on a recurring basis to let you determine if they should be paid on a regular schedule. Use this feature to ensure that you've paid all your recurring bills each month.

1. Click the **Cash Flow** menu, and click **Go To Cash Flow Center**.

2. Scroll to the **Scheduled Bills & Deposits** section at the bottom of the screen.

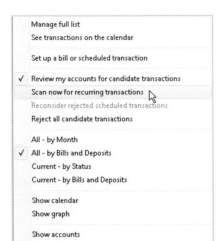

3. Click the **Show** down arrow, and click **All - By Bills And Deposits**.

4. Click **Options** to the right of the Scheduled Bills & Deposits title bar, and click **Scan Now For Recurring Transactions**. A dialog box appears stating that a list of transactions is listed at the bottom of Scheduled Bills & Deposits. Click **OK** to close the dialog box.

5. Scroll to the bottom of the list. Click the **Yes** button for each bill you want to include as a scheduled transaction, or click the **No** button if you don't want it included in the list.

Schedule These?				
	10/10/2006	Jack Fisherman	-156.25	Yes No
	3/1/2007	Balancing Cash Adjustment	1,071.87	Yes No
Add Bill or Deposit	Show Full List	Set Up Paycheck		Show Full Calendar

If you click **Yes** for a bill you want scheduled, the Edit All Future Transactions dialog box will appear so that you can make any changes you want to the transaction. Click **OK** when finished.

If you click **No** for a bill, you will be asked to confirm that decision by clicking **OK**.

If a newly scheduled transaction causes you to exceed your budget, you will be notified of that and given the opportunity to update your budget. (See Chapter 9 for a discussion of budgeting.)

Schedule a Transaction

You can schedule payments and deposits at any time.

1. Click **Add Bill Or Deposit** at the bottom of the Scheduled Bills & Deposits tab of the Quicken Home page.

–Or–

Click **Cash Flow** on the Quicken menu bar, and click **Scheduled Transaction List**. The Bills & Deposits dialog box will appear. Click **Create New** on the menu bar, and then click **Scheduled Transaction** to display the Add Scheduled Transaction dialog box, as shown in Figure 5-3.

NOTE

You may see a dialog box stating that Quicken did not find any recurring transactions other than the ones you already have scheduled or rejected in the past. If so, click **OK** to return to the Cash Flow Center.

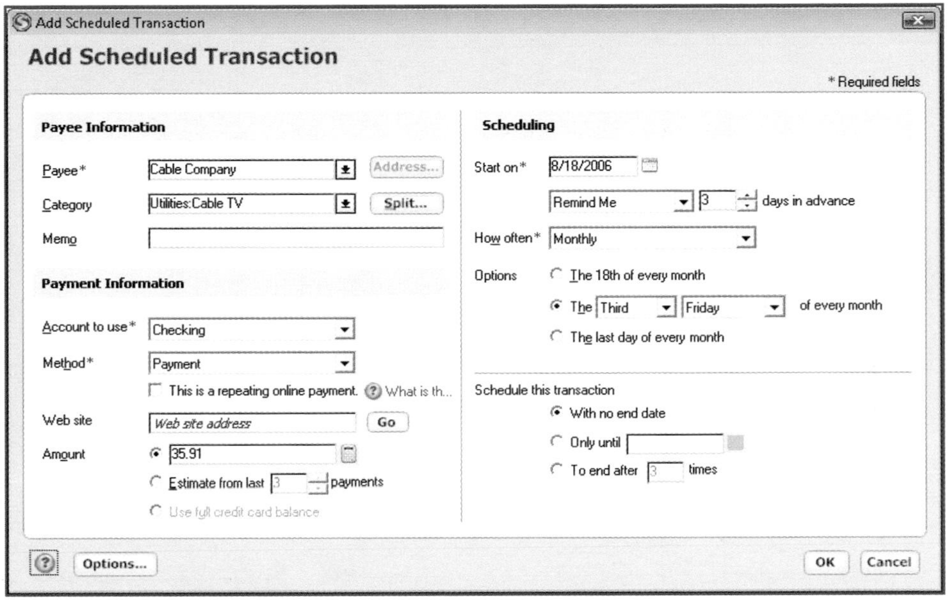

Figure 5-3: The Add Scheduled Transaction dialog box lets you determine how and when to pay your bills.

2. Click in the **Payee** text box to enter the name of the company (or person) that you are paying or, in the case of a deposit, who pays you. Press **TAB**.

3. If you pay with a printed check, you can use the Address button to enter an address. Press **SPACEBAR** or click **Address** to open the Address Book, and then enter the information. Click **OK** to close the dialog box, and press **TAB** to continue.

4. Type the category name in the Category field or click the down arrow to choose one from the drop-down list. Press **TAB**.

5. Click **Split** if this transaction is divided into several categories, such as your house payment with principal, interest, and insurance. Enter the appropriate data, and then click **OK**. Press **TAB** to continue.

6. Enter any memo information you want to appear on each check, such as an account or contract number. Press **TAB**.

7. Enter the account from which you want to pay or, in the case of a deposit, the account into which the money is to be deposited. Press **TAB**.

8. Enter the method by which you pay this bill, or choose one from the drop-down list. Press **TAB**.

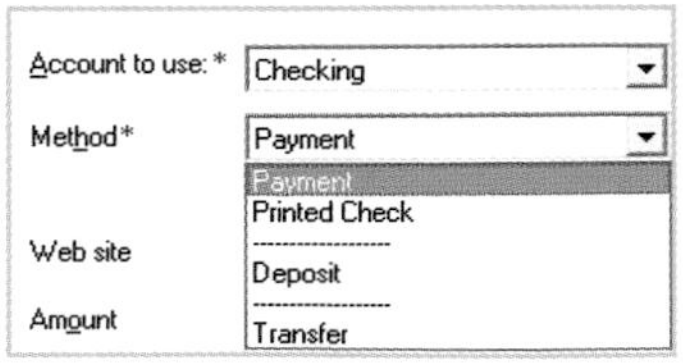

9. Enter the Web site address of your payee, if you choose. (You can click **Go** to use your Internet connection to connect to that Web site.) Press **TAB** if you clicked Go, or press it twice if you didn't.

10. You have several choices for specifying the amount of the payment or deposit:

   - Enter the amount if it is the same each time. You can type <u>0</u> and Quicken will prompt you each time for the amount. This works well for bills you pay regularly that are not the same amount, such as your telephone bill.

     –Or–

   - Click **Estimate From Last ... Payments** if you want Quicken to determine the amount of this bill based on the number of payments you determine. You will always be able to edit the check when you actually enter it to be paid.

     –Or–

   - Click **Use Full Credit Card Balance** if you want Quicken to compute your credit card balance from your downloaded transactions and make the payment amount equal to that.

11. Press **TAB** and enter the date on which this payment starts. You can also use the small calendar icon on the right side of the date field to choose the date. Press **TAB**.

12. Click the **Remind Me** down arrow to tell Quicken whether to remind you to enter the transaction or to automatically enter it. Press **TAB** and enter the number of days in advance of the payment you want to be reminded or the number of days before the payment will be made. Press **TAB**.

13. Select how often this transaction occurs in the Frequency field. The default is **Monthly**, but you have other choices, as shown in Table 5-1. Press **TAB**.

14. Choose how the date of the next payment is to be calculated. Your choices are:

   - The day of the month of the start payment date

   - The day of the week of the start payment date

   - The last day of the month

15. Your last option is to set the schedule for this transaction:

   - Click **With no end date** to have the transaction occur forever.

   - Click **Only Until** and enter the ending date for this transaction.

   - Click **To End After**, and enter the number of times this transaction will be repeated.

16. Click **OK** to close the dialog box and return to the Cash Flow Center.

QUICKFACTS

UNDERSTANDING SCHEDULED TRANSACTION METHODS

Quicken provides nine different methods for completing a scheduled transaction. These methods are based on the type of account the transaction affects and what version of Quicken you use, so not all choices are available for every transaction.

OUTGOING TRANSACTIONS

Scheduled disbursements can be used in all types of accounts. The methods for completing outgoing transactions vary, depending on the type of account, whether it is enabled for download, and so forth. These methods are:

- **Payment** is used by Quicken for all transactions that pay money out of an account without using printed checks, including handwritten checks and direct charges, such as the deduction for your annual safe-deposit box fee.

- **Printed Check** is a check that is printed with Quicken.

- **Online Payment From Quicken** is the option you select when you use an online bill-paying service through your financial institution or Quicken Bill Pay. You can repeat this online payment automatically.

- **Business Bill** schedules a regular bill, such as rent or telephone, when you use Quicken Home & Business edition.

INCOMING TRANSACTIONS

The methods for completing incoming transactions are:

- **Deposit** is used by Quicken to indicate any transaction that puts money into an account.

Continued . . .

FREQUENCY FOR SCHEDULED TRANSACTION	EXPLANATION
Only Once	This is for transactions that will only happen once, such as an upcoming balloon or final payment.
Weekly	Use this if the transaction occurs every week. Quicken uses the starting date of the transaction to determine which day of the week it will occur. With all frequencies other than Only Once, you have the option to set the date on which this transaction will end, the number of times it will occur, or no ending date.
Every Two Weeks Every Four Weeks	You have the same options as with the Weekly occurrence. The transaction repeats every two or four weeks from the start date.
Twice A Month	You tell Quicken on which two days each month to schedule this transaction.
Monthly	This is the default setting, since most recurring transactions happen monthly. You can designate a specific date or a specific day, such as the third Tuesday of each month.
Every Two Months	This option repeats the transaction bimonthly from the originally scheduled date. This frequency is often used for utility payments.
Quarterly	Use this if you have something that occurs every three months, such as estimated income tax payments.
Twice A Year	This option allows you to choose two days per year on which to schedule the transaction. Auto insurance and property tax payments are often paid twice each year.
Yearly	This option is for annual payments. You can set a specific date, such as August 10 or the second Wednesday of August.
Estimated Taxes	You can schedule four equal payments on your selected dates when you choose this option.
Variable Weeks	This option lets you schedule the transaction every set number of weeks. For example, if you choose to save $100 every 7 weeks on Tuesday, you would select this option.
Variable Months	This option repeats the transaction every specified number of months. You have the same day and date choices as you do for the Monthly option.

Table 5-1: Choices for the Frequency of Scheduled Transactions

UNDERSTANDING SCHEDULED TRANSACTION METHODS

(Continued)

- **Transfer** is the method used when you move funds from one account to another, for example, from your checking account to your savings account each month.

- **Interest** is the method used when recording a repeating payment of interest, such as from a security.

- **Dividend** is used when you are scheduling a transaction in an Investment Center account.

- **Invoice** is a method available to users of Quicken Home & Business edition that allows you to schedule invoices that are billed to your customers on a regular basis.

Create a Scheduled Transaction

You can create a scheduled transaction directly from a transaction in a register or by opening the Scheduled Transaction List.

SCHEDULE A TRANSACTION FROM ITSELF

1. With a register open, right-click the transaction you want to memorize to display a context menu.

2. Click **Schedule Bill Or Deposit**. The Add Scheduled Transaction dialog box appears, as shown earlier in Figure 5-3. Follow the instructions under "Schedule a Transaction" earlier in this chapter.

USE THE ADD SCHEDULED TRANSACTION OPTIONS

In the Add Scheduled Transaction dialog box, you have several options for your transactions.

1. Click **Options** in the lower-left corner to display the Add Scheduled Transaction Options dialog box.

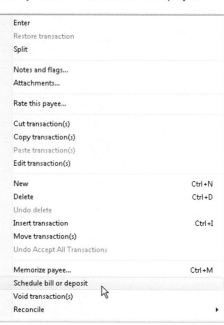

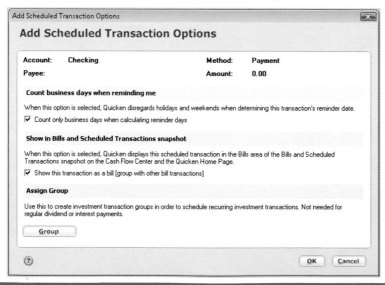

2. Click **Count Only Business Days When Calculating Reminder Days** if you want Quicken to ignore weekends and holidays when determining which day to remind you about a scheduled transaction.

3. Clear **Show This Transaction As A Bill** if you do not want Quicken to display this transaction in the Bills And Scheduled Transactions area on both the Cash Flow Center and Quicken Home page.

4. Click **Group** to assign a group to an investment transaction. *"Group"* is a term used by Quicken to help you track your expenses. Quicken provides three by default: Discretionary, Income, and Mandatory Expenses. You can create your own groups. See Chapter 8 for more information about investment groups.

5. Click **OK** to return to the Create Scheduled Transaction dialog box.

Use the Calendar

Sometimes, it's helpful to see events on a calendar to reinforce them in your mind. The Calendar in Quicken lets you see at a glance your financial events for each month, as shown in Figure 5-4.

1. Press **CTRL+K**.

–Or–

Click the **Tools** menu, and then click **Calendar**.

–Or–

Click the **Cash Flow** menu, and then click **Calendar**.

In all instances, the Calendar window opens.

2. Click the arrows to the left and right of the month on the menu bar to move between months. The current month is displayed by default.

3. In the **Go To Date** text box, type a date or click the calendar icon on the menu bar to open a small calendar from which

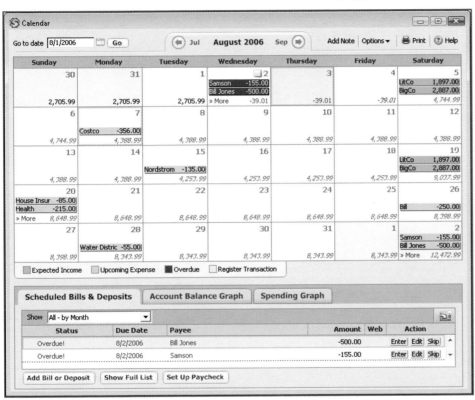

Figure 5-4: *Quicken's Calendar helps you organize your financial transactions.*

you can select any specific date you want to view. Use the right and left arrows to go to other months. Click **Go** to display that date in the large calendar.

NOTE

You can also double-click any Calendar date to display the Transactions Due: *this date* dialog box.

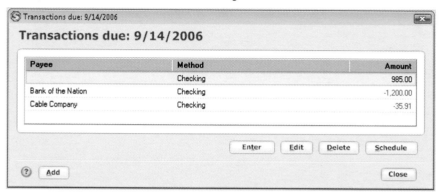

NOTE

The Enter Transaction dialog box displays the current balance in this account as well as the balance after the transaction you are entering.

WORK WITH SPECIFIC DATES

To work with a specific date:

1. Right-click the date on the Calendar to display a context menu. Click **Transactions** to display the Transactions Due: *this date* dialog box:

Payee	Method	Amount
	Checking	985.00
Bank of the Nation	Checking	-1,200.00
Cable Company	Checking	-35.91

a. Click **Add** to display the Add Transaction dialog box. This dialog box is similar to the Scheduled Transactions dialog box, except it asks if you would like to schedule or enter this transaction. If this is a one-time transaction, click **No, I Would Like To Enter It**. If you want to schedule this transaction, click **Yes, I Would Like To Schedule This Transaction**, fill in the applicable transaction fields, and click **OK** when you are finished.

b. Click **Enter** to enter a scheduled transaction into the register for that day. The Enter Transaction dialog box appears. Fill in the applicable fields, and click **Enter Transaction** when you are finished.

c. Click **Edit** to edit a scheduled transaction. The Edit All Future Transactions dialog box appears. This dialog box requires the same information as the Create A Scheduled Transaction dialog box (see "Create a Scheduled Transaction" earlier in this chapter). Click an existing transaction, and click **Edit** to change it for the future. Make the needed changes, and click **OK** to close the dialog box.

d. Click **Skip** to skip this scheduled transaction for this month.

e. Click **Close** to close the Transactions Due: *this date* dialog box.

2. Click **Note** on the context menu to add a reminder note to the date. The Add Note dialog appears:

a. Type the note you want on that date.

NOTE

To delete a note from a specific date, right-click the date on the Calendar, click **Note**, and then click **Delete Note**

NOTE

You can also add a note to a specific date from the **Add Note** menu choice on the Calendar menu bar. This option adds a note to the current (today's) date, which is the default date on the Calendar.

CAUTION

Each date can hold only one note; however, you can combine several reminders into one note.

NOTE

You can also choose which accounts to display on the Calendar from the Calendar menu bar. Click **Options** and click **Select Calendar Accounts**.

b. Select the color of the note from the drop-down box if you want a color other than the default color of yellow.

c. Click **OK** to close the dialog box.

3. Click **Previous Month** or **Next Month** on the date's context menu to see this account's Calendar for the previous or next month.

4. Click **Calendar Accounts** on the context menu to select the accounts to include on this Calendar:

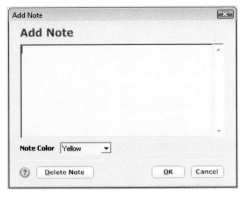

a. Click **Mark All** to have scheduled transactions for all accounts display on the Calendar.

b. Click **Clear All** to clear all selected accounts.

c. Click **OK** to close the Calendar Accounts dialog box.

USE THE CALENDAR OPTIONS

The Options menu on the Calendar toolbar allows you to tailor the Calendar to meet your needs.

1. Click **Show Recorded Transactions In Calendar** to display all of the transactions for each date.

2. Click **Show Scheduled Transactions In Calendar** to display upcoming expenses or income that you have scheduled.

3. Click **Show Daily Balances In Calendar** to display the total balance each day for all of the accounts you have selected.

4. Click **Show Snapshots Below Calendar** to display the Scheduled Bills & Deposits, Account Balance, and Spending Graphs areas below the Calendar.

SHOWING TRANSACTIONS ON YOUR CALENDAR

When you are using your Calendar, you can easily add memorized transactions to any date on your Calendar. From your Calendar:

1. Click **Options** and click **Edit Memorized Payee List**. The Memorized Payee List appears.

2. Click in the **Show On Calendar** column to tell Quicken to display a particular transaction on your Calendar.

3. Close the Memorized Payee List.

4. Click **Options** and click **Show Memorized Payee List** to display the list of memorized items displayed on the right side of your Calendar.

5. Drag any item on the list to the date on which you want the transaction to take place. The Add Transaction dialog box appears.

6. Complete any changes and click **OK**.

7. The transaction now appears on your Calendar on the date you chose.

NOTE

In the Monthly Bills & Deposits List, transactions in black with check marks are paid transactions, transactions in red are past due, and transactions in black without check marks are due in the future. The account that is affected is shown in blue.

5. Click **Show Memorized Payee List** to display a list of your memorized transactions that you can drag onto specific dates on your Calendar. See the "Showing Transactions on Your Calendar" QuickSteps at left for further information.

6. Click **Edit Memorized Payee List** to display the Memorized Payee List so that you can make necessary changes.

7. Click **Select Calendar Accounts** to choose which account information you want to display on your Calendar.

IDENTIFY THE COLOR CODES USED ON YOUR CALENDAR

Quicken color-codes information on your calendar, as seen in Figure 5-4.

- Deposits or payments that have been recorded in your account register are displayed in black text on a clear background.

- Pending transactions you have scheduled appear in black text on a grey background.

- Any scheduled transaction that is overdue displays with a red background.

- Income items scheduled in the future display on a green background.

- Payment items scheduled in the future display on an orange background.

RECOGNIZE THE MEANING OF THE NUMBERS ON EACH CALENDAR CELL

Quicken displays a daily balance of the selected Cash Flow accounts at the bottom of each Calendar cell:

- The balances shown for the current date, as well as all past dates, are actual balances for that date.

- Future balances are based on your future scheduled transactions.

The information displayed on your Calendar is the same as what is displayed in the Cash Flow section of the Account bar.

Use the Scheduled Transaction List

Quicken displays scheduled transactions on the Calendar, on the Quicken Home page, on the Cash Flow Center, and at the bottom of each cash flow check register that has scheduled transactions. The Bills & Deposits List displays scheduled transactions for all of your accounts, for several accounts, or for only one. In addition, you can add, edit, and delete transactions to, on, or from the list, as well as enter a transaction into the check register or skip it for this time period.

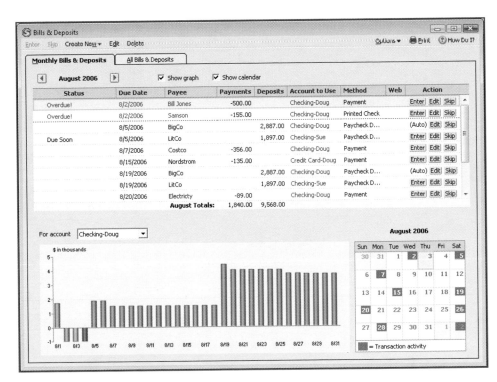

Figure 5-5: *Scheduled transactions help you plan and account for your income and expenses.*

1. Press CTRL+J.

   –Or–

   Click the **Cash Flow** menu, and click **Scheduled Transaction List**.

   In either case, the Bills & Deposits window opens. One view of it is shown in Figure 5-5.

2. If it is not already selected, click the **Monthly Bills & Deposits** tab to display the payment and deposit transactions you have scheduled for the current month. Click the arrow to the right or left of this month's name to move to other months.

3. Click **Show Graph** to display a graph showing the balances each day in all, some, or one of your accounts.

4. Click **Show Calendar** to display a small calendar of the current month. Days on which you have paid transactions or have scheduled transactions are shown in blue.

5. Click **Options** to choose how the transactions are sorted: by description, by amount, or by the next payment date.

6. Click **Print** to print a list of the scheduled transactions.

WORK WITH AN EXISTING SCHEDULED TRANSACTION

An existing scheduled transaction—one that has not been handled and entered on a register—can be changed in the Bills & Deposits dialog box in either the Monthly Bills & Deposits or the All Bills & Deposits tab. When you click a transaction, the Enter, Skip, Edit, and Delete buttons become available on the menu bar. Until a transaction is selected in the Bills & Deposits dialog box, these options are unavailable.

TIP

The account graph shown in the Bills & Deposits List uses colored bars so that you can easily differentiate between the days. Yellow is used for previous dates, green for today's date, and blue for future dates. Quicken uses color coding in several locations, including the calendar, to help you.

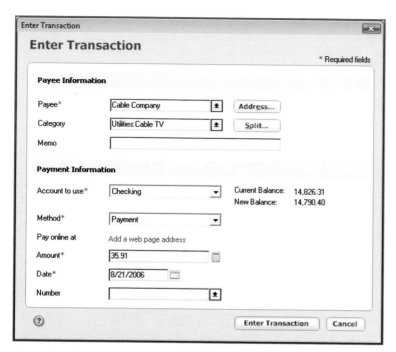

Figure 5-6: *The Enter Transaction dialog box allows you to change the payment method, payee, category, date, and amount before recording a scheduled transaction.*

CAUTION

When using scheduled transactions, remember that you still actually have to go to the bank to make the deposit or physically mail the handwritten or printed checks. It is easy to think that because you have made the transaction happen in Quicken that it has actually happened.

1. Click an existing scheduled transaction, and click **Enter**, either on the menu bar or to the right of the transaction, to enter that transaction into its register. The Enter Transaction dialog box appears, as shown in Figure 5-6:

   - Make your desired changes and move through the dialog box using the **TAB** key.

   - Click **Enter Transaction** to record the transaction.

2. Click **Edit**, either on the menu bar or to the right of the transaction, to modify the transaction. The Edit All Future Transactions dialog box appears. Make any changes necessary, and click **OK** to close the dialog box.

3. Click **Skip**, either on the menu bar or to the right of the transaction, to skip the scheduled payment this time only. A dialog box appears asking you to verify that you are skipping this transaction. Click **Yes** to confirm the skip. Click **No** to keep the transaction available for the current month.

4. Click **Delete** on the menu bar to remove the transaction. This only removes the scheduled transaction so that it won't be displayed in the future; it has no effect on transactions that have already been recorded. A dialog box appears warning you that you are about to delete a scheduled transaction. Click **OK** if you mean to delete the transaction, or click **Cancel** to save the scheduled transaction.

5. Click **Close** to close the Bills & Deposits List.

WORK WITH TRANSACTIONS ON THE CASH FLOW CENTER

You can access your scheduled transactions from both the Cash Flow Center and the Quicken Home page. Each location offers different options. The options available on the Quicken Home page are discussed in Chapter 2. To work with the Cash Flow Center:

1. Click **Cash Flow Center** on the Account bar.

   –Or–

   Click **Cash Flow** on the Quicken menu, and click **Go To Cash Flow Center**.

QUICKSTEPS

SCHEDULING REPEATING ONLINE PAYMENTS

When you schedule your transactions using the Online Payment From Quicken option, you can send the first set of instructions and then tell the bill-paying service to repeat that payment a certain number of times on specific dates. This way, the financial institution does not need to receive instructions every time.

1. Click the **Quicken** menu, click **Tools** and then click **Go To Quicken Home**. You may need to scroll down to view the Scheduled Bills & Deposits section.

2. Click **Show Full List**.

3. Click **Create New** on the menu bar, and then click **Scheduled Transaction**. The Add Scheduled Transactions dialog box appears.

4. Enter the payee, category, and memo, and choose the account from which you want to make the payment.

5. Click the **Method** down arrow, and click **Online Payment From Quicken**. If this option does not appear, you must activate the account for online bill payment before you schedule the transaction.

6. Click **Repeat This Payment Automatically Even If I Don't Go Online** to set up the repeating online payment.

7. Enter the amount and the first payment date, and schedule the number of times and frequency of this payment.

8. Click **OK**. The instruction is listed in the Scheduled Transaction List as a repeating online payment.

9. To send the instruction, click the **Quicken** menu, click **Online**, and then click **One Step Update**. Then click **Update Now** to complete the setup.

2. You may need to scroll to the bottom of the Activity Center to display the Scheduled Bills & Deposits section.

Scheduled Bills & Deposits					Options ▼
Show [All - by Bills and Deposits ▼] ☐ Show graph ☐ Show calendar					
Status	**Due Date**	**Payee**	**Amount**	**Web**	**Action**
Bills					
Overdue!	7/28/2006	Electric Company	-84.37		Enter Edit Skip
	8/21/2006	Cable Company	-35.91		Enter Edit Skip
Deposits and Other Scheduled Transactions					
	10/1/2006	MegaFirm	3,935.58		Enter Edit Skip
Schedule These?					
	10/10/2006	Jack Fisherman	-156.25		Yes No
	3/1/2007	Balancing Cash Adjustment	1,071.87		Yes No
Add Bill or Deposit	Show Full List	Set Up Paycheck			Show Full Calendar

3. Click the **Show** down arrow, and click one of the following:

- **All – By Month** displays both recurring bills and scheduled transactions for each month. You can move between months by clicking the right and left arrows.

- **All – By Bills And Deposits** shows all scheduled transactions by the due dates. Use this view to ensure that you have not missed any scheduled transactions.

- **Current – By Status** displays a list that is sorted according to transactions that are overdue, due today, and due soon.

- **Current – By Bills And Deposits** displays bills that are due first, then deposits, and then gives you possible transactions to schedule.

4. Click the **Show Graph** and **Show Calendar** check boxes to activate the Calendar and Graph (clear these check boxes if you do not want these items displayed).

5. Click **Options** to open a menu that offers more choices when working with scheduled transactions.

Repeating online payments do not appear in your account register or the transaction lists until they are processed by your financial institution.

Use Reports and Graphs

After you have been working with Quicken for a while, it may be easier to see information in a report or graph format rather than viewing the various Centers, lists, or registers. You can create reports directly from registers or transactions, use one of the many standard reports included with Quicken, customize an existing report in a number of ways, and memorize the reports you use regularly. You can

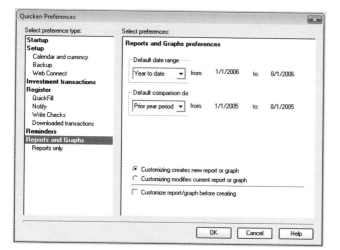

print reports and graphs, and you can copy or transfer the data on a report to other programs, such as Microsoft Excel, TurboTax, or Microsoft Money. By setting your preferences, you can change how reports use color and display information, and you can set the default date range for your reports. In this chapter we discuss some of the standard reports and graphs available. In later chapters we discuss ways you can customize and change reports, and you'll learn about reports you can create regarding your investments, taxes, and net worth.

Set Report Preferences

You can determine how each report displays your data from two different locations in Quicken: the Reports menu and the Preferences menu.

1. Click the **Reports** menu, and click **Reports & Graphs Center**. The Reports & Graphs window opens, as shown in Figure 5-7. Click **Preferences** on the right of the menu bar.

   —Or—

   Click the **Edit** menu, click **Preferences**, click **Quicken Program**, and click **Reports And Graphs**.

   In both cases, the Quicken Preferences dialog box appears (shown left, top illustration) displaying reports and graphs preferences:

   - Click the **Default Date Range** down arrow to choose the range you will most often use when running reports. Year To Date is selected by default.

   - Click the **Default Comparison Date Range** down arrow to choose the range that you will compare the current data to when creating a report. Prior Year Period is selected by default.

   - In the Customizing Reports And Graphs area, click **Customizing Creates New Report Or Graph** or **Customizing Modifies Current Report Or Graph**. Customizing Creates New Report Or Graph is selected by default. You can also click **Customize Report/Graph Before Creating** to customize reports or graphs before creating them.

Figure 5-7: The Reports & Graphs window allows you to choose from the many standard reports and graphs supplied in Quicken.

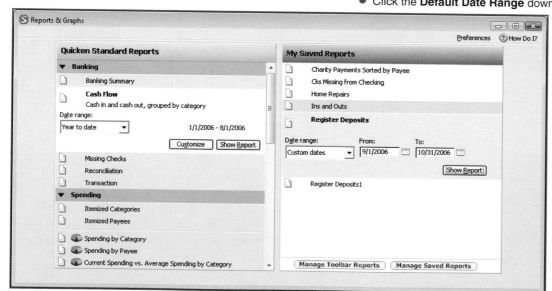

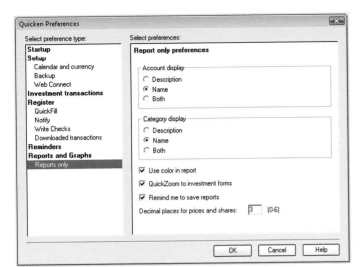

2. Click **Reports Only** to view the options for how reports will display information. For the display of both accounts and categories:

- Click **Description** to include each account's or category's description in your reports.

- Click **Name** (selected by default) to include the name of an account or category.

- Click **Both** to include the name and description in each report.

3. For other display options:

- Clear the **Use Color In Report** check box if you want to print your report in black and white.

- Click **QuickZoom To Investment Forms** to have the capability of seeing what information makes up each line of data on an investment report.

- Clear the **Remind Me To Save Reports** check box if you don't want Quicken to remind you to save any reports you have created.

- Type a number in the **Decimal Places For Prices And Shares** field if it is different from the default choice of 3.

4. Click **OK** to close the Quicken Preferences dialog box.

Create a Standard Report

To create a standard report in Quicken:

1. Click the **Reports** menu, and click **Reports And Graphs Center** to display the Reports & Graphs window (see Figure 5-7).

2. Click the small triangle icon in the area from which you want the report created. The standard reports available in this area are displayed in the window.

3. Click the report you want to create.

4. Choose the date range if it is different from the default range you set under Preferences.

5. Click **Customize** to open the Customize dialog box for this report (see Chapter 6 for more information).

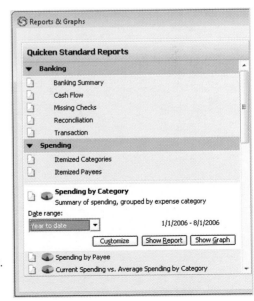

> **TIP**
>
> QuickZoom is a Quicken feature that allows you to see more detail about items in a report or graph. In some reports and graphs, this feature opens the original transaction.

QUICKSTEPS

CREATING A MINI-REPORT

Quicken's standard reports are designed to give you broad information about your accounts and activities. However, sometimes you might only want to find out how much you have paid to one payee to date or how much money you have spent eating out during the last three months. You can create a mini-report from any register regarding a payee or a category.

1. Open a register that has either the category or the payee on which you want your mini-report.

2. Click in either the **Payee** or the **Category** field.

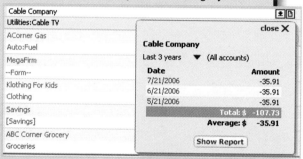

3. Click the mini-report icon (it looks like an orange square with one corner folded down). You will see a small report on your screen displaying the last few transactions for this category or payee.

4. Click **Show Report** to see a full report. In the Transaction Report window, a standard report appears about this payee or category. From this window, you can:

   ● Change the date range from the default settings

   ● Determine how the report calculates subtotals

   ● Edit individual transactions within the mini-report

5. Click **Close** to close the Transaction Report window.

6. Click **Show Report** to see the report.

7. Click **Print Report** on the menu bar to print the report.

8. Click **Save Report** on the menu bar to save the report and close the Reports & Graphs window.

Create a Standard Graph

Quicken supplies you with several standard graphs for each report area, some of which can be customized. On the Standard Reports List, if there is a standard graph associated with a report, you will see both a report and a graph icon by the report name. To create a graph:

1. Click the **Reports** menu, and then click **Graphs**. A list of available graphs appears.

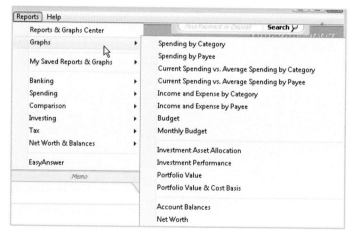

2. Click the graph you want. The standard graph will appear.

3. If you want to customize the graph, click **Customize**. (Customizing graphs is discussed further in Chapter 6.)

4. Click **Print Graph** on the menu bar if you want to print the graph.

5. Click **Close** to close the graph.

Chapter 6
Tracking Your Assets and Liabilities

In the last chapter you learned how to memorize and schedule transactions and were introduced to reports and graphs. In this chapter you use those skills as you work with transactions in the Property & Debt Center. This chapter will teach you how to link your assets with the related liabilities, enter information that affects the value of your assets, track your loans, and record other liabilities or payments. You'll learn how to customize reports, set alerts, and display your net worth. You'll also learn how to create a listing of your other assets, such as furniture and sports equipment, and use that list in Quicken.

Work with Asset and Liability Accounts

When you used Quicken New User Setup (see Chapter 1), you probably set up your house and its accompanying mortgage accounts. It is a good idea to track the asset value in one account and the liability, or amount you owe, in another. While you may not have an asset account for every liability account, review

LOAN TYPE	DESCRIPTION
Mortgage	A long-term loan, secured by real property, such as your house. A mortgage can have a *fixed* or an *adjustable* interest rate. Fixed rate means the amount of interest you pay is set at the beginning and stays at that rate for the life of the mortgage. Adjustable rate means that the rate of interest is adjusted at regular intervals throughout the life of the mortgage. Adjustable-rate mortgages are sometimes called variable-rate or floating-rate mortgages.
Home Equity	This type of loan is secured by the equity in your house. It is sometimes called a *second mortgage*. In some cases, the interest you pay on this type of loan may be tax-deductible. Consult with your tax professional for more information. Home equity loans can also have either fixed or variable interest rates.
Reverse Mortgage	This type of loan allows homeowners with no mortgage to borrow against the equity in their home. This type of loan pays the homeowner regular monthly payments and is paid off when the home is sold. This type of loan is often used by people on a fixed income to provide additional income, such as during retirement.
Vehicle Loan	This type of loan uses a vehicle—such as a boat, automobile, or recreational vehicle—as the *collateral* for the loan. Collateral is property used as security for a loan. The interest is normally not tax-deductible, but check with your tax professional to be sure.
Personal Loan	This type of loan usually requires no collateral, and interest is often charged at a higher rate than with the other types of loans.

Table 6-1: **Types of Loans You Can Track in Quicken**

your accounts now to ensure that you include all the assets you want to watch. Quicken can track any loan type you may have, as described in Table 6-1.

For most of us, our biggest asset is our home, so much of the information in the following section is focused on that. However, you can make adjustments to any asset in the same way as described here.

Link an Asset to a Liability Account

If you have created your mortgage account but not the asset account, create the asset account now and then link them. If you have not yet created your house or mortgage account, do it now, following the directions in Chapter 3. If you have created both accounts but not yet linked them, you can link them quickly.

1. Click the **Tools** menu, and click **Account List**.

   –Or–

   Press **CTRL+A** to see the Account List.

2. Click the asset account with which you want to work.

3. Click **Edit** on the menu bar. The Account Details dialog box appears, as shown in Figure 6-1.

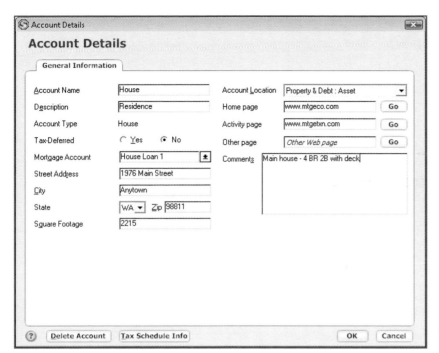

Figure 6-1: *The Account Details dialog box can be used to link an asset account with a liability account, as well as to enter other information.*

4. Click the **Mortgage Account** down arrow to see a list of liability accounts.

5. Click the relevant liability account, and click **OK**.

Adjust the Value of an Asset

As time passes, you will probably add improvements to your home, thereby increasing its value. Furthermore, in many areas, real-estate market values increase over time. You may want to record this information in your Asset Account register.

RECORD IMPROVEMENTS

An improvement, such as remodeling a bathroom or adding a garage, is called a *capital* improvement and adds to the value of your home. For example, if you purchased your home for $180,000 and added a garage for $25,000, the adjusted basis, or cost, of your home is $205,000. For additional information on how capital improvements may affect you, consult your tax professional. To record an improvement in your Asset Account register:

1. Open the account from which you want to pay for the improvement, for example, **Checking**.

NOTE

The account-linking feature is available in Quicken Deluxe, Premier, and Home & Business versions.

LINKING MULTIPLE LIABILITY ACCOUNTS TO ONE ASSET ACCOUNT

If you have a second mortgage or line of credit secured by your home, you can track this information in Quicken.

1. Press **CTRL+A** to open the Account List.

2. Click the liability account you want to link with your asset account.

3. Click **Edit** on the menu bar.

4. Click the **Linked Asset Account** down arrow to open a list of assets.

5. Click the asset to which this liability is to be linked.

6. Click **OK** to close the Account Details dialog box.

7. Click the asset account you just linked.

8. Click **Edit** to open the Account Details dialog box. Note that the mortgage account now reads "Multiple," indicating that there are more than one liability accounts associated with this asset.

9. Click **OK** to close the dialog box.

10. To unlink a liability account, reverse this process.

CAUTION

With any transaction that may have significant tax implications, consult your tax professional for the best way to handle the transaction for your particular situation.

2. Enter the transaction in the normal manner.

3. Select the **Transfer To/From** category, and select the name of the asset account.

4. The transaction appears in the Checking Account register, and the improvement is automatically added to the value of the house in the House Asset register.

| 9/18/2006 | 4801 | Kitchens Unlimited [House] | kitchen remodel-materials deposit | 12,150 00 | | 18,803 56 |
| 9/18/2006 | | Kitchens Unlimited [Checking] | | | 12,150 00 | 257,150 00 |

USE THE UPDATE BALANCE DIALOG BOX

As your real estate assets increase in value and your other assets, such as cars and boats, decrease in value, you may want to adjust the account balances to ensure your financial net worth shows properly in Quicken. To access the Update Account Balance dialog box:

1. Click the **Property & Debt** menu, and click **Go To Property & Debt Center**.

2. Double-click the account you want to update. The Account register displays.

3. Click **Update Balance** on the register menu bar to open the Update Account Balance dialog box.

4. Enter the new total value of the asset in the **Update Balance To** field.

5. Enter the adjustment date if it is different from today's date.

6. Click the **Category For Adjustment** down arrow to open a list of categories for this adjustment. Quicken uses "Misc" as the default category. Consult your tax professional for a recommendation if needed. Personal net worth statements often show the market value of assets, as opposed to business balance sheets which, by business accounting standards, show the historical cost of an asset.

7. Click **OK** to close the dialog box.

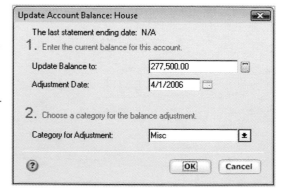

QUICKFACTS

UNDERSTANDING DEPRECIATION

If you rent out an asset, gain income from it, or use an asset in business, your tax advisor may want you to depreciate that asset. *Depreciation* is the amount that a property's value declines because of general wear and tear, heavy use, or becoming outdated. There are several instances when you may want to track depreciation in Quicken:

- You rent out part of your home.
- One or more of your assets is a rental property.
- You rent out your motor home or houseboat.
- Part or all of your home or other asset is used for your business.

In all cases, consult your tax professional for advice on whether depreciation should be recorded in your situation. You should understand both the type of depreciation used—since there are a number of different types—and the amount to enter every year. Once you know the amount to be entered, you can schedule this transaction, as described in Chapter 5.

Work with Loans

Whether you used Quicken New User Setup to set up your loans or manually entered the information regarding your debts (other than credit cards), you may have to change interest rates or otherwise work with your loan information on occasion.

Adjust the Interest Rate on a Loan

From time to time, interest rates on loans may be adjusted by your lender. The rate change may take effect at some future date, or it may be effective immediately with the next payment.

CHANGE THE INTEREST RATE IN THE FUTURE

To adjust your loan when the change takes effect with future payments:

1. Click the **Property & Debt** menu, and click **Loans**.

   –Or–

   Press **CTRL+H** to open the View Loans dialog box.

2. Click **Choose Loan** on the menu bar to display a list of all of your loans. Click the loan whose rate you want to change.

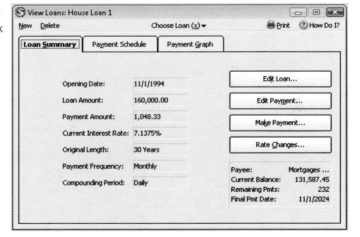

3. Click **Rate Changes**. The Loan Rate Changes dialog box appears.

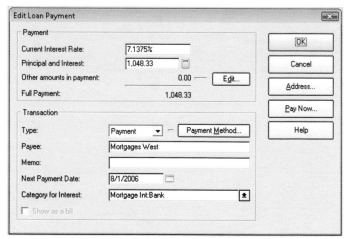

Insert an Interest Rate Change

Effective Date: 10/3/2006

Interest Rate: 7.725%

Regular Payment: 1,094.85

OK   Cancel   Help

4. Click **New** to open the Insert An Interest Rate Change dialog box.

5. Type a date in the **Effective Date** field. Press **TAB** to move to the next field.

6. Type the new interest rate in the **Interest Rate** field. Press **TAB**, and Quicken calculates the new payment amount without changing the length of the loan.

7. Click **OK** or **Close** to close the Insert An Interest Rate Change dialog box, and click **Close** to close the Loan Rate Changes dialog box. Finally, click **Close** to close the View Loans dialog box.

CHANGE THE INTEREST RATE FOR THE NEXT PAYMENT

If your new interest rate is effective with the next payment:

1. Open the **View Loans** dialog box, and select your loan, as described in the first two steps of "Change the Interest Rate in the Future."

2. Click **Edit Payment** to open the Edit Loan Payment dialog box.

3. Type the new rate in the **Current Interest Rate** field.

Quicken calculates the principal and interest payment for you using the next payment date as the effective date of the change without changing the length of the loan. However, if you change the payment amount (Principal And Interest field), Quicken changes the loan's length to accommodate the new payment.

Edit Loan Payment

Payment

Current Interest Rate: 7.1375%

Principal and Interest: 1,048.33

Other amounts in payment: 0.00   Edit...

Full Payment: 1,048.33

Transaction

Type: Payment — Payment Method...

Payee: Mortgages West

Memo:

Next Payment Date: 8/1/2006

Category for Interest: Mortgage Int:Bank

☐ Show as a bill

OK   Cancel   Address...   Pay Now...   Help

4. Click **OK** to close the Edit Loan Payment dialog box, and click **Close** to close the View Loans dialog box.

Handle Other Loan Functions

In addition to changing the interest rate, you may need to handle other loan functions, including changing the loan balance, making additional principal payments (including tax and insurance payments), handling interest-only or balloon payments, and printing a loan summary.

CHANGE LOAN BALANCES

Periodically, you may get statements from your lender showing the current balance of a loan or the balance as of a specific date. If you want to change the loan balance in Quicken to match the lender's record:

1. Click the **Property & Debt** menu, and click **Loans**.

   –Or–

   Press **CTRL+H** to display the View Loans dialog box.

2. Click **Choose Loan** and click the loan with which you want to work.

3. Click **Edit Loan** to open the Edit Loan dialog box.

4. Click **Next** in the lower-right corner.

5. Type the balance shown by the lender in the **Current Balance** field.

6. Click **Done** to close the dialog box, and click **Close** to close the View Loans dialog box.

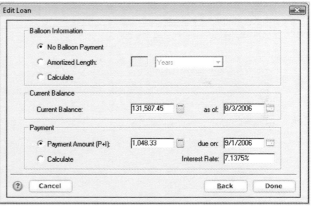

INCLUDE TAX AND INSURANCE PAYMENTS

Many mortgages, and some home equity loans, include other amounts with each payment, such as property taxes, *PMI* (private mortgage insurance), or homeowners' insurance. The property taxes and insurance payments are then paid by the lender directly to the taxing authority and insurance company. If these amounts are changed, you should reflect that information in your loan payment.

1. Press **CTRL+H** to open the View Loans dialog box.

2. Click **Choose Loan** and click the loan with which you want to work.

3. Click **Edit Payment** to open the Edit Loan Payment dialog box.

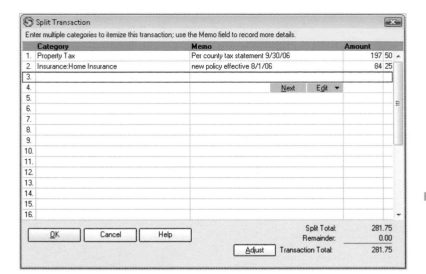

TIP

Some lenders send periodic escrow account statements. If you have entered the escrow amounts of insurance and taxes as split transactions, you can easily compare your records to that of the lender's.

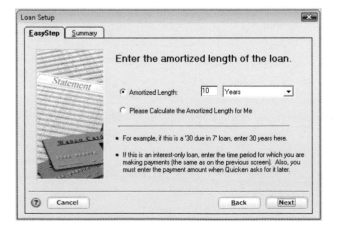

4. Click **Edit** to open the Split Transaction window.

5. Fill in the **Category** and **Amount** fields for each of the fees included in your payment:

   a. You may want to use the standard Quicken category of Insurance:Home Insurance for the insurance portion of your payment.

   b. Quicken's standard category for property taxes is Taxes - Property.

6. Click **OK** to close the Split Transaction window, click **OK** once more to close the Edit Loan Payment dialog box, and click **Close** to close the View Loans dialog box.

HANDLE INTEREST-ONLY OR BALLOON PAYMENTS

Some mortgages are interest-only loans, with the full amount of the loan payable at the end of the loan's term. In this way, consumers have a lower monthly payment and can make principal payments whenever they choose. To enter a new loan of this type:

1. Press **CTRL+H** and click **New**. The Loan Setup Wizard starts. Click **Next**.

2. Click **Borrow Money**, click **Next**, and enter an account name. Click **Next**, tell Quicken if payments have been made on this loan by clicking **Yes** or **No**, and click **Next** again.

3. Enter the date of the loan and the original balance, and click **Next**.

4. You are asked if this loan includes a balloon payment at the end. Click **Yes** and then click **Next**.

5. In the **Original Length** field, enter the length of time in which payments are to be made on the loan, *not* the length of time over which it is amortized, and click **Next**.

6. Enter the number of years over which the loan is to be amortized in the **Amortized Length** field. If you are not sure of the amortized length, click **Please Calculate The Amortized Length For Me**, and Quicken will compute the amortization period based on the amount of the payments and the interest rate. Click **Next** to continue.

7. Enter the payment period for this loan:

   a. Click **Standard Period** if you make regular payments—usually monthly. If you will be making payments other than monthly, use the drop-down list to choose the interval at which you will be making the payments.

   b. Click **Other Period** if you will not be making regular, periodic payments. Enter the number of payments per year you will be making.

MAKING ADDITIONAL PRINCIPAL PAYMENTS

Making additional principal payments can reduce the amount of interest you pay over the term of a loan. To record these additional payments:

1. Press **CTRL+H** to open the View Loans window.

2. Click **Choose Loan** and click the loan with which you want to work.

3. Click **Make Payment**. The Loan Payment dialog box appears. Click **Extra**.

4. Click the **Account To Use** down arrow, and select the account you want.

5. Click the **Type Of Transaction** down arrow, and choose how you want to make the payment.

6. Type a value in the **Amount** field, click the **Number** down arrow, and select how you will reference the payment.

7. If you want to include your account number or other information on the check, enter it into the **Memo** field.

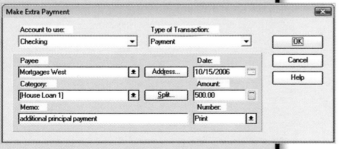

8. Click **OK** to close the dialog box, and click **Close** to close the View Loans dialog box.

   The transaction is entered in the relevant checking account and is reflected as an additional principal payment in the Liability Account register.

8. Click **Next**. Enter the compounding period for this loan. This describes the way your lender calculates interest owed. Many institutions compound interest daily; however, "Monthly" is the default. Click **Next**.

9. If you answered "Yes" in step 2, that payments have been made on this loan, you are asked if you know the current balance. If you know it, click **Yes**; if you do not know the current balance, click **No**. In either case, click **Next** to continue.

10. If you answered "Yes," that you know the current balance, you are asked to:

    a. Enter the date of the current balance in the **Current Balance Date** field.

    b. Enter the amount of the current balance in the **Current Balance Amount** field.

    c. Click **Next** to continue.

11. If you answered "No," that you do not know the current balance, you are asked to enter the date of the next payment.

12. If you answered "No" in step 2, that no payments have been made on this loan, you are asked to enter the date of the first payment if it is different than a month from today. Click **Next**.

13. You are asked if you know the amount of either the first payment (if no payments have been made on this loan) or the next payment (if payments have been made on this loan). Click either **Yes** or **No**.

14. If you chose Yes, enter the amount in the **Payment Amount** field, and click **Next** to enter the interest rate for this loan.

15. Independent of whether you answered "Yes" or "No" to knowing the payment amount, the Interest Rate dialog box will appear. Enter the interest rate as a percent (you don't need to include the percent sign), and click **Next**.

16. The first Summary dialog box will appear. Confirm the information it contains, and click **Next**. A second Summary dialog box will appear. Again, confirm the information it contains, and click **Next**.

17. The third Summary dialog box will appear. Confirm the information it contains, and click **Done**. Depending on how you entered the information, Quicken may display a message stating that it has calculated either the amortization period or the payment.

18. The final Summary dialog box displays the information you have entered or that Quicken has calculated. Click **Done** to display the Set Up Loan Payment dialog box.

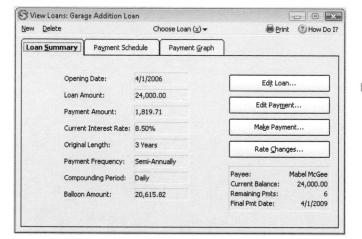

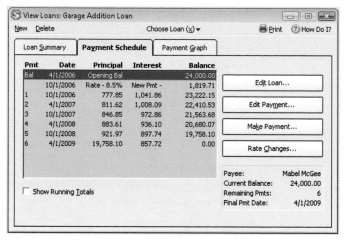

19. Enter the payee information in the Set Up Loan Payment dialog box, and click **OK**. Click either **Yes** or **No** when asked if you want to create an asset account for this loan. If you click **No**, you will see a summary of your loan. Click **Close** to close the View Loans dialog box.

PRINT A LOAN SUMMARY

The View Loans dialog box allows you to print a summary of each loan, the payment schedule, and a graph that shows the progress of the loan repayment. To access this dialog box:

1. Press **CTRL+H** to open the View Loans dialog box. Click **Choose Loan** and select the loan you want to print.

2. Click **Print** on the menu bar to open a Windows Print dialog box.

3. Click **Preview** to see how the report will look when it is printed. Figure 6-2 shows an example of this report.

4. Click **Print** to print the report, or click **Close** to close the Print Preview dialog box without printing the report.

Figure 6-2: **Printing a loan schedule report shows not only the payment schedule, but also a summary of the loan itself.**

The payment graph allows you to see the history of your loan, interest, and future balance displayed in a line graph. While you cannot print this directly, it is a useful tool. To see the payment graph:

1. Press **CTRL+H** to open the View Loans dialog box. Click **Choose Loan** and select the loan you want to view.

2. Click the **Payment Graph** tab to view it. The colored legend on the bottom of the graph shows what each line means.

3. Click **Close** to close the View Loans dialog box.

Understand Alerts

One of the most powerful features in Quicken Premier and Home & Business editions is the ability to set up *alerts*, or reminders. Not all alerts are available in Quicken Deluxe, and some may be called Reminders or Billminders in Quicken Basic. Alerts remind you to download transactions, pay bills, know when your credit card balance is nearing its limit, know when an account is near its minimum balance, or know when your auto insurance is approaching its renewal date, among other things. With Quicken.com, you can create a Watch List for securities you want to track. Chapter 7 discusses investments and securities in further detail. There are four major categories of alerts:

- **Cash Flow alerts** let you monitor minimum or maximum balances, credit card limits, monthly expenses, and savings goals. You can even check your financial institutions for new services they offer.

- **Investing alerts** remind you to download quotes and prices, notify you when earnings fail to meet or exceed projections, tell you when mutual funds increase their fees, give you useful information about mutual fund distributions, and identify the holding periods for your securities.

- **Tax alerts** notify you when you have either over- or under-withheld income tax from your paycheck, remind you about upcoming tax dates, and provide useful tax information about personal deductions.

- **General alerts** remind you to download transactions and notify you that scheduled transactions are soon due, that insurance policies are approaching renewal dates, and that a mortgage interest rate may be changing.

QUICKSTEPS

DELETING AN ALERT

To delete an alert:

1. Click the **Tools** menu, and click **Show All Alerts**.

   –Or–

   Click **Quicken Home**, choose an Activity Center, and click **Show All Alerts**.

   In either case, the Alerts Center window opens with the Show All tab displayed.

2. Click the check box next to the alert you want to delete, and click the **Delete** button at the bottom of the window. A dialog box will appear warning that you are about to delete an alert. Click **OK** to verify the deletion.

3. Click **Close** to close the window.

Set Up Alerts

To set up an alert:

1. Click the **Tools** menu, and then click **Set Up Alerts**.

   –Or–

   Click **Quicken Home** and select any of the Activity Centers. Click **Set Up Alerts** in the chosen Center.

2. If the **Setup** tab is not already displayed, click it.

3. Select the type of alert you want to set, and click the plus sign (+) to the left of it.

4. Click the check box corresponding to the alert you want. The values that can be entered appear on the right side of the window.

5. Click the individual categories for which you want to receive alerts, and enter the required information.

6. Click either **Text In The Alert List** or **Urgent (Pop Up Dialog Box)** to tell Quicken how you want the alert displayed.

7. Click the **Keep The Alert In The List For** down arrow, and choose how long you want the alert to remain in the list, as shown in Figure 6-3.

8. Click **OK** to save the alert and close the window.

Tools	Online	Cash Flow	Investing	Property & I
Go to Quicken Home				
Go to Net Worth Center				
Edit Personal Information				
Account List				Ctrl+A
Category List				Shift+Ctrl+C
Scheduled Transaction List				Ctrl+J
Memorized Payee List				Ctrl+T
Class List				Ctrl+L
Calendar				Ctrl+K
Show All Alerts				
Set Up Alerts				
Address Book				
Calculator				
Add Business Tools				
Quicken Services				

Create Custom Reports

In Chapter 5 you learned how to create standard Quicken reports and graphs. The following sections will discuss how to customize reports so that they provide exactly the information you want. You can review your spending, know your net worth, and get ready for taxes. You can save reports, or you can tell Quicken to save new reports automatically. You can export your reports to the Clipboard in Windows or to Microsoft Excel. You can also export them to a PDF file format that can be read with Adobe Acrobat Reader on any computer, even if Quicken is not installed.

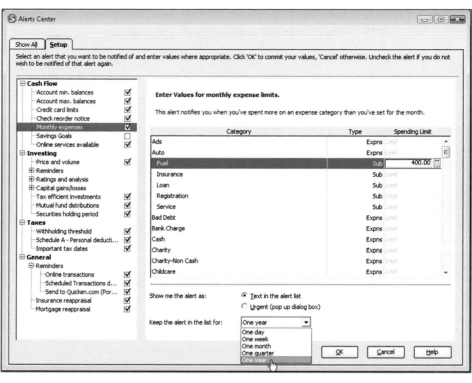

Figure 6-3: *You can set a wide variety of alerts and customize them further by selecting various options.*

Customize an Existing Report

The easiest way to make a report your own is to start with an existing report and customize it to meet your needs. We'll start with one report (the Transactions Report) and create a report based on what we want to know. Each standard report may have slightly different options.

1. Click **Reports** on the menu bar, and then click **Reports & Graphs Center**.

2. In the left pane of the Reports & Graphs window, click the arrow to the left of **Banking** to display the standard reports available in that area.

3. Click **Transaction**. Year To Date is shown as the time period on which you want the report based.

Reports & Graphs

Quicken Standard Reports

- Missing Checks
- Reconciliation
- **Transaction**
  Transactions from your accounts

Date range: Custom dates
From: 1/1/2006
To: 9/30/2006

Customize   Show Report

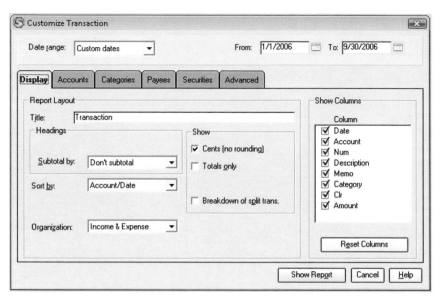

4. Click **Customize** to open the Customize Transaction dialog box:

   a. Click the **Date Range** down arrow, and choose from a list of preset periods.

   b. Click **Custom Dates** from the Date Range list to set your own date range.

5. Click the **Display** tab to tell Quicken how to lay out your report:

   a. Click in the **Title** field, and type a new title.

   b. Click the **Subtotal By** down arrow, and choose to subtotal by one of several time periods or by category, class, payee, account, or tax schedule.

   c. Click the **Sort By** down arrow, and choose how you want your data sorted.

   d. Click the **Organization** down arrow, and choose whether the report is organized with income at the top and expenses at the bottom or with income items interspersed with expense items to show the cash flow at any period of time.

   e. Click **Cents (No Rounding)** if you want to see transactions to the nearest penny, or clear this check box to round items to the nearest dollar.

   f. Click **Totals Only** if you want only the summary categories displayed. Clear this check box if you want all transactions displayed.

   g. Click **Breakdown of Split Trans.** if you want to show how split transactions were categorized.

   h. Click the columns you do not want displayed in the Show Columns area; by default, all columns are displayed. To reselect all the columns, click **Reset Columns**.

6. Click the **Accounts** tab to choose the accounts included in the report. You can choose to use all accounts or specific accounts within each Center:

   a. Click **Mark All** to choose all accounts.

   b. Click **Clear All** to clear all accounts and select the ones you want to use. This is the quickest way to select only one or two accounts.

   c. Click **Show (Hidden Accounts)** to include accounts that normally aren't displayed in Quicken.

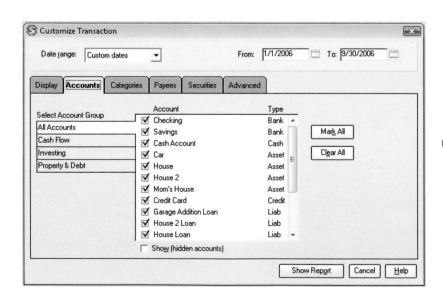

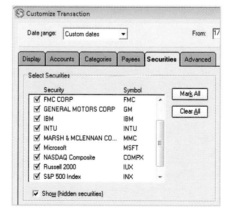

7. Click the **Categories** tab to select the categories included in your report:

   a. Click **Mark All** to choose all accounts.

   b. Click **Clear All** to clear all accounts and select the ones you want to use.

   c. Click **Expand All** if you want details about subcategories included, or click **Collapse All** if you want only the main category information to be displayed.

   d. Enter information into the **Category**, **Payee**, or **Memo Contains** fields if you want to include only those transactions that contain specific information in the Category and/or Memo fields.

8. Click the **Payees** tab to select the payees to include in the report. Type a payee name, or choose one from the list. Click **Clear All** to clear the payee check boxes and select the ones you want.

9. Click the **Securities** tab to choose the securities included in the report.

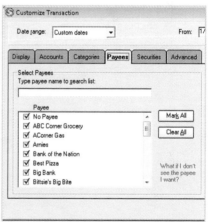

NOTE

It may be confusing why you can enter a payee in the Reports & Graphs Customize Transaction Categories tab or enter a category in the Payees tab. The answer is that the Categories tab allows you to select all the categories in the report and to select a single payee in those categories. Step 7 allows you to select all the payees in the report and to select a single category for those payees. In most instances, the payee is left blank in the Categories tab and the category is left blank in Payees tab so you can create a report with both multiple categories and multiple payees.

TIP

Expand the date range if your payee name does not appear and you are sure you have paid this payee.

TIP

If the payee name does not appear, review the list again. You may have misspelled the name the first time you entered it.

10. Click **Show (Hidden Securities)** to include securities you have chosen not to display in your report, or clear the check box if you do not want them included.

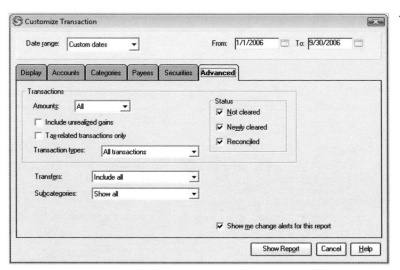

11. Click the **Advanced** tab to further refine your report:

    a. Click the **Amounts** down arrow, and click a criterion for selecting the amounts you want to include.

    b. If you choose a criterion other than All, enter an amount to use with the criterion.

    c. Click **Include Unrealized Gains** if you have set up investment accounts and want to include paper gains and losses in your report (see Chapter 8 for more information).

    d. Click **Tax-Related Transactions Only** to include only those transactions that relate to income tax.

    e. Click the **Transaction Types** down arrow, and choose **All Transactions** (selected by default), **Payments**, **Deposits**, or **Unprinted Checks**.

    f. Clear the check boxes in the **Status** area to limit your report to transactions that have cleared and are not reconciled transactions.

12. Click **Show Report** to display the report after you have finished customizing it.

13. Click the **Print Report** icon on the toolbar to print the report.

Save a Customized Report

After you have created your custom report, you can save it to your My Saved Reports folder, recall it, revise it, and resave it with either a new name or as a replacement for the original saved report.

To save a customized report when you first create it:

1. Click the **Save Report** icon on the toolbar to open the Save Report dialog box.

2. Type a name in the **Report Name** field to identify this report, press TAB, and type a description if you want. The description will appear in your list of saved reports under the title of the report.

TIP

A "paper" gain or loss is an unrealized gain or loss that you might have realized if you had sold the security at today's price. The word "paper" comes from getting today's price from the newspaper.

Save Report

CAUTION

The Description field in the Save Report dialog box holds only 21 characters, including spaces. If you choose to create a description for a saved report, make it short.

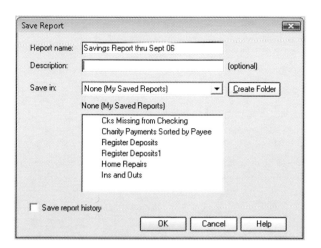

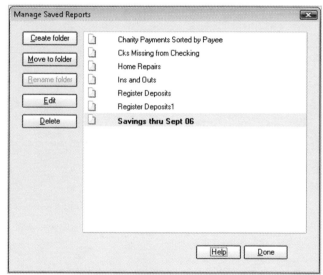

3. Click the **Save In** down arrow, and click the folder in which you want your report stored. If you do not create a separate folder, the report will be displayed on the right side of the Reports & Graphs window under My Saved Reports.

4. Click **Save Report History** if you want to save all versions of this report. By default, Quicken does not save this history.

5. Click **OK** to save the report, and click **Close** to close the Reports & Graphs window.

Manage Custom Folders for Saved Reports

You might want to organize your saved reports into different folders so that you can easily retrieve them. To create a folder:

1. Click the **Reports** menu, and then click **Reports & Graphs Center**. The Reports & Graphs window opens.

2. Click **Manage Saved Reports** on the bottom of the window. The Manage Saved Reports dialog box appears.

3. Click **Create Folder**. The Create New Report Folder dialog box appears.

4. Type a new folder name, and click **OK**.

5. In the Manage Saved Reports dialog box, click a folder, click **Rename Folder**, type a new name, and click **OK**.

6. Click a report within a folder, or click **No Folder**, and click **Edit** to change a report's name or description.

7. Click a report or a folder, and click **Delete** to delete the report or folder.

8. Click a report and click **Move To Folder** to move a report to another folder.

9. Type or select the name of the folder, and click **OK**.

10. Click **Done** when you have finished organizing your saved reports. Click **Close** to close the Reports & Graphs window.

Add a Report to the Quicken Toolbar

In addition to saving your reports to folders, you can save your reports or your report folders to the toolbar. To save a report to the Quicken toolbar:

1. Click the **Reports** menu, and click **My Saved Reports & Graphs**.

NOTE

You cannot delete a folder from your Saved Reports screen without moving or deleting all of the reports in that folder.

2. Click **Add Reports To Toolbar** at the bottom of the submenu. The Manage Toolbar Reports dialog box appears.

3. Click the small arrow to the left of each folder's check box to display the reports in that folder.

4. Click the check box of the reports (or folders) you want to appear on the Quicken toolbar.

In Toolbar	My Saved Reports
☑	**Nick's Reports**
☐	Charity Payments Sorted by Payee
☐	Cks Missing from Checking
☐	Home Repairs
☐	Ins and Outs
☐	Register Deposits
☐	Register Deposits1

Manage Toolbar Reports
Select the items you want to display in the Quicken toolbar.

5. After you have made your selections, click **OK** to close the dialog box.

6. Your selections appear on the Quicken toolbar.

Create a Net Worth Report

Your *net worth* is the difference between the value of what you own (your assets) and what you owe (your liabilities). From time to time, you may want to print a report of your net worth, and Quicken makes this easy to do. An example of a Net Worth Report is shown in Figure 6-4.

1. Click **Reports** on the toolbar. The Reports & Graphs window opens.

2. Click the arrow to the left of **Net Worth & Balances** to display the related reports.

3. Click **Net Worth**. In the **Report Balance As Of** text box, enter the as-of date for which you want the report, and click **Show Report**.

4. Click the **Date Range** down arrow, and choose from a list of preset periods. The default is from the earliest date to today's date.

5. Click **Interval** to choose the period of time that this report will cover. There may be times that creditors or others will ask for a "Net Worth Statement" covering just a specific period. When that is the case, use this option.

6. Click **Print** on the Report toolbar to print your report.

7. Click **Customize** to change the date or other items within the report, as described in "Customize an Existing Report" earlier in this chapter.

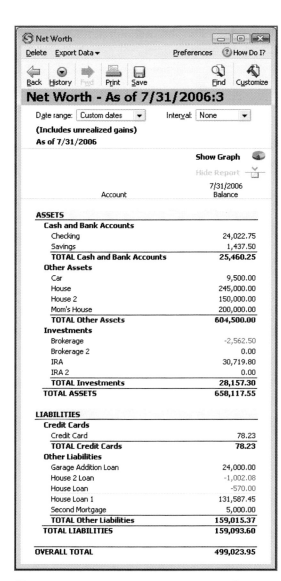

Figure 6-4: *A Net Worth Report shows all of your assets minus all of your liabilities for a "net" financial "worth."*

8. Click **Save Report** to open the Save Report dialog box, as described in "Save a Customized Report."

9. Click **Close** to return to Quicken.

Use Quicken Home Inventory

The Quicken Home Inventory, which is only available in Quicken Deluxe, Premier, and Home & Business editions, allows you to maintain an inventory of your belongings. With this feature you can:

● Maintain an itemized list of your goods for insurance purposes.

● Provide a list of where items are located. This is especially useful if you have a vacation home or boat, or even a storage unit.

● Keep a list of your heirs and what you plan to give them.

● Help determine your true net worth.

Set Options for Quicken Home Inventory

To start working with the Quicken Home Inventory:

1. Click the **Property & Debt** menu, and then click **Quicken Home Inventory Manager**. The Quicken Home Inventory window opens displaying a welcome message. Click **Continue**.

2. Click the **Edit** menu, and then click **Options**. The Options dialog box appears.

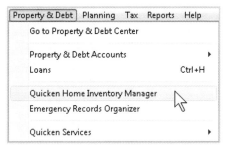

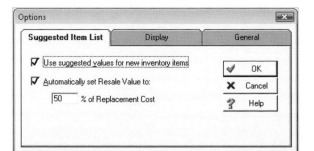

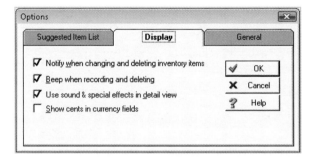

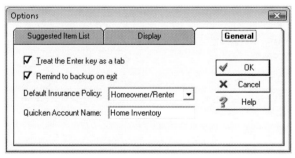

3. Click the **Suggested Item List** tab to see the default settings for your inventory:

   a. Clear the **Use Suggested Values For New Inventory Items** check box if you do not want Quicken to use its database to suggest values for items you choose from its Suggested Items List.

   b. Click **Automatically Set Resale Value To** if you want Quicken to set a resale value at the percentage you enter in the text box. Otherwise, Quicken uses the replacement cost for the item as its resale value.

4. Click the **Display** tab to set how the inventory is displayed and associated sounds:

   a. Clear the **Notify When Changing And Deleting Inventory Items** check box to stop a warning prompt from appearing when you change or delete an item.

   b. Clear the **Beep When Recording And Deleting** check box to turn off the sound when you record an item.

   c. Clear the **Use Sound & Special Effects In Detail View** check box to turn off the sound of a page turning when you click either Prev Item or Next Item.

   d. Click the **Show Cents In Currency Fields** check box to include exact amounts.

5. Click the **General** tab to set the inventory name, type of insurance, and other options:

   a. Clear the **Treat The Enter Key As A Tab** check box if you want to use ENTER to complete an entry, as it does by default in a Quicken register. Otherwise, pressing ENTER moves the cursor between fields like pressing the TAB key does.

   b. Clear the **Remind To Backup On Exit** check box if you don't want to be reminded to back up your data each time you leave Quicken Home Inventory.

   c. Click the **Default Insurance Policy** down arrow, and click which type of policy covers your goods. You can choose **Unassigned** and move items later to other types if you want.

   d. Enter the name of the account in the **Quicken Account Name** field where you want your information sent if you have more than one Quicken file.

   e. After you have entered all of your choices, click **OK** to close the dialog box.

Understand Quicken Home Inventory

Quicken Home Inventory comes preset with locations, categories, suggested items, and suggested replacement costs. You determine which way you want to view your possessions—either by location, such as the living room—or by

NOTE

A companion product from Quicken, called Quicken Home Inventory Manager, allows you to integrate your inventory with photo documentation. For more information go to www.quickenhomeinventory.com

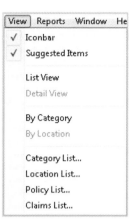

category, such as furnishings. There are several combinations of views available. To see them, click the **View** menu. Depending on the view you are currently in, there may be only one choice available to you:

- If you are in Category view, your only choice is **By Location**.
- If you are in Location view, your only choice is **By Category**.
- If you are in List view, your only choice is **Detail View**.
- If you are in Detail view, your only choice is **List View**.

Each time you enter an item, it is included in the total for that category and location. You can change, delete, or move items between locations and categories.

The tools on the toolbar are useful shortcuts to summary lists and other dialog boxes. Use the tools to open their respective dialog boxes, and then click **Close** to put them away.

1. Click **Locations** to open a list of your inventory items listed by locations in your home. You may add new locations and edit and delete locations from the Quicken default list. To edit the location of your items:

   a. Select the location you want to edit.

   b. Click **Edit** and type the new name of the location.

   c. Click **OK** to close the Edit Location dialog box.

2. Click **Categories** to open a list of the Quicken default inventory categories, such as Furnishings, Electronics, Office Equipment, and so forth. You may change the category of your items in the same manner as changing locations.

3. Click **Policies** to both open the list of default insurance policies provided by Quicken and enter new policies. The display shows any differences between your coverage on each policy and the replacement cost of your items. If there is a negative difference, consider obtaining more insurance, as policies should cover at least the replacement value of insured items.

4. Click **Claims** to open a list of all your insurance claims or to enter a claim on your inventory items.

5. Click **Find** to display the Find Item dialog box. You can search for a specific item using the information you have entered in the Item Description field, the Item Notes field, or both:

   a. Enter the item for which you are looking.

b. Click **Item Description** to have Quicken search for the name you entered in the Item Description areas of your inventory.

c. Click **Item Notes** to include your notes in the search.

d. Click **Find All** to find all occurrences of this item in your Quicken Home Inventory.

e. Click **Close** to close the dialog box.

6. Click **Move Item** to change the location of individual items or groups of items. You can view the items by both current location and insurance policy:

a. Click the **Current Location** down arrow to choose the location to which you are moving the item.

b. Select the item you want to move. If you want to move several items, hold down **SHIFT** to select the first and last item in a contiguous list, or hold down **CTRL** to select noncontiguous items.

c. Select the new location from the list on the right side of the dialog box.

d. Click **Move** to change the location of the inventory item.

e. Click **Item Info** to see a summary of the information about a selected item.

f. Click **Close** to close the dialog box.

Start a Home Inventory

To start a Home Inventory, you begin by entering your belongings. You can use the List view to enter each item and use the default values supplied by Quicken. For a more accurate record, use Detail view. As you can see in Figure 6-5, you can track a lot of information about each item.

1. Click the **Property & Debt** menu, and click **Quicken Home Inventory Manager**.

2. Click the **View** menu, and click **By Location** if it isn't already selected (it will appear dim if it is already selected). If necessary, click the **View** menu again, and click **Detail View**. The window that opens looks similar to the one pictured in Figure 6-5.

3. Click **Description** and enter the name of your item, or choose it from the **Suggested Items List** on the right side of the window.

4. Press **TAB** and enter the make and model of this item. Press **TAB** again and enter the serial number.

5. Press **TAB**, enter where the item was purchased, press **TAB** again, and enter the purchase date.

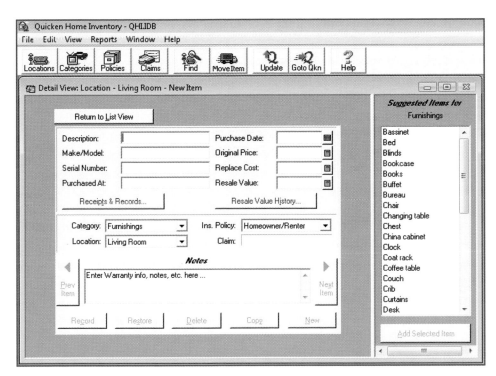

Figure 6-5: *The Detail view of Quicken Home Inventory allows you to keep a complete and accurate record of all your possessions.*

6. Press **TAB**, enter the original price, and press **TAB** again. If you chose an item from the Suggested Items List, Quicken will enter a replacement cost and a resale value based on the percentage you entered in the Edit menu options (see "Set Options for Quicken Home Inventory" earlier in this chapter).

7. Click **Receipts & Records** to record what type of receipt you have for this item and where the receipt and other records pertaining to this item are located. Click **OK** to close the Receipts & Records dialog box.

8. Click **Resale Value History** to open the Resale Value History dialog box. This window shows the chronological resale value history of this item. As the value of most items decreases over time, it is a good idea to periodically review the current resale value of your items and adjust them as necessary. Click **Close** to close the Resale Value History dialog box.

9. Click the **Category** down arrow, and choose the category from the drop-down list.

10. Click the **Location** down arrow, and choose the location from the drop-down list.

11. Change the **Insurance Policy** field if necessary, and make any needed changes.

12. Enter any notes pertaining to this item.

13. Click **Record**.

14. Click **Next Item** and repeat steps 3–14 to enter another item.

15. Click **Return To List View** to display all items in this location or category.

Create and Print Reports in Quicken Home Inventory

Quicken Home Inventory provides a number of reports for you to view and print.

TIP

If an item does not appear on the Suggested Items List in one category, check another category.

NOTE

In Quicken Home Inventory, click **Goto Qkn** on the toolbar to return to Quicken at any time. Quicken Home Inventory will still be available in the Windows taskbar at the bottom of the screen.

QUICKSTEPS

PROTECTING YOUR INVENTORY DATA WITH PASSWORDS

As you use your Home Inventory, you might want to protect your work by creating a password so that no one can inadvertently access or change your information. You can change or delete this password at any time.

CREATE A PASSWORD IN QUICKEN HOME INVENTORY

1. In the Quicken Home Inventory window, click the **File** menu, and click **Password**. The Password dialog box appears.

File	Edit	View	Reports	Window	Help
New...					Ctrl+N
Open...					Ctrl+O
Close					
Print...					Ctrl+P
Print Preview					
Print Setup...					
Backup...					
Restore...					
Import					▸
Password...					
Update Quicken...					
Goto Quicken					Ctrl+Q
1 C:\Users\...\Quicken\QHI.IDB					
Exit					

2. Type your new password in the **Password** field.

3. Press **TAB** and type the password again in the **Confirm Password** field.

4. Click **OK** to close the dialog box. Make a note of your password, and keep it in a safe place. If you lose the password, you will not be able to get into this file again.

Continued . . .

1. Click the **Reports** menu, and choose the report you want to see. An Inventory Report can be viewed by category, location, or insurance policy. An Insurance Report can be viewed by policy and sorted by either category or location. The Insurance Claim Summary and Detail Reports are not available unless you have entered insurance claim information.

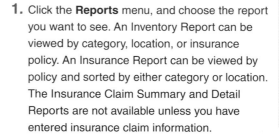

Reports	Window	Help
Inventory Value Summary		
Inventory Detail		
Insurance Coverage Summary		
Insurance Coverage Detail		
Insurance Claim Summary		
Insurance Claim Detail		

2. Click **Inventory Value Summary** to open a summary report.

3. Click the **View** down arrow, and click **Category** to display each item in each category. This type of report shows a subtotal by category and a grand total.

4. Click the **View** down arrow, and click **Location** to display the same information subtotaled by location.

5. Click the **Reports** menu, and click **Inventory Detail** to display a detailed report of each inventory item with the same fields displayed as indicated in Detail view.

6. Click **Select Items**. The Select Items For Inventory Detail Report dialog box appears.

7. Click **Clear All** to deselect all items and choose the items manually.

8. Click **Select All** (which is selected by default) to display all your inventory items.

9. Click **OK** to close the dialog box.

10. Click **Preview** to display how the report will look when it is printed and how many pages it will be.

11. Click **Next Page** or **Prev Page** to move between the pages.

12. Click **Close** to close the preview.

13. Click **Print** to open the Windows Print dialog box.

14. If needed, select the printer name, and change the number of copies.

15. Click **OK** to print the report.

Send Quicken Home Inventory Data to Quicken

You can add your Quicken Home Inventory resale value to a Quicken asset account and more accurately reflect your net worth and financial position. From Quicken Home Inventory:

1. Click the **Update** icon on the toolbar. You are asked to click **Yes** to send your inventory data to your Quicken file. It will be displayed as "Home Inventory" in the Property & Debt Activity Center on the Account bar.

Update

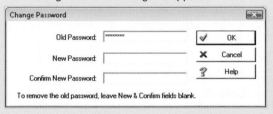
PROTECTING YOUR INVENTORY DATA WITH PASSWORDS *(Continued)*

CHANGE OR DELETE A PASSWORD IN QUICKEN HOME INVENTORY

1. Click the **File** menu, and click **Password**. The Change Password dialog box appears.

Change Password	
Old Password:	✔ OK
New Password:	✘ Cancel
Confirm New Password:	❓ Help
To remove the old password, leave New & Confirm fields blank.	

2. Type your current password in the **Old Password** field.

3. Press **TAB** and type your new password in the **New Password** field, or leave the field blank to no longer use a password.

4. Press **TAB** and enter your new password again, or leave the **Confirm Password** field blank.

5. Click **OK**.

CAUTION

If you lose the password for a file and you must have access to it, you can contact Quicken Product Support. They will instruct you to send them the file, and they will recover the data and send it back to you. Quicken charges a fee for this service.

---

2. Click **Yes**. The resale value of your inventory is sent to Quicken.

3. To verify that the information is in Quicken, click the **Goto Qkn** icon on the toolbar.

4. Click **Quicken Home** and then click the **Property & Debt Center** to see the accounts there. Your Home Inventory Account should be listed.

Back Up Quicken Home Inventory

After you have completed all of your inventory entries and have sent the inventory information to Quicken, click **Close** to close the Quicken Home Inventory. A backup message appears asking if you want to back up your information at this time. If you choose **Don't Backup**, Quicken Home Inventory closes and you are returned to Quicken. If you choose **Backup** to create a backup of this file, the Backup dialog box appears.

1. Click the **Backup Drive** down arrow to designate the location of your back up.

2. Enter a file name if you do not want to use the default name provided by Quicken. If you have used this file name before, you will see a dialog box asking if you want to overwrite that file. Click **Yes** to use the same file name as before. Overwriting the backup will update the file to your current information. If you click **No**, you are returned to the Backup dialog box to enter a new name.

3. Click **OK** to run the backup.

4. Quicken Home Inventory closes and you are returned to Quicken.

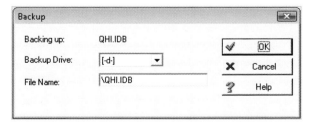

Chapter 7
Keeping Your Records Up to Date

What does it mean to reconcile an account? Why should you do it? *Reconciling* is the process of verifying that what is in your Quicken register is the same as what the bank or other financial institution shows in their records. Reconciling, or *balancing*, your checking and other accounts ensures that you have entered any fees and charges, that all deposits have been credited to your account (banks do make errors), and that your records accurately reflect what has happened during the period since you last balanced your account. This chapter will discuss how to reconcile and update checking and savings accounts, credit card statements, and investment accounts from paper statements as well as from online ones. In addition, you'll learn how to set up and maintain records information your family may need in an emergency.

7

Reconcile Checking and Savings Accounts

You are probably familiar with the checking and savings account statements sent by your bank. They show the balance at the beginning of the month, all of the transactions for the account that occurred since the last statement, any fees charged to your account, and the bank's balance for the account at the end of the month. This section will show you how to reconcile your Quicken checking and savings accounts with your bank's paper statements and online information. It will also discuss how to deal with items that appear on the bank statement that aren't recorded in Quicken, what to do if the account doesn't balance the first time, and how to find discrepancies.

Reconcile Quicken with Your Bank's Paper Statement

One of the great features of Quicken is its ability to quickly reconcile or balance your bank's statement to your Quicken account. To reconcile an account with the bank's paper statement:

1. Click the name of the account you want to reconcile in the Account bar to open its register.

2. Click **Reconcile** on the register menu bar to open the Statement Summary dialog box. You can also click the **Cash Flow** menu, and click **Reconcile**. If you see the Reconcile Online Account window, click **Paper Statement** to open the Statement Summary dialog box.

3. Confirm the amount in the **Opening Balance** field. If the statement opening balance is not what Quicken shows, type the statement amount. Press TAB to continue.

4. Type the amount from your bank statement in the **Ending Balance** field, and press TAB.

5. Change the date in the **New Statement Ending Date** field to the date of the bank statement, if the two are different. Press TAB to continue.

6. Enter any service charge shown on the bank statement in the **Service Charge** field, and enter the date on which it was charged. Press TAB.

7. In the **Category** field, enter or select the category for the service charge. By default, Quicken uses **Bank Charge**. Press TAB.

NOTE

The first time you reconcile a Quicken account, Quicken uses the starting account balance as the opening balance. After you have used Quicken once to reconcile the account, Quicken uses the ending balance from the last time you reconciled as the opening balance.

Statement Summary: Checking

The last statement ending date: 7/10/2006

1. Enter the following from your bank statement.

Opening Balance: 915.22

Ending Balance: 24,122.75

New Statement Ending Date: 7/31/2006

2. Enter and categorize your interest and bank charges, if any.

Service Charge: | Date: 7/10/2006

Category: Bank Charge

Interest Earned: 2.57 | Date: 7/31/2006

Category: Interest Inc

OK | Cancel

NOTE

"Interest Inc" in Quicken is an abbreviation for "Interest Income."

TIP

If most of the transactions have cleared, click **Clear All** and then click the transactions that haven't cleared to deselect them.

8. In the **Interest Earned** field, enter the amount of interest shown on the bank statement. Press **TAB** and enter the date the bank credited the account in the second **Date** field. Press **TAB**.

9. In the **Category** field, enter or select the category for the interest. By default, Quicken uses **Interest Inc** as the category.

10. Click **OK** to close the dialog box and open the Statement Summary window. All of the transactions you have entered into this Quicken account that have not yet been cleared appear in this window, an example of which is shown in Figure 7-1.

11. Click **Clr** (for "cleared") by each deposit and check that appears on the bank statement. After you have selected all the cleared checks and deposits, the difference shown in the bottom-right corner of the window should be zero. If it does, you're done reconciling. If you don't have a zero difference, see "Make Corrections in the Statement Summary Window" next in this chapter.

12. Click **Finished** to open the Reconciliation Complete dialog box.

13. Click **Yes** to create a Reconciliation Report, or click **No** if you don't want to create one. If you do not want to be asked this question again, click **Don't Show Me This Screen Again**. If you click Yes, the Reconciliation Report Setup dialog box appears.

14. Type a title in the **Report Title** field if you want. If you leave this field blank, Quicken uses the default title "Reconciliation Report."

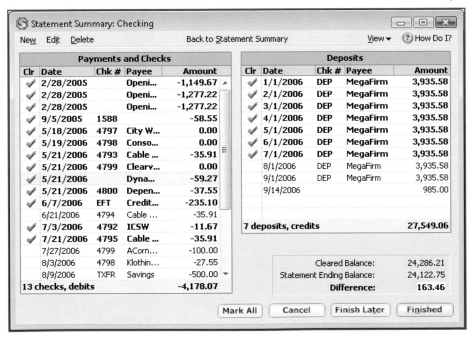

Figure 7-1: **The Statement Summary window allows you to quickly reconcile an account.**

15. Change the date in the **Show Reconciliation To Bank Balance As Of** field if you want it to be the statement date instead of today's date.

16. Click either **All Transactions** or **Summary And Uncleared** to tell Quicken what to include on the report. The default selection, Summary And Uncleared, makes for a shorter, more concise report.

17. If you have established savings goals and want to include them in the report, click the **Show Savings Goal Transactions** check box. Chapter 9 discusses savings goals and other financial-planning matters in more detail.

18. Click the printer icon to open a Windows Print dialog box. Click **Preview** to see how the report will appear when printed, and then click **Print** in the Preview window or click **OK** in the Print dialog box to print the report.

Make Corrections in the Statement Summary Window

If your transactions do not immediately balance, you can make corrections in the Statement Summary window to eventually reconcile the account:

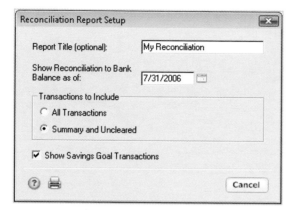

- Click **New** to enter a transaction into the register that appears on the bank statement but that has not been entered into the register. This could be a charge for new checks or money withdrawn using a cash machine or a debit card. See "Deal with Unrecorded Items" next in this chapter.

- Select a transaction and click **Edit** to make changes to that transaction in the register. This is great for fixing transpositions or penny errors.

- Select a transaction and click **Delete** to permanently remove a transaction from the register.

- Click **Back To Statement Summary** to go back to the Statement Summary dialog box to make changes to service charges or interest.

- Click **View** to change how Quicken sorts the transactions in this window.

- Click **How Do I?** to display a Help screen.

- Click **Mark All** to mark all of the transactions displayed in the window. If it has already been clicked, **Clear All** is displayed on the menu bar to perform the reverse operation.

- Click **Cancel** to stop the reconciliation. This opens a dialog box that asks if you want to save your work or close the window without saving it. Click **Yes** to close the window without saving your work.

NOTE

If you have turned off the Reconciliation Report message, you can still obtain a Reconciliation Report. Click the **Reports** menu, click **Banking**, and click **Reconciliation**. The Reconciliation Report Setup dialog box will appear.

QUICKFACTS

RECONCILING FOR THE FIRST TIME

Before you reconcile a Quicken account for the first time, you may have to enter checks or deposits that occurred before you started using Quicken. When you entered the beginning balance of your account from last month's ending bank statement, the bank's balance did not include outstanding checks or deposits. Before you reconcile, enter any of those checks or deposits that had not cleared the bank as of last month's statement, even though you made the transaction before the opening date of your account. That way, these transactions will be available to you during the reconciliation process.

NOTE

You might want to use a split transaction for cash withdrawals so that you can keep track of how much money you are paying, if any, to use the cash machine.

Cleared Balance:	27,079.15
Statement Ending Balance:	27,079.78
Difference:	**-0.63**

Cancel	Finish Later	Finished

- Click **Finish Later** to save what you have done so far. When you return to the register, you will notice that any transactions you have selected now display a "c" in the Clr column. When you have finished the reconciliation, the "c" turns into an "R," and, if you have set the preferences to their default setting, the entire transaction will be grey.

- Click **Finished** to complete the reconciliation and open the Reconciliation Complete dialog box.

Deal with Unrecorded Items

Items may appear on your bank statement that do not appear in Quicken. Some examples can be automatic withdrawals, such as payments for your safety deposit box, or withdrawals from the cash machine you forgot to record. To enter an item from the Statement Summary window:

1. Click **New** on the menu bar to open the account register.

2. Enter the date on which the transaction occurred. The default is today's date, but you probably want to use the actual transaction date.

3. Enter the type of transaction in the **Num** field, and then fill in the **Payee**, **Category**, and **Amount** fields.

4. Click **Enter** and then click **Return To Reconcile** to return to the Statement Summary window.

Return to Reconcile	Enter	Edit	Split	☆ Rate	📎 Attach
Insurance Company				450 00	*Deposit*
Insurance:Home Insurance					

FIND STATEMENT DISCREPANCIES

Several things need to be considered when trying to find a discrepancy between a bank statement and your Quicken account register:

- Ensure you are working with the right account. It's easy to click the wrong name if you have several accounts.

- Verify that the "Deposits, Credits" total amount and the "Checks, Debits" total amount displayed at the bottom of the Statement Summary window match the total amounts shown on the bank statement.

- Check the **Difference** amount in the lower-right corner of the window. If the difference is evenly divisible by nine, you may have transposed an entry. For example, if the difference is $.63, you may have entered a check into Quicken as $29.18 and written the actual check for $29.81.

NOTE

Using Quicken's Scheduled Transactions feature can ensure that all of your transactions are entered into your check register.

CAUTION

Working back and forth between reconciling online and with a paper statement can be confusing. Transactions that appear on your paper bank statement may not appear in the Statement Summary window, since Quicken has already reconciled them.

TIP

When you pay your credit card or other bills, take the envelopes directly to the post office rather than leaving them in the mailbox. This ensures that anyone stealing mail from the boxes cannot get your information.

- If the difference is not a transposition, you may have neglected to enter a transaction, or you entered a deposit as a check or vice versa. If the difference does not equal a check amount on either your bank statement or your register, look in both for a transaction equaling half the amount of the difference. You may have entered a deposit as a payment or vice versa.

- Determine if the difference is positive or negative. If the difference is negative, the bank shows more money than your register does. The bank may have a deposit you haven't entered, or you may have cleared checks the bank hasn't received. If the difference is positive, the bank shows less money than your register does. You may have neglected to enter a fee or an automatic withdrawal in your register.

- Watch for pennies. If your handwriting is not clearly legible, the automated machinery used by the bank for clearing checks may not read the amount correctly, for example, it might mistake an eight as a three.

- Take a time out. If you've been looking at your account for some time and can't locate the discrepancy, walk away for a few minutes. Often, when you come back after a break, the difference seems to appear as if by magic.

Reconcile Online

Before you reconcile online, ensure that all of your transactions have been downloaded and that you have reviewed and accepted them. When you update your Quicken register, the transactions can be automatically reconciled (see the QuickSteps "Activating Automatic Reconciliation"). There are two methods for reconciling online:

- You can update several times during a month and then reconcile to the paper statement at the end of the month.

- You can reconcile each time you download transactions.

- Whichever method you use, stick to that method.

To perform the online reconciliation after you have downloaded and accepted all of the transactions:

1. Open the register of the account with which you want to work.

2. Click **Reconcile** to open the Reconcile Online Account dialog box.

3. Click **Online Balance**. This option lets you reconcile to the balance that was last downloaded for this account.

USING A QUICKEN ADJUSTMENT

If you do not want to locate a discrepancy between the bank and your Quicken register, Quicken will enter an adjusting entry for you.

Adjust Balance

The total of the items you have marked is $0.63 less than the total of the items shown on your bank statement.

You may have Quicken enter a balance adjustment in your register for this amount, or click Cancel to go back to reconciling.

Adjustment Date 8/31/2006

[Adjust] [Cancel]

1. Click **Finished** in the Statement Summary window. The Adjust Balance dialog box appears.

2. Click in the **Adjustment Date** field, and enter the date of the adjustment. This can be the date of the paper statement or today's date, whichever makes more sense to you.

3. Click **Adjust**.

4. A Reconciliation Complete dialog box appears. Click **Yes** if you want to create a reconciliation report; click **No** if you do not. If you click No, the dialog box closes and you are returned to the register.

Reconciliation Complete

The items you have marked have been reconciled in your register. A Balance Adjustment has been entered to make it agree with your bank statement.

Would you like to create a reconciliation report?

[Yes] [No]

5. In your register, locate the balance adjustment that Quicken just created, and, if you want, change the category by clicking in the **Category** field and entering a new one. Click **Enter** to save the change.

Balance Adjustment	R	0 63
Misc		

4. Click **OK** to open the Statement Summary window. Items you have already accepted are selected by default.

5. Verify any unselected transactions that are more than a few days old. If a transaction is on your register and is not included with your downloaded transactions, you may have made an error entering that transaction into your Quicken register, or the transaction may have been lost.

6. Complete the reconciliation process by clicking **Finished**.

Reconcile Credit Card Statements

Reconciling your credit card statement is similar to reconciling your checking or savings account statement, especially if you enter your credit card purchases as you make them. If you wait until the credit card statement arrives to enter the charges and categorize them, however, the process takes a bit longer.

RECONCILE A PAPER CREDIT CARD STATEMENT

To reconcile your credit card account to a paper statement:

1. Click the **Cash Flow** menu, click **Cash Flow Accounts**, and click the account with which you want to work.

   –Or–

   Click the name of the account on the Account bar to open the register.

2. Click **Reconcile** to open the Credit Card Statement Summary dialog box.

3. Enter the total from the statement in the **Charges, Cash Advances** field.

4. Click in the **Payments, Credits** field, and enter the total from the statement.

5. Click in the **Ending Balance** field, and enter the balance due on the statement.

6. Click in the **New Statement Ending Date** field, and enter the ending date of the statement.

7. Click in the **Finance Charges** field, and enter the amount of finance charges, if any. Click in the **Date** field, and change the date of the charges from the default of today's date if needed.

8. Click in the **Category** field, and either choose a category from the drop-down list or type the category for the finance charges.

QUICKSTEPS

ACTIVATING AUTOMATIC RECONCILIATION

When you have activated the downloading of transactions from your bank accounts, you can use a Quicken feature that makes reconciling automatic each time you download.

1. Open the register of the account you want to use.

2. Click **Reconcile** on the toolbar.

3. Click **Online Balance**.

4. Click **Auto Reconcile After Compare To Register**.

The setting takes effect after the next time you go online. Quicken will automatically reconcile the downloaded transactions after you have accepted them. If the balances do not match, Quicken displays a Statement History dialog box to help you find the problem.

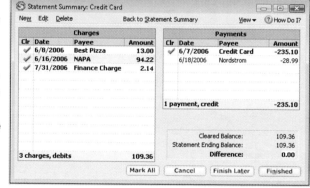

9. Click **OK**. The Credit Card Statement Summary window opens.

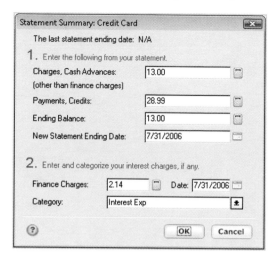

10. Proceed as described in "Reconcile Quicken with Your Bank's Paper Statement" earlier in the chapter.

11. If zero appears in the Difference field, click **Finished** to open the Make Credit Card Payment dialog box. You are asked if you want to make a payment on the balance now. If so:

    a. Click **Bank Account** to choose the account from which to write the check.

    b. Choose the method of preparing the check, and click **Yes**.

    - If you click **Printed Check**, a check facsimile opens for you to fill in. The default category is the credit card account.

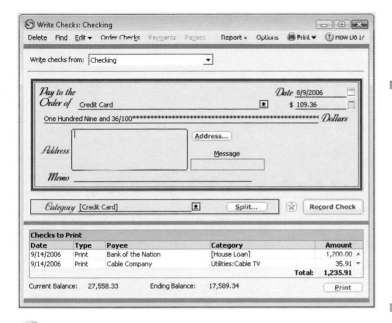

- If you click **Hand Written Check**, the check is entered into the register and pauses for you to enter the check number.

- If you click **No**, the window closes and you are returned to the register.

RECONCILE A CREDIT CARD ONLINE

As with reconciling bank accounts, if your credit card company offers it, downloading and reconciling transactions directly into your credit card register is the most efficient way to reconcile your account. However, if you want to keep track of your spending by category, you must remember to enter the category for each downloaded transaction, although if your transactions are to the same establishment for the same purpose, the category will carry over from transaction to transaction. The process for performing an online reconciliation of your credit card account is the same as described in "Reconcile Online" earlier in the chapter.

MAKE CREDIT CARD STATEMENT ADJUSTMENTS

Sometimes, you just don't want to take the time to find all the discrepancies in a credit card register. Perhaps you've just started entering transactions and some of the beginning balances aren't right. Quicken can help you fix these problems.

1. When you have completed the reconciliation as far as you want, click **Finished** in the Statement Summary window. The Adjusting Register To Agree With Statement dialog box appears.

2. In the **Register Missing One Or More Payments** area, if there is one in your dialog box, click in the **Category** field, and change the category from the default "Misc" if you choose.

3. In the **Register Missing One Or More Charges** area, if there is one in your dialog box, click in the **Category** field, and change the category.

4. Click **Adjust** to have the entries recorded in the credit Card Account register.

5. If you want to apportion each entry between several categories, make no changes to the categories in the Adjusting Register To Agree With Statement

TIP

If you want to keep track of your credit card spending by category, you will need to enter each transaction separately, both charges and credits, so that you can categorize them.

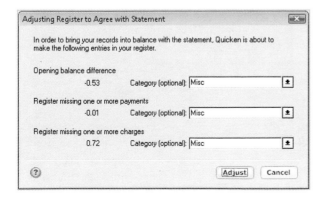

FINDING AND RESOLVING CREDIT CARD ERRORS

Using Quicken to reconcile your credit card statements may help you find errors in your account. To ensure there are no errors on your statement and that your account is protected:

- Check each item on the statement as soon as you get it.

- Ensure that each charge is the amount you expected.

- Know the date on which your statement usually arrives. Set an alert in Quicken to remember that date. If your statement has not arrived, call the credit card company to advise them the statement has not been delivered.

- If the credit card company provides online access to your account, go online on a regular basis to ensure that each charge to your account is valid.

RESOLVE CREDIT CARD ERRORS

If you do find an error, or if you have a dispute with a seller, take the following steps:

- Call the seller that charged you to see if the issue can be resolved between the two of you. Document the call; the name of the seller's agent; and the date, time, and nature of the problem.

- Call the credit card company to tell them of the problem. Document the call as to date, time, and the name of the person with whom you spoke.

- Write a letter to the credit card company explaining the same information. The Fair Credit Billing Act requires that you notify your credit card company in writing. Make sure it is addressed to the correct address for billing inquiries. This address is usually

Continued . . .

dialog box. When you return to the register, locate each adjustment and select the first one with which you want to work:

- Click **Split** to open the Split Transaction window, and assign the categories you choose.

- Select the other adjustments you want to change, and assign categories to them.

Reconcile Investment Accounts

You use the same process to reconcile an investment account as you do with a checking account, except you have to balance to both a cash balance and a share balance. If your financial institution offers it, the easiest way to reconcile each account is to sign up for their download services. That way, you can download each transaction directly from your broker and use Quicken's Compare To Portfolio feature to monitor the account.

Reconcile an Investment Account to a Paper Statement

The process of reconciling an investment account is the same as described in "Reconcile Quicken with Your Bank's Paper Statement" earlier in the chapter. To reconcile an investment account to a paper statement:

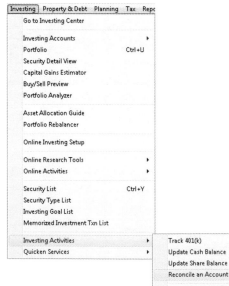

1. Click **Investing Center** on the Account bar. Click the account you want to reconcile.

2. When the Activity Center for the account displays, click the **Summary** tab if it is not already selected (see Figure 7-2). Under the **Account Status** section, click **Options** and then click **Reconcile This Account**.

   –Or–

   Click the **Transactions** tab, click the **Investing** menu, click **Investing Activities**, and then click **Reconcile An Account**.

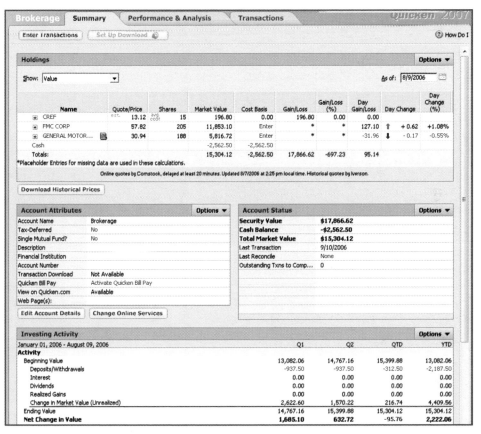

QUICKSTEPS

FINDING AND RESOLVING CREDIT CARD ERRORS (Continued)

listed on the back of your credit card. Include any supporting information. For further protection, send this letter via certified mail and ask for a return receipt as proof. This verifies both that you sent the letter within 60 days of the statement date and that your credit card company received the letter.

- Your credit card company must respond to your dispute letter, in writing, within 30 days. The credit card company then has two billing cycles, or 90 days—whichever is less—to determine if the charge was in error. They are required to notify you in writing of their determination. If the charge was correct but there is still a dispute, write the credit card company again. They are not allowed to charge interest or require payment until the issue has been resolved.

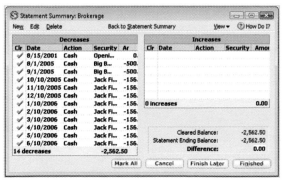

Figure 7-2: *The Summary section of the Investing Activity Center shows the holdings, account attributes, account status, and investing activity of this investment account.*

In either case, the Statement Summary dialog box appears.

3. Click in the **Starting Cash Balance** field, and enter the beginning balance amount from your statement.

4. Click in the **Ending Cash Balance** field, and enter the amount from your statement.

5. Click in the **Statement Ending Date** field, and type the date.

6. Click **OK**. The Statement Summary window opens. This is similar to the Statement Summary window for your checking account. The only difference is that instead of checks and deposits, you see decreases and increases to the account.

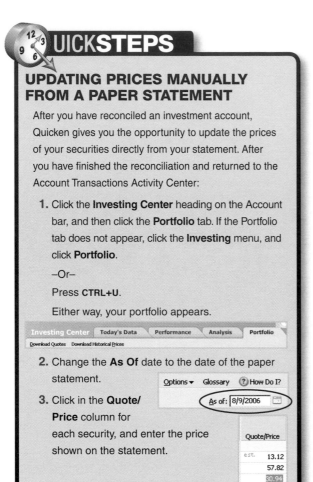

UPDATING PRICES MANUALLY FROM A PAPER STATEMENT

After you have reconciled an investment account, Quicken gives you the opportunity to update the prices of your securities directly from your statement. After you have finished the reconciliation and returned to the Account Transactions Activity Center:

1. Click the **Investing Center** heading on the Account bar, and then click the **Portfolio** tab. If the Portfolio tab does not appear, click the **Investing** menu, and click **Portfolio**.

   –Or–

   Press **CTRL+U**.

   Either way, your portfolio appears.

2. Change the **As Of** date to the date of the paper statement.

3. Click in the **Quote/ Price** column for each security, and enter the price shown on the statement.

7. Click each transaction to note that it has cleared.

8. Click **Finished** to complete the reconciliation. The Reconciliation Complete dialog box appears. Click **Yes** to create a reconciliation report. Click **No** to close the dialog box and return to the Account Transactions Activity Center.

Reconcile a Single Mutual Fund Account

Since single mutual fund accounts have no cash balances, you reconcile only the share balances. There are two ways of updating this type of account: with and without transaction detail.

USE A STATEMENT THAT SHOWS TRANSACTION DETAIL

If your mutual fund statement includes the transaction detail:

1. Click **Investing Center** on the Account bar, and click the account with which you want to work.

2. Click either the **Summary** or the **Transactions** tab. Click the **Enter Transactions** button to open the Buy - Shares Bought dialog box, which is displayed in Figure 7-3.

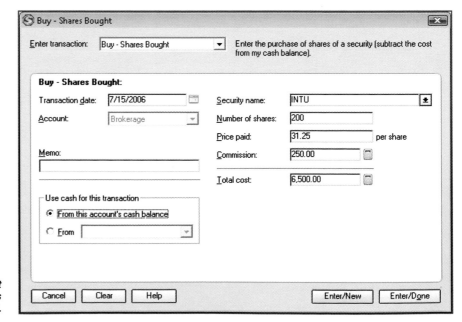

Figure 7-3: **The Buy - Shares Bought dialog box is used to enter transactions into your investment account.**

3. Enter each transaction listed on your statement. Click **Enter/New** to move to a new transaction. Click **Enter/Done** when you have entered all of the transactions shown on the statement. You are returned to the Center from which you started, either Summary or Transactions.

4. If you started from the Transactions Activity Center, click the **Summary** tab to see the Account Status section. Click **Options** on the Account Status title bar, and click **Reconcile This Account**.

5. Follow the procedure in "Reconcile an Investment Account to a Paper Statement" earlier in the chapter.

USE A STATEMENT WITHOUT TRANSACTION DOLLAR DETAIL

Some brokerage and mutual fund statements only show transactions in terms of shares and not the dollars relating to those shares. To reconcile that type of statement:

1. Click the account with which you want to work.

2. Click **Options** on the Account Status menu bar, and click **Reconcile This Account**. The Reconcile Mutual Fund Account dialog box appears.

3. Enter the starting share balance and ending share balance from the statement in the relevant fields.

4. Enter the statement ending date.

5. Click **OK**. The Reconcile Mutual Fund Account window opens.

6. Click each transaction that appears in the window. Note that the balance is displayed in number of shares rather than in dollars. The ending balance in the Reconcile Mutual Fund Account window should be the same as the ending balance on the statement.

7. Click **Finished** when you have reconciled the account. The Reconciliation Complete dialog box appears. Click **OK** to close the dialog box.

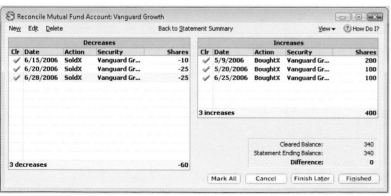

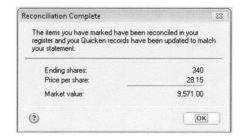

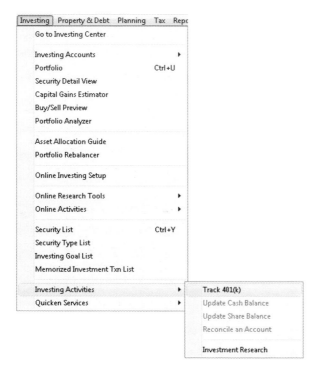

Update 401(k) Accounts

401(k) accounts are tracked a bit differently from other investment accounts. If you have Quicken Deluxe, Premier, or Quicken Home and Business editions, you can track actual shares or dollar amounts. If your financial institution offers it, you can even download your transaction details. You can also manually enter the information from a paper statement or use the 401(k) Update Wizard. The easiest method to use is the download option; however, the 401(k) Update Wizard lets you track the performance of funds in your 401(k).

USE THE 401(K) UPDATE WIZARD

1. Click the **Investing** menu, click **Investing Activities**, and click **Track 401(k)**.

2. Click **Update An Existing 401(k) Account**, and then click **OK**.

3. Select the 401(k) account with which you want to work, and click **OK**. The 401(k) Update Wizard starts.

4. Enter the date of the statement in the **This Statement Ends** field.

5. Click either **Yes** or **No** in response to the question Does Your Statement Show How Many Shares Of Each Security You Own?, depending on which is correct.

6. Click either **No** or **Yes** in response to the question Did You Take Out A New Loan Against This Account During The Last Statement Period?, and then click **Next**.

7. Enter the amount in the **Employee Contributions** field, as shown on the statement.

8. Enter the amount in the **Employer Matching Contributions** field, as shown on the statement.

9. If needed, click in the **Other Contributions And Payments** field, and enter those amounts from the statement. Quicken adds all of these transactions, which should match your paper statement.

10. Click **Next**. The **Total Withdrawals This Period** dialog box appears.

11. Enter the amount in each of the fields applicable to you from the statement. Quicken shows the total, which should match the statement. Click **Next**.

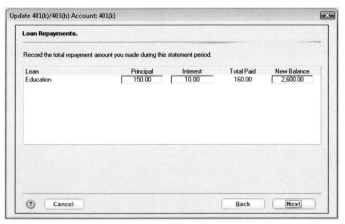

12. If you took out a loan during this period, you are asked to enter the purpose of the loan and the loan amount. You may also choose to set up an account to track the loan balance. Enter the relevant information, and click **Next**.

13. The Loan Repayments dialog box appears. Enter the amount of principal and interest paid, as shown on the statement, and then click **Next**.

14. The name of each security held in the account is displayed in the next dialog box. Click **Add New Security** if there is a security on the statement that does not appear on this list. Otherwise, click **Next**.

15. Click either **No** or **Yes** in response to the question Did You Move Any Money From One Security To Another?

16. If you clicked Yes, enter the number of transfers on the statement in the **How Many Transfers Appear On Your Statement?** field. Click **Next**.

17. If you selected Yes in step 5, enter the number of ending shares shown on your statement. If you selected No in step 5, you do not have that option. Enter the value in the **Market Value** field from the statement for each security in the account. Click **Next**.

18. Verify that the amount in the **Total Market Value** field shown on the statement matches the 401(k)/403(b) Update Summary page.

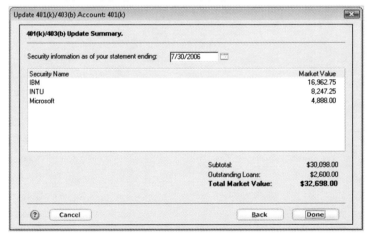

19. Click **Done**.

QUICKFACTS

UNDERSTANDING HOW QUICKEN WORKS WITH 401(K)/403(B) ACCOUNTS

When you add a 401(k)/403(b) account in Quicken Deluxe, Premier, and Home and Business editions, Quicken adds a special tax impact account. This account is not visible on the Account List, but you can see it on tax reports. (Learn more about taxes in Chapter 10.) This tax account tracks any transaction in this retirement account that may have an effect on your income taxes, such as early withdrawal of funds. Quicken uses the information in this hidden account in both reports and its tax planning tools. To ensure your tax planning tools and reports are as accurate as possible, do not change or remove any of the transactions in this account, nor the account itself.

NOTE

Some companies allow loans of up to 50 percent of your 401(k) account. However, the interest on these loans is not deductible on your income tax.

Reconcile Property & Debt Accounts

Property & Debt Center accounts can be reconciled or updated in much the same way as accounts in the other Centers. If you choose to update an asset account based on current market value, you can use documentation such as a property tax statement or valuation summary from a commercial appraisal. As you acquire and enter new items in your Home Inventory, that asset will be updated automatically when you transfer the information into Quicken. You may get monthly statements from a financial institution showing loan balances and loan payments due so that these accounts can be updated. While you can update these accounts without documentation, it is usually best to wait until you have written proof of your change before you make it. You can include the written proof as an attachment in Quicken, as described in Chapter 4.

Update an Asset or Liability Account

You use the same process to reconcile either an asset or a liability account.

1. Click **Property & Debt** on the Account bar.
2. Click the account you want to reconcile. That account's Activity Center appears.
3. If it is not selected, click the **Overview** tab.
4. Click **Reconcile Account**. The Update Account Balance dialog box appears.

5. In the Update Account Balance dialog box, click in the **Update Balance To** field, and enter the balance from the statement or other documentation. For an asset, this is the current value of the asset. For a loan, this is the balance due on the loan.
6. Click in the **Adjustment Date** field, and enter the date of the documentation.
7. Click the **Category For Adjustment** down arrow, and choose the category in which the adjustment will be entered. You might choose **Interest Exp** to reflect additional interest being added to a loan.
8. Click **OK** to return to the Activity Center. The adjustment has been added to the account.

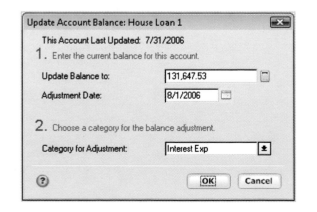

NOTE

If your home has increased in value or your boat's value has decreased and you want to enter the increase or decrease, check with your tax professional for a category.

USING THE FIND AND REPLACE DIALOG BOX

When you need to locate a number of transactions for one payee, one category, or one amount, Quicken has a useful Find utility.

1. Click the **Edit** menu, click **Find & Replace**, and click **Find/Replace**. The Find And Replace dialog box appears.

2. Click the **Look In** down arrow, and click the field where Quicken is to look for the data (you can also click **All Fields**).

3. Click the **Match If** down arrow, and click the type of match.

4. Click in the **Find** text box, and enter the information for which you want to search, which will depend on the field you are searching.

5. Click **Find All**. A list of all matching transactions is displayed in the Found List.

6. Click **Show Matches In Split** if you want Quicken to include information shown in the Split Transactions window.

7. Click **Mark All** to select all the items on the list, or choose only the transactions you want to change.

8. Click the **Replace** down arrow, and choose a field whose contents you want to replace.

9. Click in the **With** text box, and type the replacement text, or choose it from the drop-down list. Then click **Replace** to change the transactions.

10. Click **Done** to close the dialog box.

Watch for Escrow Discrepancies

If your financial institution pays real estate taxes or insurance premiums from the payments you send them each month, you may get an escrow statement from them each year. If you have set up your mortgage loan account using the Split Transactions window and have been tracking the portion of each payment that goes to insurance and the portion that goes to real estate taxes, as well as the portion that goes to principal and interest, it is an easy task to reconcile the escrow statement you receive.

1. Click the **Reports** menu, click **Banking**, click **Transaction**, and click **Customize** on the far right of the toolbar. The Customize Transaction dialog box appears.

2. Click the **Date Range** down arrow, and click the date range of the escrow statement. Click the **Display** tab if it is not already selected.

3. Click the **Subtotal By** down arrow, and click **Category** from the list.

4. Click the **Accounts** tab, click **Clear All**, and click the account from which you pay this loan.

5. Click the **Categories** tab, click **Clear All**, and click the categories that are on the escrow statement. Click the **Payee** down arrow to select the payee.

6. Click **OK** to return to or if you want to save this report, click **Save** in the Save Report dialog box that appears on the toolbar. Otherwise, click **Don't Save**. If you click Save, you will be prompted to name the report and designate the folder into which it should be saved.

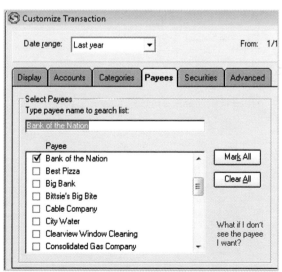

Match the totals on the report to your paper escrow statement, and make any changes to the loan account.

7. Click **OK** to close the Customize Transaction dialog box, and click **Close** in the Transaction window.

Prepare for Emergencies

Just as you are building a complete set of financial records with Quicken, it is a good idea to have a complete set of family-related information should it be needed in an emergency. In the Deluxe, Premier, and Home & Business editions, Quicken provides an Emergency Records Organizer to keep important personal and legal information in the same place as your financial data.

With the Emergency Records Organizer, you can:

- Organize all information about you and your family that might be needed during a time of crisis
- Create reports about this information by an entire topic or using selected areas of the Organizer
- Print customized reports for family members or others, such as legal or medical professionals
- Record insurance policy numbers, coverage, and policy locations; Social Security numbers of family members; medical information, such as shots or allergies; and even wishes for funeral arrangements

Use the Emergency Records Organizer

To enter information in the Emergency Records Organizer:

1. Click the **Property & Debt** menu, and then click **Emergency Records Organizer**. The Emergency Records Organizer Introduction window opens.

2. Click the **Create/Update Records** tab.

3. Click the **Select An Area** down arrow, and click one of the 11 areas in which to enter information.

4. Click an option under **Select A Topic**. The records pane on the right will display text boxes to enter information pertaining to that topic. Figure 7-4 gives an example of the first record under the Medical History topic of the Children's Emergency Info.

5. Enter the relevant information in each field. Press **TAB** to move between fields.

CAUTION

When you first open the Emergency Records Organizer and select Accounts, all of the accounts you currently have set up in Quicken are included in the Topic List. No new accounts can be added to this list through the Emergency Records Organizer. However, as you add new accounts, you can use the generic Other Accounts or add the new record to an existing account.

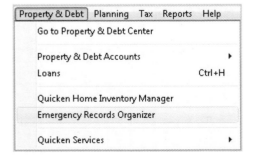

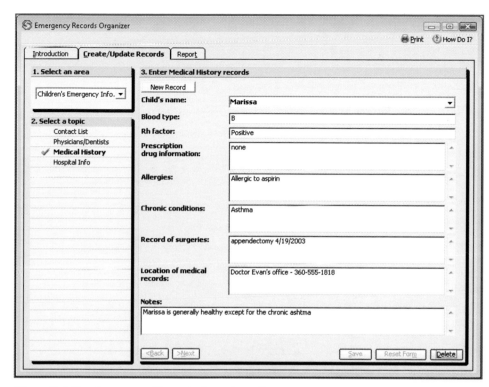

Figure 7-4: *The Emergency Records Organizer allows you to have a wide variety of personal, legal, and emergency information in one location.*

NOTE

The Notes area can hold up to 199 characters, including spaces.

6. Click **Save** to save the record when finished.

7. Click **New Record** to add another record in this topic.

Create Reports in the Emergency Records Organizer

One of the best uses of the Emergency Records Organizer is to create reports that may be needed by various professionals in case of an emergency.

1. With the Emergency Records Organizer displayed, click the **Report** tab, click the **Report Type** down arrow, and choose which report you want.

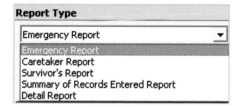

2. Click **Sort By Family Members** to include all information about each family member separately. Otherwise, it will be displayed by area.

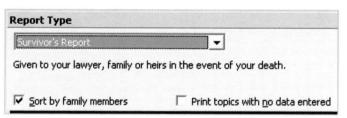

3. Click **Print Topics With No Data Entered** to show that data has not been entered about this topic as yet.

4. Click **Print** to print the report. If you need more than one copy, you must click Print for each copy.

5. Click **Close** to exit the Emergency Records Organizer.

Protect Your Data

As with your other valuable data, the information in the Emergency Records Organizer should be protected. Quicken suggests several ways to do this, each method offering a different level of protection.

Basic security can be provided by making a copy of your Quicken data on a CD or floppy disk and storing that media in a secure location, which might be a bank safety-deposit box.

Moderate security can be gained by assigning a password to protect your entire Quicken data file. To create such a password:

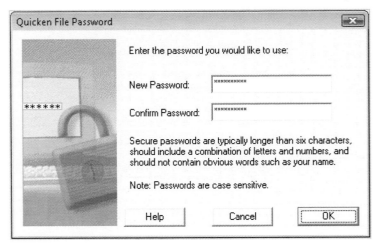

1. Click the **File** menu.
2. Click **Passwords** and click **File**. The Quicken File Password dialog box appears.
3. Type your new password in the **New Password** field. Press **TAB**.
4. Confirm your password by typing it again in the **Confirm Password** field.
5. Click **OK** to close the dialog box.

The highest level of security for this information is obtained as follows:

1. Create a new Quicken data file that will contain only the Emergency Records Organizer information by clicking the **File** menu and clicking **New**.
2. Choose **New Quicken File**, and click **OK**. Type a name for the file in the **File Name** field, and click **OK**.
3. Enter your emergency information into this file, not the one with your financial records.
4. Assign a password to this file. Copy or back up the file to a CD, floppy disk, DVD, or Flash drive. Make two copies as additional insurance in case one external media becomes unusable.
5. Delete the data file from your hard disk.

Chapter 8
Managing Your Investments

Your investments help shape your financial future. Whether you are saving for a new home, your children's education, or your own retirement, Quicken can help you with your investments in many ways. You can obtain a quick online quote for a specific security or learn the historical value of your portfolio. You can use Quicken to monitor prices on securities you already own or are thinking about purchasing. You can download information from your broker, analyze your asset allocation, estimate your capital gains, or use other sophisticated analysis tools included with Quicken. Whatever your financial position today, Quicken can help you strengthen it for tomorrow. The Investing Center not only gives you access to all of your investment accounts, it also provides links for downloading transactions, online quotes, and other investment services. You can set alerts and establish a Watch List, track the performance of both individual securities and your mutual funds, and get an analysis of your entire portfolio. The Investing Center displays two or more tabs (depending on the version of Quicken you are using). Each tab contains different views of your information in the form of graphs, charts, and tables, some of which are customizable.

8

Understand the Today's Data Tab

The Today's Data tab provides an Internet link so you can download quotes, gives you a way to set alerts for your investment accounts, provides information about your individual investment and retirement accounts, lists the securities you have told Quicken to watch for you, includes links to investing services, and updates all of your accounts in one step. To open the Investing Center:

1. Click **Investing Center** on the Account bar. Click the **Today's Data** tab if it isn't already selected.

   –Or–

   Click the **Investing** menu, and click **Go To Investing Center**.

2. The Investing Center opens with the Today's Data tab displayed, as shown in Figure 8-1.

Download Quotes

If you have an Internet connection, Quicken provides the means to download the most current *quotes*, or prices, for all of the securities in your portfolio. (A quote is the highest price being offered by a buyer or the lowest price being asked by a seller for a security at a given point in time.) To download quotes from the Today's Data tab:

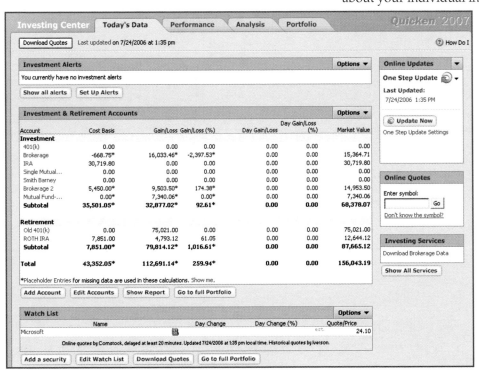

Figure 8-1: ***The Today's Data tab in the Investing Center displays your portfolio, Watch List, account data, and gives you useful tools with which to track and evaluate your investments.***

1. Click the **Download Quotes** button in the upper-left corner of the Investing Center.

   –Or–

   Click **Download Quotes** in the Watch List area of the Activity Center.

2. Once you are connected to the Internet, the Quicken One Step Update Status dialog box appears. Quotes for your selected securities are downloaded to your computer.

QUICKSTEPS

GETTING A QUOTE FOR A SECURITY

If you are considering the purchase of a security and have Internet access, you can use the Online Quotes feature.

1. On the right of the Investing Center, under **Online Quotes**, click in the **Enter Symbol** field.

Online Quotes

Enter symbol:

INTU [Go]

Don't know the symbol?

2. Enter the ticker symbol for the security, and click **Go**.

3. If you don't know the symbol, click **Don't Know The Symbol?** to display Quicken's online database. Type the name of the security to see the ticker symbol. Type or copy and paste the symbol into the **Online Quotes** field, and click **Go**.

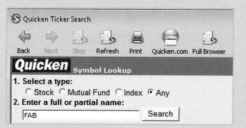

4. After you have gotten the information you wanted about the ticker symbol you entered, click **Close** to close the window.

---

3. If you are having trouble connecting and downloading, click **Help** to display Quicken Help.

4. Click **Stop Download** to stop the download before it is complete.

5. When all of your quotes have been downloaded, the Quicken One Step Update Status dialog box closes and you are returned to the Today's Data tab in the Investing Center. You may be returned to the One Step Update Summary dialog box. If so, click **Close** to return to the Investing Center.

Set Up Quicken.com

When you registered Quicken, you may have created a Quicken.com account. With this account, you can keep an eye on your Quicken data from any computer with Internet access. You can even update your account information from your Quicken.com account, including alerts. To use Quicken.com for your investment information:

1. From the Quicken toolbar or from the Today's Data tab in the Investing Center, click the **One Step Update** icon to open the One Step Update Settings dialog box.

2. In the upper-right corner of the One Step Update Settings dialog box, click Select Quotes. The Customize Online Updates dialog box will appear.

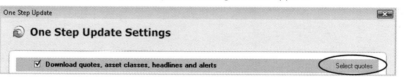

3. If it is not already selected, click the Quotes tab, and select the securities for which you want to download quotes.

4. Click the **Portfolio** tab, and then:

   - Click to select each investment account you want included. A green check mark appears.

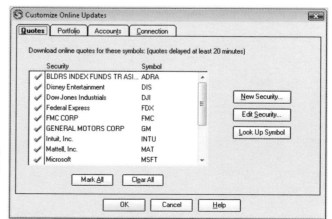

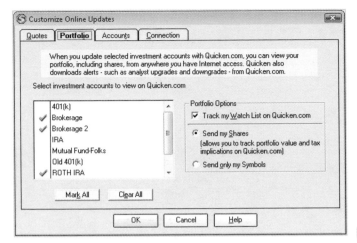

- Click **Track My Watch List On Quicken.com** if you want to see Watch List information on your Quicken.com account. (See the QuickSteps "Working with Your Watch List" later in this chapter.)

- Click **Send My Shares** to track the value of your portfolio and any tax implications.

- Click **Send Only My Symbols** to download only the current price of your securities.

5. Click the **Accounts** tab, and select the cash flow, asset, and liability accounts you want to see using Quicken.com.

6. Click the **Connection** tab to select how online updates will be run.

7. Click **OK** to close the Customize Online Updates dialog box, and then click **Close** to close the One Step Update dialog box.

Use Quicken WebEntry

If you have registered with Quicken.com, you can use WebEntry to enter transactions in the accounts you set up in the section "Set Up Quicken.com."

1. Click **Quicken.com** on the Quicken toolbar.

   –Or–

   Open your Internet browser, connect to the Internet, and go to **www.quicken.com**.

2. Click **My Quicken**.

3. Click **Investing Center Log In** in the left column. If you have a broadband Internet connection and have previously entered your member ID and password, the Investing Center may open immediately. If you have a dial-up connection, you may have to re-enter your information.

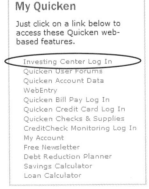

4. If the sign-in screen appears, type your member ID and password, and then click **Sign In**. The Investing Center home page is displayed, as shown in Figure 8-2.

5. Scroll to the **Tools** section of the page, and click **WebEntry** to display the WebEntry data form. Quicken WebEntry is also available at the bottom of the page to the left of **Buy Software Online**.

6. Enter the name of the Quicken account you want to use. Enter the relevant information in each field.

7. Click **Enter Transaction** to save the transaction for the next time you download to your Quicken account.

8. Click **Clear Form** to delete what you just entered.

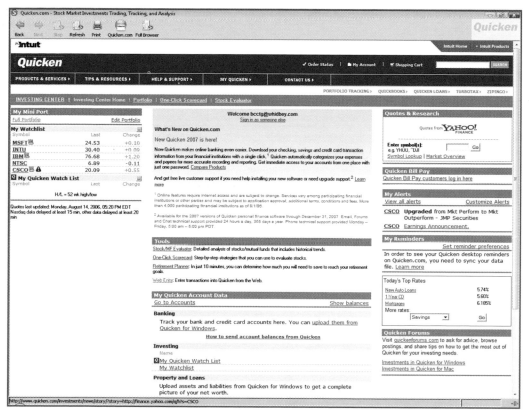

Figure 8-2: *The Investing Center at Quicken.com provides a number of resources for you to learn more about your investments.*

9. Download the transaction from Quicken.com to Quicken on your computer:

a. On your computer, open the Quicken Home page. Under **Online Updates** on the right, click **One Step Update** to open the One Step Update dialog box.

b. If necessary, in the Quicken.com checklist, click **Download WebEntry Transactions From Quicken.com**.

c. Click **Update Now**. The Online Update Summary dialog box appears. Review the contents, making sure your transactions are there, and then click **Done**. Downloaded transactions appear at the bottom of the register for the account to which they relate.

d. Accept each transaction individually by selecting it and clicking the **Accept** button on the line; or you can accept all your transactions at once by clicking **Accept All**.

10. Click **Sign Out From Quicken.com** to sign out. This is especially important if you are using a computer accessible to the public.

Work with Investment Alerts

You can set three different alerts for your investments. Depending on the version of Quicken you are using, your dialog boxes may look different from the ones described. Some alert features are not available in Quicken Basic or Deluxe editions.

1. Click the **Investing Center** on the Account bar to open the Investing Center.

2. Click the **Today's Data** tab, and then, under the **Investment Alerts** section, click **Set Up Alerts**. The Alerts Center dialog box appears.

NOTE

For security purposes, only the Category List, Account List, and Class List (if any) are sent to Quicken.com. No other information, such as account numbers or descriptions, is transmitted. If you want to delete this information, click **Remove My Categories, Accounts And Classes From The Web**.

SCHEDULING ONE STEP UPDATES

The One Step Update utility allows you to download your quotes at the same time you update information from your financial institutions. You can schedule the updates so that Quicken will update your information at a time most convenient for you.

1. Click the **Online** menu, and click **Schedule Updates**. The Schedule Updates dialog box will appear.

2. Click **Download Quotes, Asset Classes, Headlines And Alerts** to instruct Quicken to download the most current quotes for your securities, along with headlines and alerts.

Schedule Updates

Check the items you would like to update and choose schedule options.

Items to Schedule

Quotes   Select quotes
☑ Download quotes, asset classes, headlines and alerts

Financial Institutions

Quicken.com   Select Quicken.com data to update
☑ Update my portfolio on Quicken.com
☐ Update my banking accounts on Quicken.com
☑ Update my reminders on Quicken.com
☐ Download WebEntry transactions from Quicken.com

Note: Use One Step Update to send online payments, transfers or emails. More info

---

3. Click **Financial Institutions** to choose the banks, credit card companies, and other financial institutions for which you have activated online services.

4. Select the Quicken.com data to update by clicking **Update My Portfolio On Quicken.com**, **Update My Banking Accounts On Quicken.com**, **Update My Reminders On Quicken.com**, or **Download WebEntry Transactions From Quicken.com** in the relevant check boxes. Continued . . .

3. Click **Price And Volume** to ask Quicken to notify you if a price goes over or under a value or a percentage you set. You can also direct Quicken to advise you of any announcements or "industry buzz" about the security. Click the **Go To Quicken.com To Customize Price And Volume Alerts** link. If necessary, enter your Quicken.com member ID and password, and click **Continue**. The Alerts Set Up dialog on the Web is displayed, as shown in Figure 8-3. Depending on the version of Quicken you are using, you may have to select an account before you go online.

4. For an individual security, click in the **Drops Below** text box, and enter the price below which you want to receive an alert; or click in the **Rises Above** text box, and enter the price above which you want to receive an alert. Continue through the dialog box to choose what alerts you want to receive.

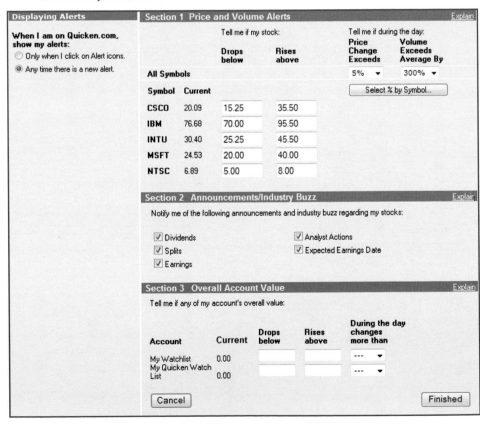

Figure 8-3: *The Alerts Set Up dialog box at Quicken.com allows you to schedule alerts for many changes in your investments.*

SCHEDULING ONE STEP UPDATES

(Continued)

5. Click the relevant check boxes for the day or days on which you want Quicken to do the update.

6. Enter the time in the **At** field.

7. If you are asking Quicken to update from your

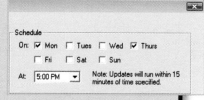

financial institutions, you must have stored your password for each institution in the Quicken Vault. To ensure proper security, select the time when Quicken will ask for your Vault password:

a. Click **Before Each Scheduled Update** to be prompted as the scheduled update begins.

b. Click **At Windows Startup** to have the password available the entire time you are working in Quicken.

8. Click **OK** to close the Schedule Updates dialog box.

5. Click **Finished** to open the Standard Portfolio window in Quicken.com. Scroll to the bottom of the Standard Portfolio window, and, opposite Investing Center, click **Sign Out** to end the session. A message appears, indicating that you have signed out.

6. Click **Close** to end the Quicken.com session and close your browser. You are returned to the One Step Update Summary dialog box. Click **Close** to close the dialog box. You are returned to the Alert Center Setup tab dialog box.

7. Under **Reminders**, if it isn't already selected, click **Download Quotes** to create an alert reminding you to download quotes from Quicken.com and update your portfolio.

8. If it isn't already selected, click **Maturity Date** to be reminded of the maturity date of a CD.

9. If it is available, click the plus sign to the left of **Ratings And Analysis** to display your choices. Click **Stock** to set an alert for information about your stocks, and click **Mutual Funds** for information about the mutual funds you hold.

10. If it is available, click the plus sign to the left of **Capital Gains/Losses** to see and set the options in this section.

11. Click **OK** to close the dialog box.

Manage Your Security List

Once you have entered your investment accounts, you may want to work with the individual securities in your accounts. When you created your investment accounts and told Quicken which securities were included in them, Quicken created a list of these accounts in its data file. To access your Security List:

1. Click the **Investing** menu, and click **Security List**.

   –Or–

   Press **CTRL+Y**.

   The Security List dialog box appears. From this list, you can add, edit, hide, and delete specific securities or add securities to your *Watch List*. (The

Security	Symbol	Type	Asset Class	Watch
BLDRS INDEX FUNDS TR ASIA...	ADRA	Stock	Unclassified	☑
Disney Entertainment	DIS	Stock	Large Cap Stocks	☑
Dow Jones Industrials	DJI	Market Index	Unclassified	☑
Federal Express	FDX	Stock	Large Cap Stocks	☑
FMC CORP	FMC	Stock	Small Cap Stocks	☑
GENERAL MOTORS CORP	GM	Stock	Large Cap Stocks	☑
INTERNATIONAL BUSINESS MAC...		Stock	Large Cap Stocks	☑
Intuit Inc-401K		Stock	Large Cap Stocks	☐
Intuit, Inc.	INTU	Stock	Large Cap Stocks	☑
Mattell, Inc.	MAT	Stock	Large Cap Stocks	☑
Microsoft	MSFT	Stock	Large Cap Stocks	☑
Microsoft-401K		Stock	Large Cap Stocks	☐
NASDAQ Composite	COMPX	Market Index	Unclassified	☐
Russell 2000	IUX	Market Index	Unclassified	☐
S&P 500 Index	INX	Market Index	Unclassified	☐
TIAA-CREF INSTL EQUITY INDEX R	TIQRX	Mutual Fund	Unclassified	☑
United Parcel Service	UPS	Stock	Large Cap Stocks	☑
Washington Mutual	WM	Stock	Large Cap Stocks	☑

8

Watch List is a special snapshot in the Investing Center that allows you to track the performance of securities you own or may purchase on a daily basis. See the QuickSteps "Working with Your Watch List" next in this chapter.)

2. To add a new security to your Security List, click **New**. The Add Security To Quicken dialog box appears:

   a. Click in the **Ticker Symbol** field, and type the ticker symbol for this security. If you don't know the symbol and have Internet access, enter the company name, and click **Look Up**.

   b. Click **Include This Security On My Watch List** if you want to monitor its daily performance.

   c. Click **Next** to continue. The Quicken One Step Update window opens briefly, and information about this security is downloaded into Quicken.

   d. A summary window displays the name of your security, its ticker symbol, security type, asset class, and whether you have chosen to include this security on your Watch List. If the information is correct, click **Done**. The new security is displayed on your Security List in alphabetical order by name.

CAUTION

It is better to use the Look Up button to change the symbol of a security rather than typing it yourself in the Symbol field to ensure you have correctly entered the new symbol.

CAUTION

It is usually better to hide a security than to delete it. Before you delete a security, you must first find and delete all transactions related to it.

3. To edit an existing security, click the security name to select it, and then click **Edit**. The Edit Security Details dialog box appears. Click in and edit the fields you want to change.

4. To permanently delete a security, click the security and click **Delete**. A warning dialog box appears, telling you that you are about to permanently delete a security. Click **OK** if you want to continue.

5. To hide a security so that its information is available but not included in totals or reports, click its name and then click **Hide**. To include hidden securities in the Security List, click **Options** and then click **View Hidden Securities**. To restore a hidden security, select it and click **Hide** again.

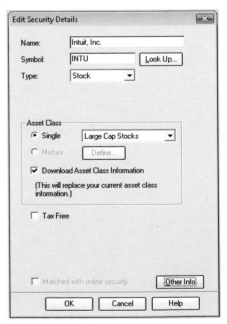

WORKING WITH YOUR WATCH LIST

The Watch List in the Today's Data tab provides a convenient way to see the short-term performance of securities you currently hold, as well as securities you may want to purchase in the future, and compare them to various market indicators. From the Watch List, you can add a new security to your Security List, edit the Watch List, download quotes, see your entire portfolio, research a stock or mutual fund with your Quicken.com account, set up a price alert, and display ticker symbols rather than names in the Watch List. To work with the Watch List:

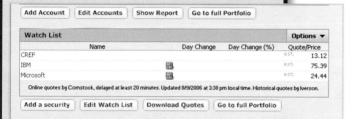

1. Click **Investing Center** on the Account bar, and click the **Today's Data** tab.

2. Scroll to the bottom of the Watch List, and click **Add A Security** to open the Add Security To Quicken dialog box.

3. Enter a ticker symbol or a company name for the new security, click **Look Up** for the security you want to track, and then click **Next**.

4. Confirm that the information that appears is for the correct company, and then click **Next**. A dialog box appears, notifying you that the new security has been added to Quicken.

5. If you want to add another security, click **Yes**, click **Next**, and repeat steps 3–5. When you are finished, click **Done** to return to the Today's Data tab in the Investing Center. *Continued . . .*

6. Click **Choose Market Indexes** to display a list of market indexes, which you can include as part of your Security List and your Watch List. By including these indicators, you can compare their short-term performance to those of your securities:

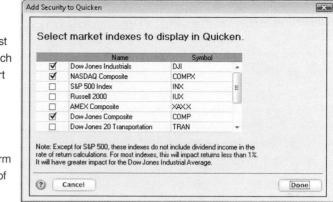

a. Click in the check box of each index you want to include. A small check mark is displayed.

b. Click **Done** to close the dialog box.

7. To create a report about a security, click the name of the security, and click **Report**.

8. Click **Print** to print the Security List.

9. Click **Close** to close the Security List.

Work with the Analysis Tab

The Analysis tab allows you to break down your portfolio by account, asset class, or security. You can then analyze its performance with several useful analysis tools, including the Asset Allocation Guide, the Portfolio Analyzer, and the Capital Gains Estimator. If you are using Quicken Premier or Home & Business edition, the Morningstar Mutual Fund Ratings appear in the Activity Center.

Choose Accounts to Analyze

Depending on the version of Quicken you are using, you will see three or four ways to analyze your portfolio in the Analysis tab, as well as several links to analysis tools. The choices at the top of the Analysis tab for determining the accounts on which to do the analysis are:

QUICKSTEPS

WORKING WITH YOUR WATCH LIST
(Continued)

6. At the bottom of the Watch List, click **Edit Watch List** to display the Security List. Click the security you want to work with, click **Edit** on the menu bar, make any desired changes, and click **OK**; or click the **Watch** check box to include or exclude the security or market index in the Watch List. Click **Close** to close the Security List.

7. Click **Download Quotes** to download the latest quotes for your holdings. The last date and time you downloaded appears as a note to the right of the download quotes under the Today's Data tab.

8. At the bottom of the Watch List, click **Go To Full Portfolio** to display the Portfolio tab. See the discussion in "Work with the Portfolio Tab" later in this chapter. Click the **Today's Data** tab to return to it.

9. In the Watch List title bar, click **Options** and click **Research A Stock Or Mutual Fund** to use your Quicken.com account to research a specific security. You may be prompted for your user name and password, and are then directed to enter the ticker symbol for the stock or mutual fund you want to research. The Quicken Security Evaluator window opens. Review the research findings on six different pages. When you're finished, click **Sign Out** at the bottom of the page to return to the Watch List, and then close the Quicken.com page.

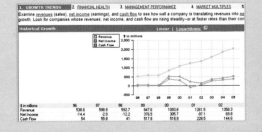

1. Click the **Analysis** tab, and click **All** to view information for all of your investment accounts.

   –Or–

   Click **Investment** or **Retirement** to include only the investment or retirement accounts.

   –Or–

   Click **Multiple Accounts** to select the accounts with which you want to work:

2. Click the drop-down list box to open it, and then click Multiple Accounts to open the Customize dialog box with a list of your investing accounts.

3. Select the check box to the left of each account you want to include, or click Mark All to include all accounts.

4. Click Clear All to clear all check boxes and select individual accounts.

5. Click Show Hidden Accounts to include them in the analysis.

6. Click OK to close the Customize dialog box.

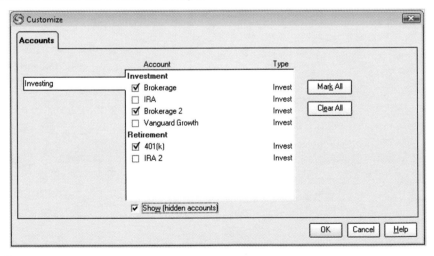

–Or–

Click Choose Securities to select individual securities to analyze. This also opens the Customize dialog box, but it now lists all your securities. Use the same steps as with the Multiple Accounts option.

Allocate Your Assets

Quicken provides an Asset Allocation Guide to help you structure your portfolio. In the Asset Allocation area of the Analysis tab, you see a graph that shows your current allocation and a second graph that shows your target allocation. To work with the allocation of your assets:

1. Click **Show Allocation Guide** at the bottom of the Asset Allocation area.

   –Or–

   Click **Asset Allocation Guide** in the Analysis Tools links section on the right side of the window.

   Either way, the Asset Allocation Guide displays the How Can Quicken Help With Asset Allocation? page. Click **Print** to print a page of the Guide. Figure 8-4 shows the first page. If you have downloaded quotes or other information from your brokerage firm or Quicken.com, this page displays your current asset allocation. If you don't see your asset allocation, click the **Replace It With An Example** or **Set Up Quicken So You Can** link.

2. Click **What Are Asset Classes And Why Should I Use Them?** to display a discussion of asset classes.

3. On the left side of the Asset Allocation Guide, click **How Do I Update Asset Classes?** to display the next page.

   –Or–

   On the How Can Quicken Help With Asset Allocation? page, under the graph, click **Next: How Do I Update Asset Classes?**

4. Click **Go Online And Update Asset Classes** to open the Download Security Asset Classes dialog box:

   a. Click to the left of each security name for which you want the asset class downloaded, or click **Mark All** to choose each security in the list.

   b. Click **Update Now** to update your asset classes. After the transmission window has closed, the One Step Update Summary dialog box may display what was downloaded. If you don't need to see this summary each time, click **Show This Dialog Only If There Is An Error**. Otherwise, click **Close** to return to the Asset Allocation Guide.

Figure 8-4: **The Asset Allocation Guide shows you how to determine if your securities meet your risk and return objectives.**

Figure 8-5: *The What Should My Asset Allocation Be? page of the Guide helps you set your allocation.*

CAUTION

Remember that investments in mutual funds are composed of several asset classes. While the allocation of classes within the fund changes from time to time, you really have no control over that mixture, and it may not meet your target allocation.

5. Click **Common Questions About Downloading Asset Classes** to display a list of frequently asked questions.

6. Click **Back: How Do I Update Asset Classes?** to return to that page.

7. Click **Next: What Should My Asset Allocation Be?** to continue. On this page of the Guide, two sample asset allocation graphs are displayed: a current allocation and a target allocation, as shown in Figure 8-5.

8. Click **Be Smart About Your Target** or click **See Model Portfolios** to read advice about your allocation.

9. After you have read the material, click **Set Your Target Allocation**.

10. Click **Set**. The Set Target Asset Allocation dialog box appears.

11. Click **Percentage** for each of the various asset classes to enter the percentage you want to achieve. Click **OK** when finished.

12. If this is the first time you've allocated your assets, click **How Do I Rebalance My Portfolio?** *Rebalancing* means moving money between investments so that your total investments are allocated in the best way for you to achieve your goals, as shown in Figure 8-6. Goal setting and planning is discussed in Chapter 9. Follow the directions and links on the page.

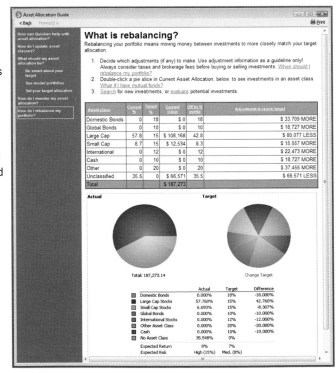

Figure 8-6: *Periodically reviewing how your investments are balanced can help you better achieve your goals and objectives.*

NOTE

Asset allocation can only be kept current if you download quotes and asset classes regularly.

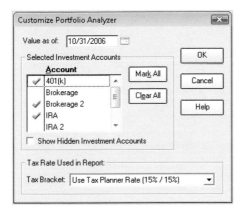

CAUTION

Before using the Capital Gains Estimator, make sure you have set up your Tax Planner. See Chapter 10 for more information on setting up the Tax Planner.

13. Click **How Do I Monitor My Asset Allocation?** to understand more about your asset allocation.

14. Click **Close** to close the Guide.

Use the Portfolio Analyzer

The Portfolio Analyzer helps you review the risks and performance of your holdings. You can customize which accounts are being analyzed.

1. On the right of the Analysis tab, in the list of links under Analysis Tools, click **Portfolio Analyzer**.

2. Click **Customize** on the menu bar to open the Customize Portfolio Analyzer dialog box. If not all of your investments appear in the list, click **Show (Hidden Accounts)**:

  a. Click to the left of each account to select it for analysis, or click **Mark All** to choose all of the accounts on the list.

  b. Click the **Tax Bracket** down arrow to select the tax rate used in the report. (See Chapter 10 for a complete discussion of tax planning.)

  c. Click **OK** to close the dialog box.

3. A discussion of your holdings' performance displays. This can include a graphic presentation of your returns, your five best and five worst performers, tips on what to look for, and actions you can take to improve performance. Figure 8-7 shows a page of the Portfolio Analyzer.

4. Click **Holdings** to go directly to the graphic representation and accompanying tips on your holdings. Continue through the Portfolio Analyzer, clicking the items you want to view.

5. Click **Close** to close the Portfolio Analyzer.

Estimate Capital Gains

The Capital Gains Estimator helps you determine how much tax you might have to pay if you sell a security.

1. On the right of the Analysis tab, in the list of links under Analysis Tools, click **Capital Gains Estimator**.

2. Click **Let's Get Started** at the bottom of the Welcome message to start the wizard.

3. You can create up to three scenarios for comparison. Click one of the scenarios, and then click **Next** to continue.

Figure 8-7: *The Portfolio Analyzer has several sections, each one designed to help you with your financial investments.*

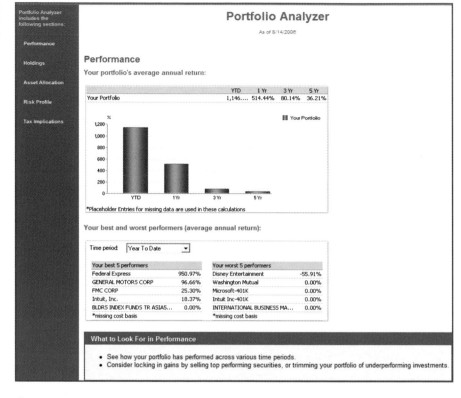

CAUTION

Investment accounts that have missing cost-basis information or that are hidden in Quicken will not appear in the Capital Gains Estimator. Also, the Estimator does not include IRA or 401(k) accounts.

4. Click to the left of the account name you want to include in the scenario. Click **Next**.

5. Continue through the Estimator by clicking **Next** and entering all relevant information.

6. Click the goal you want to achieve, such as **Maximize After Tax Returns** or **Balance My Year-To-Date Capital Gains**. The default is **Maximize After Tax Returns And Minimize Fees**.

7. Click **Search** to have Quicken find the best way to meet your goal. When the Search dialog box has reached 100%, click **View Results**. The What Should I Sell? dialog box may appear and notify you that Quicken could not complete the scenario as you requested. Click **OK** and click **Settings**. Then:

  a. Click in the **% Of Your Target Goal** text box, and enter a percent of your target goal. Ten is the default percentage.

  b. Click in the **Seconds** text box, and enter the maximum number of seconds you want Quicken to try to meet your goal.

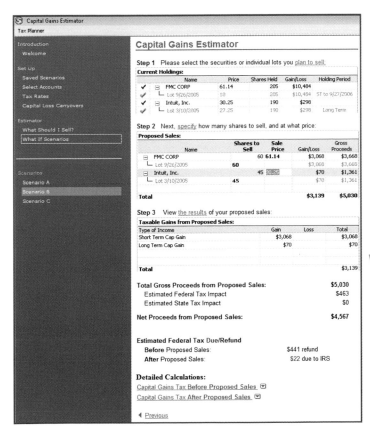

c. Click in the **Optimal Solutions** text box, and enter the maximum number of possible solutions.

d. Click **Stop As Soon As The First Acceptable Answer Is Found** to have Quicken end the search when any answer is found matching your criteria.

e. Click **Quick Search** to choose one best method, or click **Exhaustive Search** to have Quicken merge a number of searches to give you a result.

f. Click **OK** to return to the Search dialog box, and click **Start**.

8. After the search is complete, you may see a dialog box stating that Quicken was not able to complete the task. Otherwise, click **View Results** to display the Capital Gains Estimator.

9. In the Current Holdings area, click to the left of the name of the security you want to sell. A check mark appears. If you have several lots of this holding, select the lot from which you want to sell your shares.

10. In the Step 2 area, click in the **Shares To Sell** column opposite the stock you want to sell, and enter the number of shares you will be selling (see Figure 8-8).

11. In the Step 3 area, view the potential taxable gains from your proposed sales. Read the bottom of the page to see detailed information about the proposed sale.

12. Click **Close** to return to the Analysis tab.

Work with the Portfolio Tab

The Portfolio tab in the Investing Center displays all of your investment information. By customizing the way you see this information, you can make educated decisions about the performance of each investment. To view your portfolio, press CTRL+U.

Figure 8-8: **The Capital Gains Estimator lets you decide which shares to sell to reach your objectives.**

Understand Portfolio Terms

You can include several different columns of information in a custom view of your portfolio. To find what the column headings mean:

1. Click **Glossary** on the menu bar. The Help screen is displayed.

2. In the text box in the upper-left area of the Help screen, type <u>find out about investment terms</u>, and press **ENTER**, or click **List Topics**.

3. Click **Quicken Help Glossary** on the right side of the Help dialog box.

4. Click the first letter of the word you want to look up, and then scroll to the term you want to find, and click it to read the definition.

5. Close the Help window when you are finished.

Customize Your Portfolio View

Quicken has nine standard views for the portfolio, and you can customize up to nine others. All of the views can use any of a number of column headings. Before you create a customized view, make sure you download both the latest quotes and historical prices. To customize a view in your portfolio:

1. In the Investing Center Portfolio tab, click the **Show** down arrow to select the view you want to customize.

2. Click **Customize View** to open the Customize Current View dialog box (see Figure 8-9). The name of the current selected view is displayed in the Name field. Type a new name for this view if you want.

3. In the **Accounts To Include** list, click to the left of the accounts to select the ones you want to use. Click **Show (Hidden Accounts)** to include hidden accounts.

4. By default, your accounts are displayed alphabetically. If you want to change this, click an account and then click **Move Up** or **Move Down** to change that account's position in the list.

5. To choose all of the accounts in the list, click **Mark All**.

6. In the **Securities To Include** list, click to the left of the securities that you want to show. Click **Show (Hidden Securities)** to include hidden securities. You cannot change the order in which securities are displayed; they are always displayed in alphabetical order.

7. The columns that appear by default for this view are shown in the Displayed Columns list. To remove a column, click its name and then click **Remove**. The column heading moves from the Displayed Columns list to the Available Columns list.

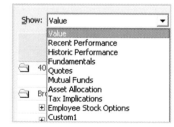

Figure 8-9: **The Customize View dialog box allows you to tailor how you view your portfolio.**

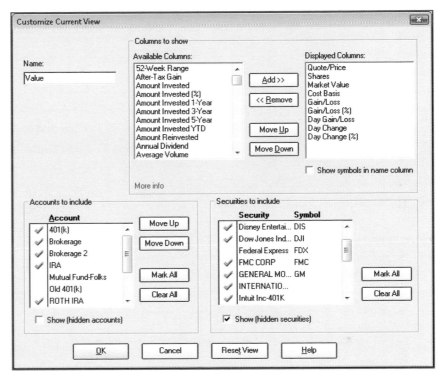

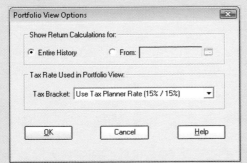

QUICKSTEPS

SETTING OPTIONS IN YOUR PORTFOLIO VIEW

The Portfolio tab in your Investing Center allows you to set options for each view you display. From your Portfolio tab:

1. Click **Options** on the menu bar, and then click **Preferences**. The Portfolio View Options dialog box appears.

2. Click **Entire History** to include all transactions for your securities. This is the default setting. The alternative is to click **From** to enter a beginning date from which to display the information. The ending date is always today's date.

3. Click the **Tax Bracket** down arrow to choose a tax rate. The tax rate for short-term gains is shown first, and the rate for long-term gains is shown second. For example, (15%/5%) indicates that short-term gains are calculated at a 15-percent tax rate and that long-term gains are calculated at a 5-percent tax rate.

4. Click **OK** to close the dialog box.

8. Click a column in the Available Columns list, and click **Add** to include it in the Displayed Columns list.

9. Click a column heading, and click **Move Up** or **Move Down** to change its position in the list.

10. Click **Show Symbols In Name Column** to display the ticker symbol rather than the name of your security.

11. Click **Reset View** if you want to return to the original default settings.

12. Click **OK** when you are finished.

Explore the Performance Tab

If you use Quicken Premier or Home & Business edition, Quicken provides additional analysis tools in the Performance tab.

Use the Growth Of $10,000 Utility

Quicken uses a utility called the Growth Of $10,000 that you can use to see how your portfolio compares to the main market indexes. This utility shows the value of $10,000 invested in your selected accounts compared to the same $10,000 invested in one or more of the market indexes over the same time period, as shown in Figure 8-10. To use and customize this utility:

1. Click the **Investing** menu, and click **Go To Investing Center**.

2. Click the **Performance** tab. At the top, you'll see a graph labeled "Growth Of $10,000."

3. At the top of the Investing Center, opposite **Show Accounts**, click one of the options—**All**, **Investment**, **Retirement**, or **Multiple Accounts**—to tell Quicken which accounts to include in the graphs in this tab.

4. Click **Choose Securities**. The Customize dialog box appears. Select the securities you want to compare in the graph:

   a. Click **Mark All** to choose all the securities on your Security List, or click **Clear All** to clear all selections and choose just a few.

   b. Click **OK** to close the dialog box and return to the graph.

5. Click **Download Historical Prices** below the chart. The Get Historical Prices dialog box appears:

   a. Click the **Get Prices For The Last** down arrow, and click **Month**, **Year**, **Two Years**, or **Five Years**, depending on the time period for which you want to download prices.

   b. Select the securities for which you want to download prices.

   c. Click **Update Now** to download the information. When the information has been downloaded, the summary screen is displayed.

   d. Click **Close** to return to the graph.

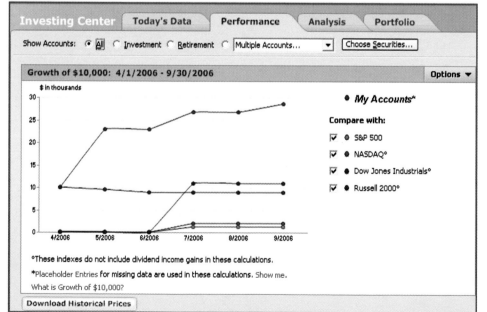

Figure 8-10: **The Growth Of $10,000 analysis tool compares your securities with the performance of several market indexes.**

QUICKSTEPS

CUSTOMIZING THE DATE RANGE

The default view for the Growth Of $10,000 snapshot is the last 12 months; however, you can customize the date range.

1. Click the **Investing** menu, and click **Go To Investing Center**.

2. Click the **Performance** tab.

3. Click **Options** on the right of the menu bar, and then click **Customize This Graph**. The Customize dialog box appears.

4. Click the **Date Range** down arrow to see the list of possibilities, or click **Custom Dates** to determine your own dates.

| Date range: | Custom dates ▼ | From: 4/1/2006 | To: 9/30/2006 |

5. Click **OK** to close the dialog box.

Filter the Average Annual Return Analysis

The second analysis tool on the Performance tab of your Investing Center is the Average Annual Return tool. This shows the return on your investments as an annualized figure. To filter and customize this:

1. At the top of the Investing Center, opposite **Show Accounts**, click **All**, **Investment**, **Retirement**, **Multiple Accounts**, or **Choose Securities** to determine which accounts or securities to include. (See "Use the Growth Of $10,000 Utility" earlier in the chapter.)

2. In the Average Annual Return title bar, click **Options** and click **Show Security Performance**. The Security Performance dialog box appears:

a. Click **Customize View** to open the Customize Current View dialog box. Follow the instructions in "Customize Your Portfolio View" earlier in the chapter, and then click **OK**.

b. Click in the **As Of field** to enter the date for which you want to see the data. The default is today's date.

c. Click **Close** when you are finished.

3. Click **Options** and click **Show Security Performance Comparisons** to work with the Security Performance dialog box. You can customize this view as well. Click **Close** when you are finished.

Use the Performance Research Tools

Quicken includes several additional research tools in its Premier and Home & Business editions, including One-Click Scorecard, Stock Screener, and Fund Finder. You will need Internet access to use these. For all three:

1. Click the **Investing** menu, and click **Go To Investing Center**.

2. Click the **Performance** tab.

Research Tools

One-Click Scorecard
See stock ratings based on market-beating strategies.

Stock Screener
Find stocks that meet your investing goals.

Fund Finder
Step-by-step screeners for mutual funds that meet your criteria.

Several firms rate mutual funds on their performance and risk. Morningstar is one of the highest regarded and is included with Quicken. There are three time periods in each Morningstar assessment: 3 years, 5 years, and 10 years (a mutual fund must have at least three years' worth of history to be included). Each fund is categorized by special classes developed by Morningstar. The risk portion is computed by calculating the fund's monthly return to the return on a Treasury bill. The result is then compared to other similar funds, and the rating shows how risky a fund is compared to the others. Each fund is rated on a basis of five stars, with five being the highest and one being the lowest.

WORK WITH THE ONE-CLICK SCORECARD

If you have registered with Quicken.com, you have yet another research tool available to you. After connecting to the Internet, from the Performance tab in the Investing Center:

1. Click **One-Click Scorecard** on the right of the Activity Center.

   a. The Quicken.com Sign In dialog box may appear. If so, enter your member ID and password, and click **Sign In**. The One-Click Scorecard window opens, shown in Figure 8-11.

   b. Click in the **Enter Symbol(s)** text box, and enter the ticker symbol of the security you want to research.

   c. Click **Go** to see the report. Quicken creates a report showing the opinion of three different industry experts about this security.

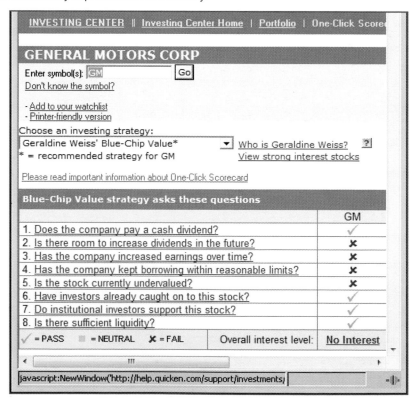

Figure 8-11: **Quicken's One-Click Scorecard** *provides extensive research from three different sources.*

d. From the report window, you can:

- Click **Add To Your Watchlist** to include this security in your Quicken Watch List.

- Click **Printer-Friendly Version** to open a report without the graphics that can be printed more easily.

- Click **Choose An Investing Strategy** to view information from one of three experts.

- Scroll down to view the grades and the reason for each grade in eight different categories.

e. Click **Sign Out** at the bottom of the window to open the Signed Out dialog box.

2. Click **Close** to return to Quicken.

USE THE STOCK SCREENER

The Stock Screener allows you to go online to research specific securities, provided you have Internet access. From the Performance tab in the Investing Center:

1. Click **Stock Screener** on the right of the Activity Center to open the Stock Screener window.

| Stock Screener | Enter Symbol(s):
 e.g. YHOO, ^DJI | [ ] GO | Symbol Lookup | Finance Search |

a. Click in the **Enter Symbol(s)** text box, and enter the ticker symbol of the stock you want to research.

b. Click **Go** to open a window displaying the relevant information.

c. If you have signed in to your Quicken.com account, click **Sign Out** at the top of the Web site, and then **Close** to return to the Investing Center. Otherwise, just click **Close**.

USE THE FUND FINDER

The Fund Finder allows you to search for a mutual fund with the performance history and characteristics that meet your objectives.

1. Under **Research Tools** on the right side of the Performance tab, click **Fund Finder**. The Overview dialog box appears. The default selection on all choices is **Any**. Click the **Category** down arrow to see a list of funds. You may have to scroll down to see the entire list.

2. Click the **Fund Family** down arrow to select a specific fund family.

QUICKSTEPS

WORKING WITH A SINGLE INVESTMENT ACCOUNT

The information available to you in the Investing Center for a specific account is similar to the information you can see in the Investing Center tabs.

1. In the Account bar, click the name of an investment account to select it. The Activity Center opens, displaying three tabs.

2. Click the **Summary** tab to view the holdings in that account, its attributes, status, and the investing activity.

| Single Mutual Fund | Summary | Performance & Analysis | Transactions |

3. Click the **Performance & Analysis** tab to view several graphs representing the performance history, allocation, and cost for that account.

4. Click the **Transactions** tab to view, add, or edit specific transactions in that account.

5. Click **Options** in either the Performance & Analysis tab or the Summary tab to customize the information.

3. Click the **Rank In Category** down arrow to choose a fund's ranking in its category. Your choices range from Any to Top 50% or Bottom 50%.

4. Click the **Manager Tenure** down arrow to select how long of a time period a manager must have managed a fund.

5. Continue through the Overview screen, making relevant selections and leaving the others with the default selection of **Any**.

6. Click **Find Funds** to see a list of available funds that meet your criteria.

7. Click **Close** to return to the Portfolio tab.

How to...

- *Understand How to Plan with Quicken*

- *Enter Information About Yourself*

- *Understanding Your Social Security Retirement Age*

- *Enter Income Information and Your Tax Rate*

- *Estimating Inflation for Your Plan*

- *Consider Savings, Investments, and Rate of Return*

- *Entering Your Expected Rate of Return*

- *Work with Homes and Other Assets*

- *Associating Income with an Asset in Your Plan*

- *Use the Loans And Debt Planner*

- *Figure Your Living Expenses*

- *Planning to Pay for College*

- *Understand the Plan Results*

- *Use the Debt Reduction Planner*

- *Using What Ifs*

- *Get Quick Answers with Calculators*

- *Create a Budget*

- *Work with Your Budget*

Chapter 9

Making Plans for Your Future

Why should you plan for your financial future? It has been said that anyone who fails to plan, plans to fail. College for your children, a house of your own, a once-in-a-lifetime cruise, retirement, a debt-free lifestyle, and a vacation cabin are all major financial events. Will you have the money to fund them? By using the Life Event Planners in Quicken, you can create a road map that will help you achieve your goals. In this chapter you will learn how to create plans in Quicken using assumptions. You will learn how to use the various Life Event Planners and how to create a budget or spending plan that will help you reach your goals. In addition, you will see the various professional planning tools available in Quicken.

Work with Assumptions

All of the Planners in Quicken are based on a set of assumptions that you create. You can change or add to these assumptions at any time. Quicken uses the data you have already entered to help you with your long-term plans, but if you have not yet entered all your data, you can enter it while you are creating your plans.

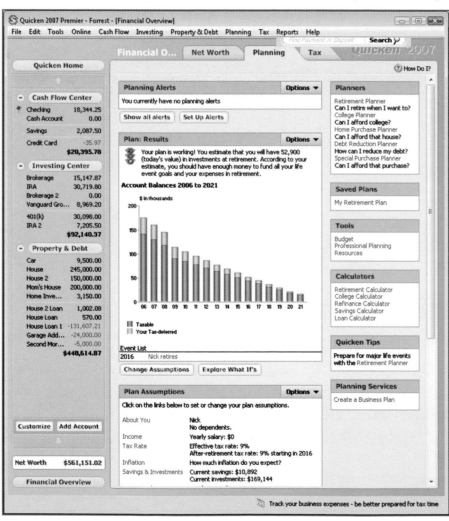

Understand How to Plan with Quicken

You begin by telling Quicken some information about yourself. Then you continue by including information about your income, tax rate, savings, investments, other assets, any debt, and living expenses. Quicken uses this information—along with the financial data you have already entered and a large database of financial resources—to help you create a plan. Within the Financial Overview Activity Center are three tabs: Net Worth, Planning, and Tax. This chapter will discuss the Planning tab (see Figure 9-1). Taxes deserve a chapter of their own and are covered in Chapter 10.

Enter Information About Yourself

All good plans start with information. This one is no exception. To begin your plan:

1. Click the **Planning** menu, and click **Go To Planning Center**. The Financial Overview Center is displayed.

   –Or–

   Click **Financial Overview** at the bottom of the Account bar, and click the **Planning** tab.

*Figure 9-1: **The Planning tab in the Financial Overview Activity Center helps you create a plan to achieve your financial goals.***

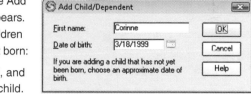

Figure 9-2: *The Quicken Planner: About You dialog box is used to enter age-related information for you and your spouse.*

TIP

You can include or exclude a spouse at any time when making your assumptions.

CAUTION

If you support a parent or other family member who was born before 1930, you must enter all four digits in the year, for example, 1929. Otherwise, Quicken will use 2029 as the date of birth.

2. If necessary, scroll down until you see **Plan Assumptions**. Click **About You** in the Plan Assumptions section to open the Quicken Planner: About You dialog box (see Figure 9-2).

3. Click **Include Spouse** if you want to include your spouse in the assumptions.

4. Under Yourself, click in the **First Name** field, and type your first name. If you are including your spouse, under Spouse, click in the **First Name** field, and type your spouse's first name.

5. Continue through the dialog box, entering all relevant information.

6. If you want to include information about children and other dependents, click **New** at the bottom of the dialog box. The Add Child/Dependent dialog box appears. This information can include children you plan to have that are not yet born:

   a. Click in the **First Name** field, and enter the first name of your child.

   b. Click in the **Date Of Birth** field, and enter the child's date of birth. You can use the format MM/DD/YY. Quicken will change the year to four digits.

   c. Click **OK** to close the Add Child/Dependent dialog box and return to the Quicken Planner: About You dialog box.

   d. Click the name of a dependent, and click **Exclude From Plan** if you don't want Quicken to include dependents in the financial assumptions.

7. Click **Done** when you have entered all of your information and are ready to return to the Planning tab of the Financial Overview Activity Center.

The Plan Assumptions section now displays your name, your spouse's name if you included one, the ages at which you and your spouse plan to retire, and the number of dependents you chose to include in your plan.

UNDERSTANDING YOUR SOCIAL SECURITY RETIREMENT AGE

Each year, you get a statement from the Social Security Administration showing your estimated benefits based on the current laws. This statement shows your benefits based on three dates: early retirement at age 62, full retirement age (which depends on your date of birth), and retirement at age 70. In addition to this annual statement, the Social Security Administration provides a Web site (www.ssa.gov) where many retirement-benefit questions are answered. The site provides benefit calculators and other tools to help you make retirement decisions based on potential Social Security benefits.

CAUTION

The Life Event Planners only support U.S. dollars. Even if you have a multicurrency Quicken file and do not use U.S. dollars as your main currency, U.S. dollars need to be in your currency list with the current exchange rate.

CAUTION

Gross annual salary should include all bonuses, commissions, and salary. It should not include any real estate income, investment income, Social Security income, or pension benefits.

Enter Income Information and Your Tax Rate

The next item in the Plan Assumptions section pertains to information about your income. This includes regular salaries; self-employment income; retirement benefits; and other income, such as child support or alimony.

ENTER SALARIES AND SELF-EMPLOYMENT INCOME

1. Click **Financial Overview** on the Account bar, and, if needed, click the **Planning** tab.

2. Scroll down, if necessary, to **Plan Assumptions**, and click **Income**. The Quicken Planner: Income dialog box appears.

3. Click the **Salary** tab to enter salary information for yourself and your spouse, if you are including a spouse in your planning assumptions.

4. Click **New** in the middle of the dialog box under Salary. The Add Salary dialog box appears:

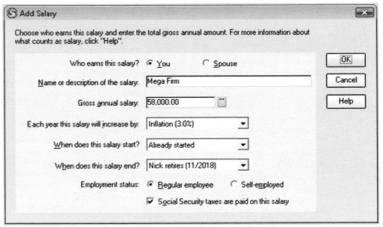

a. Click **You** or **Spouse** in response to "Who Earns This Salary?"

b. Click in the **Name Or Description Of The Salary** field, and type the relevant information.

c. Click in the **Gross Annual Salary** field, and type the amount in U.S. dollars. (Other currencies are not supported by Quicken.)

d. Continue through the questions, entering all relevant information.

e. Click **OK** when you are finished. You are returned to the Quicken Planner: Income dialog box. The information you entered for the starting and ending dates for this salary appear in the Adjustments To Salary section.

Add Salary Adjustment: Mega Firm

Choose the type of adjustment from the list on the left, then enter the information about the adjustment. For more information on which type to choose, click "Help".

- ○ Change jobs
- ○ Promotion
- ● Bonus
- ○ Unpaid leave
- ○ More hours
- ○ Fewer hours

Description: Receive bonus

Date: Specific date: ▼ 1/10/2007

○ Bonus amount: [ ]

● Percent bonus: 12.0%

[OK]
[Cancel]
[Help]

5. If you have other adjustments to your salary, such as a promotion or an expected bonus, click **New** under Adjustments. The Add Salary Adjustment dialog box appears. Enter any relevant information in the appropriate fields.

6. Click **Done** when you have entered all the information that pertains to your situation.

USE THE RETIREMENT BENEFITS TAB

If you have a retirement plan through your employer or want to include Social Security benefit information in your plan, use the Retirement Benefits tab in the Quicken Planner: Income dialog box (see "Enter Salaries and Self-Employment Income" to open this dialog box).

1. Click the **Retirement Benefits** tab to enter information about retirement income.

2. Click **Social Security Starting Age** to enter the age at which you expect to start collecting Social Security benefits. If you don't know, click the **Estimate** button. The Estimate Social Security Benefits dialog box appears.

3. Continue through the fields, entering information that pertains to your situation.

4. Select a pension benefit, and click **Edit** to change that benefit, or click **Delete** to remove it from your list. If you want to exclude a specific pension benefit from your plan, select it from the list, and click **Exclude From Plan**.

5. When you are done, click either the **Other Income** tab to enter additional, non-investment income or click **Done** to return to the Planning tab of the Financial Overview Activity Center.

ENTER OTHER INCOME

The Other Income Tab in the Quicken Planner: Income dialog box is for gifts, inheritances, royalties, and other miscellaneous income you expect to receive. (See "Enter Salaries and Self-Employment Income" to open the Quicken Planner: Income dialog box.)

1. Click the **Other Income** tab, and then click **New**. The Add Other Income dialog box appears.

2. Click the option from the list on the left that corresponds to the type of income you want to include, as shown in Figure 9-3.

3. Continue through the Planner, entering the relevant information. If you have chosen one of the specific types of income from the list on the left, this name appears in the field.

CAUTION

When entering salary starting and ending dates, you can edit the dates, but you cannot delete the dates without deleting the salary as well.

NOTE

Generally, regular employees pay half of their own Social Security and Medicare taxes, while their employer pays the other half. Self-employed persons are responsible for all of their Social Security and Medicare taxes.

TIP

Use the **Reduced Benefit Amount** text box, and type 100% if you don't want your plan to rely on Social Security benefits at all.

Add Other Income

Choose the type of income from the list on the left, then enter the information about the income. For more information on which type to choose, click "Help".

- ○ Gift
- ○ Inheritance
- ○ Trust fund
- ◉ Royalty
- ○ Alimony
- ○ Child support
- ○ Other

Description: Royalty payment

Start date: Specific date: ▾ 5/10/2007 📅

Income period: ○ One-time event
◉ Multiple-year income: [15] years

Income amount: 8,000.00 🖩 (today's value)

Annual growth: Inflation (3.0%) ▾

Tax rate: Normal rate (9%) ▾

Use for income: ○ Save it and invest in your taxable portfolio.
◉ Use it to pay expenses (none will be saved).

[OK] [Cancel] [Help]

Figure 9-3: *Other income can be a one-time event or it can span several years.*

4. Click **OK** to close the Add Other Income dialog box and return to the Quicken Planner: Income dialog box.

5. Click **Done** to close the Quicken Planner: Income dialog box and return to the Planning tab of the Financial Overview Activity Center.

DETERMINE YOUR TAX RATE

Quicken takes your tax liability into account when helping you create your plan. To tell Quicken what rate to use:

1. Click **Financial Overview** near the bottom of the Account bar.

2. Click the **Planning** tab.

CAUTION

Do not include real estate income, pension benefits, investment income, Social Security benefits, or income from a small business as other income.

3. Scroll, if necessary, to the **Plan Assumptions** section, and click **Tax Rate**. The Quicken Planner: Average Tax Rate dialog box appears.

4. Click **Demographic Average** if you want Quicken to calculate your average tax rate based on the average rate of people in your income category in your state:

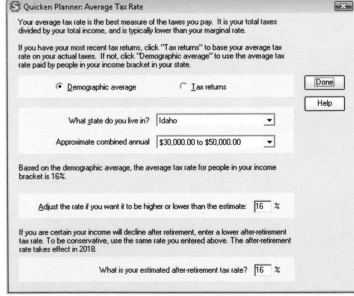

Quicken Planner: Average Tax Rate

Your average tax rate is the best measure of the taxes you pay. It is your total taxes divided by your total income, and is typically lower than your marginal rate.

If you have your most recent tax returns, click "Tax returns" to base your average tax rate on your actual taxes. If not, click "Demographic average" to use the average tax rate paid by people in your income bracket in your state.

◉ Demographic average   ○ Tax returns

What state do you live in? Idaho ▾

Approximate combined annual $30,000.00 to $50,000.00 ▾

Based on the demographic average, the average tax rate for people in your income bracket is 16%.

Adjust the rate if you want it to be higher or lower than the estimate: [16] %

If you are certain your income will decline after retirement, enter a lower after-retirement tax rate. To be conservative, use the same rate you entered above. The after-retirement rate takes effect in 2018.

What is your estimated after-retirement tax rate? [16] %

[Done] [Help]

a. Click the **What State Do You Live In?** down arrow, and click the name of your state.

NOTE

You can always enter a higher tax rate for Quicken to use in its planning calculations.

QUICKSTEPS

ESTIMATING INFLATION FOR YOUR PLAN

Quicken uses an average inflation rate of 3 percent. *Inflation* is a rise in the price of goods or services when consumer spending increases and supplies or services decreases. For the last 50 years, inflation in the United States has ranged from 0 percent to 23 percent, with an average of 2 to 3 percent per year. As you make your assumptions in Quicken, you may choose to be conservative and increase the default inflation rate of 3 percent, or be more optimistic and decrease the rate. To change the rate of inflation used by Quicken:

1. Click **Financial Overview** on the Account bar.

2. Click the **Planning** tab.

3. Scroll to the **Plan Assumptions** section, if necessary, and click **Inflation**. The Quicken Planner: Estimated Inflation dialog box appears.

4. Click in the **What Inflation Rate Do You Want To Use In Your Plan?** field, and type the number you want to use.

5. Click **Done** to close the dialog box.

---

b. Click the **Approximate Combined Annual** down arrow, and click the approximate annual income for you and your spouse.

5. Alternatively, click **Tax Returns** if you want to enter information from your most recent tax return. A different set of questions appears:

   a. Enter the total income (from Form 1040).

   b. Enter the total federal taxes (from Form 1040).

   c. If your state has a state income tax, enter the total state taxes (from your state tax form).

6. The average tax rate for your income bracket in your state appears in the **Adjust The Rate If You Want It To Be Higher Or Lower Than The Estimate** field. Enter any change in the estimated tax rate you want Quicken to use.

7. This same rate appears in the **What Is Your Estimated After-Retirement Tax Rate?** field. Enter any change you want Quicken to use.

8. Click **Done** when you have entered all of the information to return to the Planning tab of the Financial Overview Activity Center.

Consider Savings, Investments, and Rate of Return

Quicken can use the information you entered for your checking, savings, and investment accounts in its assumptions for planning. You can choose to have Quicken include or exclude any account from its computations, designate the use for each account, and indicate what contributions will be made to these accounts in the future.

INCLUDE CHECKING AND SAVINGS ACCOUNTS

To tell Quicken how to use your checking and savings accounts:

1. Click the Planning menu, and click **Go To Planning Center**.

2. In the Financial Overview Activity Center, click the **Planning** tab.

3. Scroll to the **Plan Assumptions** section, if necessary, and click **Savings & Investments**. The Quicken Planner: Savings And Investments dialog box appears.

4. Click the **Savings** tab to display a list of your checking and savings accounts. If you have not yet entered all of your accounts, now is a good time. Click the **New** button to add a new account, and follow the directions in Chapter 3.

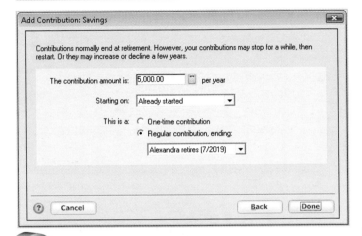

5. Click an account and click **Exclude From Plan** to exclude that account from the plan. Click **Show Excluded Accounts** if you want them to be displayed in the list even if they are not included in the plan.

6. Click **Details** to open the Account Details: Savings dialog box:

   a. Click the **Account Will Be Used For** down arrow, and select the account you want to use. If you have used any of the specific Planners, such as the Home Purchase Planner or the Retirement Planner, you will have that choice included; otherwise, your only choice is the default: **General Expenses**.

   b. Click **OK** to return to the Quicken Planner: Savings And Investments dialog box.

7. If either you or your spouse regularly put money in any of these bank accounts, click **New** underneath Contributions To Savings. The Add Contribution: Savings dialog box appears.

8. Enter the relevant information for your situation.

9. Click **Done** to return to the Quicken Planner: Savings And Investments dialog box.

INCLUDE INVESTMENT ACCOUNTS

The Investments tab shows all of the investment accounts you have entered. You can include or exclude any of these accounts from your plan and tell Quicken about any regular contributions you make to any of them.

Click the **Investments** tab, and follow the procedure in "Include Checking and Savings Accounts" earlier in this chapter.

Work with Homes and Other Assets

You can include your home and other assets in your plan, both those you currently own and those you plan on purchasing.

QUICKSTEPS

ENTERING YOUR EXPECTED RATE OF RETURN

The *rate of return* is how much you get back each year on your investments expressed as a percentage. For example, if you make $200 on a $2,000 investment, your rate of return is 10 percent ($2,000 divided by $200). You can use different rates for taxable and tax-deferred investments. Before retirement, your investments must grow enough to ensure that you have funds available to you even when you are not earning a salary. After retirement, your funds must grow to keep pace with inflation and fund your living expenses. To enter your estimated rate of return on your investments:

1. Click **Financial Overview** on the Account bar.

2. Click the **Planning** tab. *Continued . . .*

ENTERING YOUR EXPECTED RATE OF RETURN

(Continued)

3. If necessary, scroll down to display the **Plan Assumptions** section. Click **Savings & Investments**.

4. Click the **Return** tab.

5. Click **Use Separate Rates Of Return For Taxable And Tax-Deferred Accounts**, if applicable.

6. Click in the **Rate Of Return** field under Before Retirement, and enter the return you expect on your investments before you retire.

7. Click in the **Rate Of Return** field under After Retirement, and enter your expected after-retirement return.

8. If you chose to use separate rates of return in step 5, click in the **Taxable Accounts** fields, and enter the return you expect on your taxable investments, both before and after retirement.

9. Click in the **Your Tax-Deferred** fields to enter those percentages.

10. In the **How Much Of Your Taxable Return Will Be Subject To Taxes Each Year?** field, enter an appropriate percentage. In most cases, all of the return may be taxable. Check with your financial professional to learn what you should enter.

11. Click **Done** to return to the Planning tab.

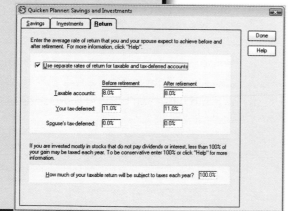

INCLUDE CURRENT ASSETS

To work with the Homes And Assets Planner:

1. Click **Financial Overview** on the Account bar.

2. If necessary, scroll down to the **Plan Assumptions** section, and click **Homes And Assets**. The Quicken Planner: Homes And Assets dialog box appears.

3. Click the **Asset Accounts** tab to display a list of the accounts you have created so far in Quicken, including homes, vehicles, real estate, and so on. The list shows a description of the asset, its purchase date, a planned sale date (if any), and its current value, as shown in Figure 9-4.

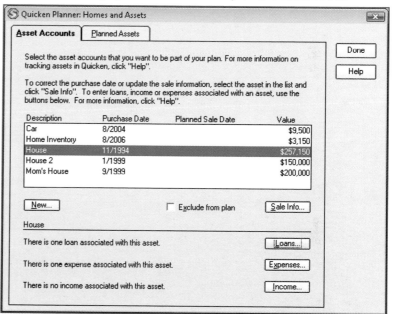

Figure 9-4: The Asset Accounts tab lists all of the asset accounts you have entered into Quicken.

4. Click **New** to add a new account, follow the directions in Chapter 3, and return to the Quicken Planner: Homes And Assets dialog box.

5. Select an asset and click **Exclude From Plan** if you want Quicken to ignore this asset in your plan.

6. Click an asset to see if there are loans, expenses, or income associated with this asset.

7. Click **Sale Info** to open the Asset Account Sale Information dialog box. Click in each of the fields, and select or type the requested information, clicking **Next** as needed.

8. Click **Done** to return to the Quicken Planner: Homes And Assets dialog box.

CONSIDER LOANS ON ASSETS

If you intend to add, pay off, or change a loan using one of your assets as collateral:

1. Click the name of the asset, and then click the **Loans** button to open the Quicken Planner: Loans And Debt dialog box.

2. Click the **Loan Accounts** tab to display the current loans associated with this asset.

3. Select a loan and click **Exclude From Plan** if you want to exclude that loan from your plan.

4. Click the **Planned Loans** tab (see Figure 9-5), and click **New**. The Planned Loans dialog box appears. Click in each of the fields, and select or type the information that is correct for your loan.

5. Click **Done** to return to the Quicken Planner: Loans And Debt dialog box. The details of this planned loan are displayed at the bottom of the dialog box. Click **Done** again to return to the Quicken Planner: Homes And Assets dialog box.

ENTER EXPENSES ASSOCIATED WITH AN ASSET

Many assets have expenses associated with them that must be included in the plan. You can include them here with their associated asset or include them later in the "Figure Your Living Expenses" section of this chapter. To include expenses with their associated asset:

1. Click **Homes And Assets** to open the Asset Accounts dialog box. Click the asset with which you want to work.

2. Click the **Expenses** button toward the bottom of the dialog box. The Quicken Planner: Asset Expenses dialog box appears.

3. Click in the **How Much Tax Do You Pay On This Asset?** field, and enter the tax amount, if any, that you pay. If the asset you selected is a house, a dialog box will appear, mentioning property taxes and providing a formula to figure the amount.

4. If there are other expenses, such as homeowner association fees, moorage fees, maintenance fees, or gardening expenses, click **New**. The Add Asset Expense dialog box appears.

*Figure 9-5: **The Planned Loans tab asks for information about future indebtedness.***

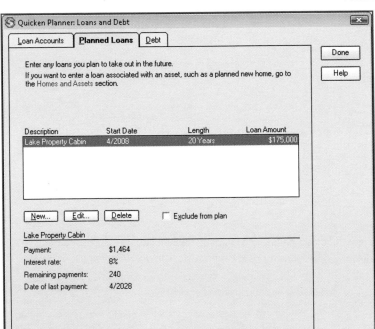

ASSOCIATING INCOME WITH AN ASSET IN YOUR PLAN

Part of your future retirement may come from income you earn by renting an asset you own, such as a motor home, boat, cabin, or real property. You can include this information in your Quicken Planner: Homes And Assets dialog box.

1. Click **Financial Overview** on the Account bar.

2. Scroll down, if necessary, to **Plan Assumptions**. Click **Homes And Assets** to open the Quicken Planner: Homes And Assets dialog box.

3. Click the name of the asset from which you earn income, and click **Income** at the bottom of the dialog box.

4. Click **New** to open the Add Other Income dialog box. Click in each of the fields, and select or type the information that is requested.

5. Click **OK** to close the dialog box.

Edit Other Income

Enter the information about this income generated by the asset "Mom's House".

Description: Income from Mom's House

Start date: Mom's House purchased (9/

Income period: ○ One-time event
○ Multiple-year income: [   ] years
● As long as you own the asset

Income amount: 15,000.00 (today's value)

Annual growth: Inflation (3.0%)

Tax rate: Normal rate (16%)

Use for income: ● Save it and invest in your taxable portfolio.
○ Use it to pay expenses (none will be saved).

[OK] [Cancel] [Help]

---

5. Click in the **Name Or Description** field, and type a name for this expense. Click **Next** to continue. Click in each of the fields, and select or type the information that is appropriate for this expense, clicking **Next** as needed and clicking **OK** to return from any subsidiary dialog box you open.

6. Click **Done** to return to the Quicken Planner: Asset Expenses dialog box. Click **Done** again to return to the Quicken Planner: Homes And Assets dialog box.

INCLUDE PLANNED ASSETS

You can include in your planning the acquisition of additional assets, such as a new home, a new weekend property, a new business or income property, and so on.

1. From the Quicken Planner: Homes And Assets dialog box (see "Include Current Assets"), click the **Planned Assets** tab.

2. Click **New** to open the Add Planned Asset dialog box, click in each of the fields, and select or type the information that is requested, clicking **Next** as needed.

3. Click **Done** to return to the Quicken Planner: Homes And Assets dialog box. See the sections, "Include Current Assets," "Consider Loans on Assets," and "Enter Expenses Associated with an Asset" earlier in this chapter, as well as the QuickSteps "Associating Income with an Asset in Your Plan," to perform the same functions with planned assets as with current assets.

Use the Loans And Debt Planner

To have a comprehensive plan, you need to include your liabilities (loans and debts), as well as your assets.

1. From the Quicken Home page, click **Financial Overview** at the bottom of the Account bar, and click the **Planning** tab. Scroll to the **Plan Assumptions** section, and click **Loans And Debt** to open the Loans And Debt Planner.

2. Click the **Loan Accounts** tab to display a list of all the loans you have entered. You can select loans and exclude them from your plan, change the payoff date, and add new loans.

3. Click the **Planned Loans** tab to display a list of any loans you plan to take out in the future. You may have entered these loans in the Quicken Planner: Homes And Assets section. You can edit, delete, and exclude these loans from the plan, as well as add new ones.

4. Click the **Debt** tab. If you have not yet used Quicken's Debt Reduction Planner, a dialog box appears with a message to that effect. See "Use the Debt Reduction Planner" later in this chapter.

5. Click **Done** to close this dialog box.

Figure Your Living Expenses

Expenses are a critical part of your plan. To figure what your expenses will be:

1. Click **Financial Overview** on the Account bar. Scroll to **Plan Assumptions** (if necessary).

2. Click **Expenses** to open the Quicken Planner: Expenses dialog box.

3. Click the **Living Expenses** tab. You are prompted to enter your regular living expenses, such as food, transportation, rent, medical insurance payments, and utility bills. Quicken offers you two methods of entering these items: by rough estimate or by category detail.

4. Click **Rough Estimate** to let Quicken base an annual estimate of your expenses based on the transactions in your registers.

5. Click **Yearly Living Expenses** and, if needed, modify the amount.

6. Click in the **What Percent Of Surplus Cash Do You Want To Sweep To Savings?** field, and enter a percentage, if you feel you will be spending less than your income. The most conservative amount to select is 0 percent.

ENTER ADJUSTMENTS

The Adjustments tab is used to enter major changes to your living expenses. This could be due to a layoff from work, a new baby, or an illness.

1. Click the **Adjustments** tab, and click **New**. The Add Living Expense Adjustment dialog box appears.

2. Click **No Specific Person** if this is a general adjustment, such as rent from an extra room in your garage. Click **A Plan Member**, and choose the member from the drop-down list, if the change affects one of the persons in your plan. The members are you, your spouse, and any dependents you listed as being included in the plan.

3. Click in the remaining fields that are applicable, and select or type the appropriate information.

Quicken Planner: Expenses

| Living Expenses | Adjustments | College Expenses | Special Expenses |

Enter your living expenses below. Do not enter expenses that are specified elsewhere in the plan, such as taxes, savings contributions, loan and debt payments, or home and asset expenses. For more information click "Help".

Select "Rough estimate" to enter an estimate of all your living expenses. Select "Category detail" to track expenses individually by category.

What method do you want to use? ⦿ Rough estimate ○ Category detail

A conservative estimate of living expenses assumes that you spend all money that does not go to loans, debt, savings or taxes.

Yearly living expenses: 48,500.00

If you have cash flow surpluses in some years, you may be able to save more. If you are confident that these are true surpluses, you may elect to "sweep" a percentage of each surplus into your savings. To be conservative, enter zero.

What percent of surplus cash do you want to sweep to savings? 25 %

Done   Help

PLANNING TO PAY FOR COLLEGE

When you are planning for your children's college education, consider the following:

- How old is the child and when will he or she actually start college? For most students, it is the fall after they graduate from high school.
- What are their options as to the type of school?
  - Consider community or junior college so that the child can complete any lower-level requirements. Some community college programs guarantee entry into a four-year state school if the student graduates with an associate's degree.
  - Community college tuition is usually much less expensive than a four-year institution.
  - State colleges and universities usually charge less tuition to residents of that state than to out-of-state students.
- Many schools are now offering a large number of classes online. This saves room and board as well as transportation costs.
- How can the student receive grants or scholarships?
- Look for scholarships or grants early. Use the Internet to search on the Web, and contact friends or family members in organizations that offer scholarships.
- Check to see if your state offers a guaranteed education account. Many universities and colleges, both state and private, now offer a prepayment plan for parents that allows you to pay over a longer period at a reduced cost and ensure a four-year education at the state or private school offering such a plan.
- Talk to your tax professional about IRAs and other savings plans designed to fund education.

The earlier you begin answering these questions, the more completely you can plan and handle this very substantial expense when it occurs.

4. Click **OK** to close the dialog box.

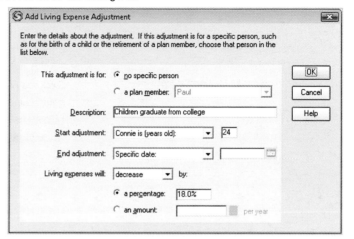

Understand the Plan Results

After you have entered all of your assumptions, the result of your hard work is displayed in graphical format in the Plan: Results section of the Planning tab. The graph shows if your plan is working and how much money you will have in retirement. A list of major events is displayed under the graph, as shown in Figure 9-6.

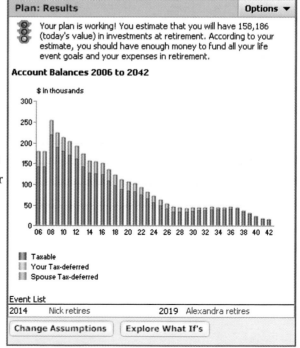

*Figure 9-6: **Your plan results tell you if your financial plan will work.***

1. Click **Options** in the upper-right corner of the Plan: Results section of the Planning tab in the Financial Overview Activity Center to see how you can change the graph.

2. Click **Show Amounts In Future Value** to display the graph in future (inflated) dollars. Click **Options** and click **Show Amounts In Today's Value** to change it back.

3. Click **Options** and click **Review Or Change Plan Assumptions** to open the Plan Assumptions dialog box. Each assumption you entered is displayed with its result. Scroll through the dialog box, or click an area on the left to ensure that you entered everything correctly. If you did not, click **Edit** in the title of each section to open the relevant dialog box, and change the information. You can also access this dialog box by clicking the **Change Assumptions** button underneath the Event List in the Plan: Results section of the Planning tab. Click **Close** to return to the Planning tab.

4. Again, click **Options** on the Plan: Results title bar, and click **What If I Did Something Different** to open the What If dialog box. This allows you to temporarily change any assumption by clicking the assumption area on the left and see the result. If you like the change, keep it; if not, close the dialog box without saving your changes. You can also open this dialog box by clicking the **Explore What If's** button to the right of the Change Assumptions button at the bottom of the Plan: Results section. Click **Close** to return to the Planning tab.

Use the Planners

On the right side of the Planning tab of the Financial Overview Activity Center are five links to Planners for specific goals designed for Quicken by the Financial Planning Association. Each link displays a thorough interview that enables you to take a comprehensive look at each goal. Using the information you entered in the Plan Assumptions section, these Planners provide additional questions for you to think about, links to resources on the Internet, and a complete list of your information in an easy-to-understand format, and then reviews each part of your plan for potential problems.

You can use these Planners to enter information rather than use the Plan Assumptions dialog boxes or to make changes to the data you entered in those assumptions. Perhaps the most important Planner in this group is the Debt Reduction Planner. It is difficult to create financial stability when you owe a large amount of debt.

Planners

Retirement Planner
Can I retire when I want to?
College Planner
Can I afford college?
Home Purchase Planner
Can I afford that house?
Debt Reduction Planner
How can I reduce my debt?
Special Purchase Planner
Can I afford that purchase?

Use the Debt Reduction Planner

With more credit card debt per person in the United States than ever in history, many people's debt load is overwhelming. Quicken's Debt Reduction Planner can help you pay less interest and take control of your debt before you are snowed under. To use the Debt Reduction Planner:

1. Click the **Planning** menu, and click **Debt Reduction Planner**.

   –Or–

   Click **Debt Reduction Planner** on the right side of the Planning tab in the Financial Overview Activity Center under Planners. Either way, the Debt Reduction Planner is displayed.

2. Click the **Start** tab if it isn't already displayed.

3. Click **Next** in the Debt Reduction dialog box to continue. The first time you use the Debt Reduction Planner, a short video explaining the Debt Reduction Planner plays for 41 seconds. Depending on the version of Windows you are using, you may be prompted to insert your Quicken CD to see this and the other videos provided in the Planner. Click **Next** to continue.

WORK WITH THE DEBTS TAB

The Debts tab lists all of the loans and credit card debt you have entered into Quicken, the interest rate for each liability, and the current balance. You may be prompted to enter additional information on one or more of your debts so that Quicken has all of the necessary information to assist you.

1. Click **Add** to add any debt you have not yet entered into Quicken. The Edit Debt Reduction dialog box appears. Click in each of the fields, and select or type the information that is requested.

2. Click **OK**. If there is no Quicken account associated with this loan, a dialog box appears and asks if you would like Quicken to set up an account for the debt. Click **Yes** to set up an account. Follow the procedure outlined in Chapter 3.

3. If you need to change or remove any of your listed loans, click the loan and click **Edit** or **Remove**. If you are editing a loan, repeat steps 1 and 2. If you are removing a loan, click **Yes** to confirm that you want to permanently remove the debt from the plan.

4. After you have entered any new loans or changed any existing loans, click **Next**. The subsequent Debt Reduction Planner page shows how much you owe and your total monthly payment. At the bottom of the page, Quicken displays when you will be debt-free and how much interest you will have paid for your total outstanding debts.

The Order tab displays the optimum plan to get you debt-free in the shortest amount of time and paying the least amount of interest.

1. Click **Next** to open the **Order** tab. Again, a short video will play. Depending on your operating system, you may need to put your Quicken CD in the disc drive. It will explain how Quicken determines the order in which debts should be paid off.

2. Click **Next** to display the order in which Quicken suggests you pay off your debt. At the bottom of the page, the Optimized Payment Plan Results are displayed, showing the new debt-free date, the total interest that would be paid, and the total savings in interest if this new plan is followed.

3. If you do not agree with Quicken, click **Change Payment Order**, and then click **Next** to manually change the order in which the debts are paid. Select a debt and click either the **Move Up** or **Move Down** button to change the order. As you make the changes, the results are displayed on the left side of the page.

4. Click **Reset To Optimized Order** to return to Quicken's order.

USE THE SAVINGS TAB

In the Savings tab, you are given the opportunity to see how making a one-time payment from your savings or investment accounts or both could reduce both your interest payments and the length of time it would take to become debt-free.

1. Click **Next** to open the Savings tab. The first time you run the Debt Reduction Planner, another video discusses using a one-time payment from your savings or investment account to reduce your debt. Click **Next** again.

2. Click in the **Onetime Amount You Would Like To Apply To Reduce Your Debt** field, and enter a dollar amount to apply towards your debt.

3. Click **Recalculate** to see what result this payment would have. The results are displayed in the lower-left area of the page.

CUT EXPENSES IN THE BUDGET TAB AND SEE YOUR PLAN

The Budget tab displays how much you spend monthly in the top four discretionary categories. Each category displays the average amount you spend each month and allows you to enter an amount you can cut back.

1. Click **Next** to see another video discussing the budgeting process. The Budget tab is displayed. Click **Next** again.

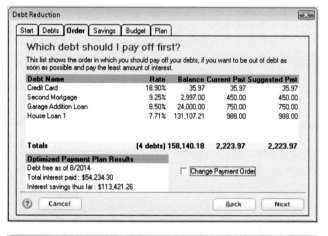

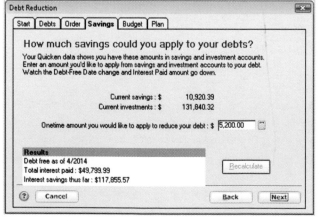

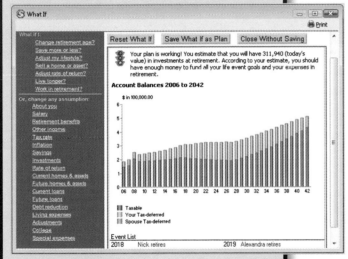

USING WHAT IFS

As you spend time creating plans for your financial future, Quicken provides a utility that allows you to quickly see the result of a possibility or a different path. The What If scenarios allow you to change assumptions or make changes in each of the four different goal types: College, Home Purchase, Retirement, and Special Expense. You can save the new scenario or close the What If dialog box without saving your changes. To use the What If dialog box:

1. Click the **Planning** menu, and click **"What If" Event Scenarios**.

2. Click the **Choose A Goal Type** down arrow, and select one of the four options. Each option has a different set of What If scenarios with which you can work.

3. Click a **What If I** option. Depending on your version of Quicken and your operating system, you may see a brief video. If so, after the video, click **Continue**. If you do not see the video, a Quicken Planner dialog box will appear.   *Continued . . .*

2. Click the first **Quicken Category** drop-down arrow, and select a category to cut. Observe the average monthly spending, and then, in the **Amount To Cut Back** text box, type how much you can decrease your spending in this category. The total amount that you will have available to apply to your debt each month is displayed at the bottom of the four categories.

3. Click in each of the fields, and select or type the information that is appropriate for this expense, clicking **Next** as needed and clicking **OK** to return from any subsidiary dialog box you open.

4. Click **Next** to play a final video. Click **Done** to see a comparison chart that shows how soon you will be debt-free with the new plan compared to the old one.

5. Click **Update Debt Balances** on the menu bar of the Debt Reduction dialog box to update any balances not being tracked in Quicken. Click **Yes** to confirm that you want to do this. Click **Done** when you have finished looking at the results.

6. Click **Payment Schedule** on the menu bar to see a detailed payment schedule. Click **Print** to print the new schedule, and click **Done** to close the dialog box.

7. Click **New Plan** on the menu bar of the Debt Reduction dialog box to redo your debt reduction plan. A dialog box appears, warning you that any new data will replace the data in your current plan. Click **Yes** to create a new plan and open the Debt Reduction Planner once again. Click **No** to close the message.

8. Click **Close** to close the Debt Reduction window.

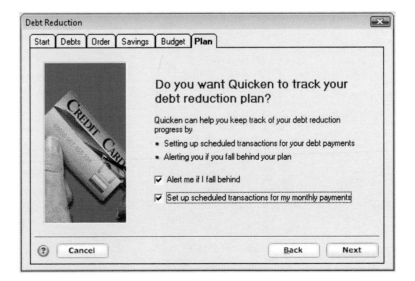

QUICKSTEPS

USING WHAT IFS

(Continued)

4. Click the area that might change, and click **Edit In The Appropriate Area**. Make any needed adjustments, and click **OK**.

5. Repeat step 4 for other What If scenarios or changes in assumptions. When you are ready, click **Done** to close the Quicken Planner dialog box. The result of this change is displayed in the Plan Results graph in the What If dialog box.

6. Click **Reset What If** to revert to your original settings or assumptions.

7. If you want, click **Save What If As Plan** to keep the change you entered and return to the Planning tab of the Financial Overview Activity Center. Otherwise, click **Close Without Saving** to return to the Planning tab of the Financial Overview Activity Center.

Calculators

Retirement Calculator
College Calculator
Refinance Calculator
Savings Calculator
Loan Calculator

Use the Calculators, Budgets, and Other Tools

Quicken provides several additional sets of tools to help you plan and achieve your financial goals. The Calculators provide a quick look at your financial situation for a particular event without having to enter all the data in plan assumptions. The Budget tool helps you create a budget manually or helps you guide Quicken to set it up automatically. The Professional Planning Resources link explains the various types of financial professionals to whom you can turn and, if one of your dreams is running your own business, Quicken has a tool to help you create a business plan for that as well.

Get Quick Answers with Calculators

The five Quicken Calculators—Retirement, College, Refinance, Savings, and Loan—help you to quickly calculate your current position without having to enter all of your assumptions. Each Calculator has different questions but performs in the same manner. This section uses the Retirement Calculator as an example.

The Retirement Calculator lets you quickly see where you stand in your retirement preparations, as shown in Figure 9-7. To use it:

1. Click **Financial Overview** on the Account bar, and click the **Planning** tab.

2. Click **Retirement Calculator** on the right side of the Planning tab of the Financial Overview Activity Center.

3. Click in each of the fields, and select or type the information that is requested.

4. Click **Done** when you have finished with your calculations.

Create a Budget

A budget is simply a formal spending plan. Whether you scribble it on the back of an envelope or create color-coded charts and graphs, a budget helps you understand where your money comes from and where it goes. Quicken provides a tool you can use to create a budget simply and quickly using the data you have already entered. There are two steps in budgeting: setting it up and then fine-tuning the income, expense, and savings information.

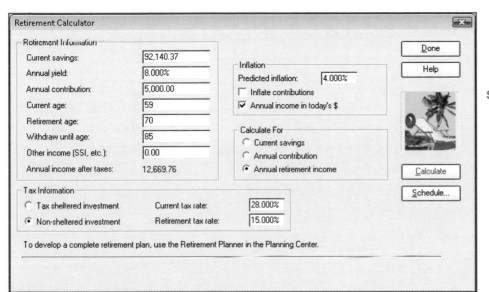

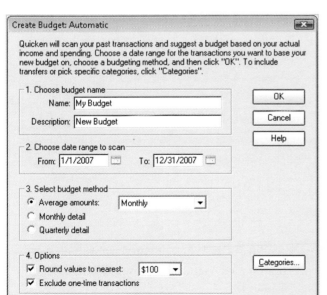

Figure 9-7: *The Retirement Calculator allows you to quickly see retirement information for you and/or your spouse.*

SET UP A BUDGET

To set up your budget in Quicken:

1. Click **Financial Overview** on the Account bar, and click the **Planning** tab.

2. In the **Tools** section, on the right, click **Budget**. The Budget window opens.

3. If it is not already displayed, click the **Setup** tab to begin.

4. If you want Quicken to use your data to create an initial budget you can modify, click **Automatic**. If you want a blank budget template into which you can enter information, click **Manual**. Then click **Create Budget**. (If you have created a budget before this, you can click **Copy Current** to create a new budget based on your original one.)

5. If you chose Automatic, the Create Budget: Automatic dialog box appears.

6. In the **Choose Date Range To Scan** area, enter a date range from which Quicken will create your budget.

7. In the **Select Budget Method** area, click the **Average Amounts** option, click the corresponding down arrow, and choose from a list of time periods for computing averages.

8. Click **Monthly Detail** or **Quarterly Detail** to have Quicken use these amounts rather than the averages.

9. In the **Options** area, click the **Round Values To Nearest** check box, click the corresponding down arrow, and choose the detail for rounding averages.

10. Click **Exclude One-Time Transactions** to eliminate these transactions from the calculation.

11. Click the **Categories** button to include or exclude accounts or categories from the calculations. Click **OK** to close the Choose Categories dialog box.

12. Click **OK** to create the budget. A dialog box appears stating the budget has been created and that you are to use the tabs at the top of the Budget window to proceed.

13. Click **OK** to close the dialog box. The Budget window opens with the income and expense categories displayed along the left side.

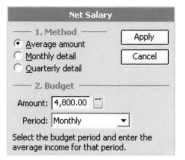

FINE-TUNE THE BUDGET

The Income, Expense, and Savings categories in the Budget window display details pertaining to your budget based on the assumptions you chose in the previous procedure. If you want to make changes:

1. Click one of the categories and/or accounts, and then click one of the options on the right—**Average Amount**, **Monthly Detail**, or **Quarterly Detail**—to change the original method. Click in each of the fields, and select or type the information that is appropriate for this expense, clicking **Next** as needed and clicking **OK** to return from any subsidiary dialog box you open.

2. Click **Close** to close the Budget window.

Work with Your Budget

After you have taken the time to create your budget, you may change its focus to create reports, print the reports, and create graphs from the results.

1. Click the **Planning** menu, and click **Budget**. The Budget window opens.

2. Click **Options** and click **Save Budget** to save your budget after you have created it.

3. Click **Options** again and select one of the three available budget views:

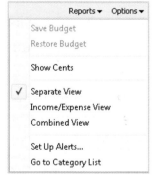

- **Separate View** shows each set of categories—Income, Expense, and Savings—as separate tabs so that you can focus on one budget area at a time.

- **Income/Expense View** includes income transfers and categories as part of the Income tab and expense transfers as part of the Expense tab.

- **Combined View** includes all categories and transfers on one tab, the Budget tab, so that you can see all categories in one list.

4. Click **Reports** on the Budget menu bar, and select one of the three report options, each of which can be customized to meet your requirements:

- **Budget Report** creates a standard report based on parameters you set.

- **Monthly Budget Report** creates a report by month rather than by annual amounts.

- **Monthly Budget Graph** graphically portrays how much over or under each item is compared to the budget for the time period you stipulate.

Chapter 10

Getting Ready for Tax Time

Tax preparation can be stressful and frustrating. You have to locate and organize your financial records, read complex publications, and fill out difficult-to-read forms. In many cases, it means writing a check to the federal and/or state government taxing authority and worrying about how much more you will owe next year. Quicken can lessen the burden. With its planning and organizational features, it can help you be ready well before the tax due date. Quicken also has a Tax Planner, a tool that helps you determine which deductions you can take, and another tool to help you decide how much withholdings you should claim. You can access additional tools online through the links provided in the Tax tab of the Financial Overview Activity Center. With Quicken, April 15 can be just another day in your smooth financial life.

Figure 10-1: The Tax Planner Summary worksheet displays information from Quicken, TurboTax, or that you enter yourself.

Use the Tax Planner

The basis for all of your tax information can be entered into the Tax Planner. The Tax Planner helps you evaluate your income tax position. It bases its estimates on numbers you give it, on the data you've entered into Quicken, or on last year's TurboTax return. It covers such areas as your employment income, interest, and dividends you earn; deductions and exemptions; withholdings; and other taxes or credits for which you may be liable. Figure 10-1 shows an example of the Tax Planner Summary worksheet. If you entered information in New User Setup, the Tax Planner starts with that information; however, you can change it at any time.

Enter the Tax Planner Options

If you did not use Quicken New User Setup to enter the information about yourself, the Tax Planner uses the default settings. These settings appear in the upper-left area of the Tax Planner.

To change these settings:

1. Click the **Tax** menu, and click **Tax Planner**. The Tax Planner is displayed. You may be asked if you want to import your TurboTax data. If so, click **Yes**. If not, you may import it later. If you do not have TurboTax data to import, or if you want to do it at another time, click **No**.

2. If "Tax Planner Options" is not displayed in the right pane, click **Year** in the left pane to display it. While you can click the **Year** down arrow to choose another year for which to plan, there are only a few instances in which you want to and can do this, such as the first quarter of a year in which you may still be working with the previous year. The default is the current year. If you change the year, a dialog box appears. Click your answer, and then click **OK** to close the Tax Year dialog box and return to Tax Planner Options.

NOTE

Most of the tasks performed with the Tax Planner and the other Quicken tax-related tools are easily done with *worksheets* in which Quicken fills in numbers it knows about, you enter other numbers or correct the ones Quicken automatically entered, and then Quicken summarizes these amounts and does the necessary calculations.

NOTE

The Tax Planner is only available in Quicken Deluxe, Premier, and Home & Business editions.

CAUTION

If you have entered information in the Tax Planner before this session, change your scenario before you make changes to either the Status or Year fields.

TIP

If you create more than one scenario, you can compare them. Click **Compare** on the toolbar in the Tax Planner after you have entered data into two different scenarios.

NOTE

Items that Quicken does not consider complete are flagged with a small magnifying glass icon, as shown in the illustration.

NOTE

If you are entering a projected-values scenario, you have the option of showing the details about where the information came from. To do this, click one of the underlined text entries, or click **Show Details**. If you are using an alternate scenario, you do not have this option.

3. Click the **Filing Status** down arrow to change your income tax filing status from the default, **Married Filing Jointly**, to your status. If you are not sure of your status, consult your tax professional.

4. Click the **Scenario** down arrow to create a new scenario. You can create up to three additional scenarios in the Tax Planner. For example, if you are thinking of starting a small business, you could enter information about your projected income in a second scenario to see how it would affect your tax situation.

5. Click **Next**. The How Can Quicken Help With Tax Planning? page is displayed. If you see the Tax Planner Summary instead, which means that the Tax Planner has been used in the past, click **How Can Quicken Help With Tax Planning?** in the left pane. If you have a previous scenario, that scenario will open in the place of How Can Quicken Help With Tax Planning?

6. Click **More Details** to open a Help window displaying information about using the Tax Planner. When you are finished, click **Close** to return to the Tax Planner.

7. Click **Let's Get Started** to display the Tax Planner Summary shown in Figure 10-1.

Enter Income into the Tax Planner

Start the Tax Planner by entering your income information.

1. If the Tax Planner isn't already displayed, click the **Tax** menu, click **Tax Planner**, and click **Wages** on the left, or click Wages And Salaries in the Tax Planner Summary. The Wages worksheet is displayed.

2. Click in the **Wages And Salaries – Self** text box. Enter the amount of wages or salary you expect to earn for the year. After you enter the information, your projected tax due or refund due is computed and displayed.

3. Click in the **Wages And Salaries – Self (Other)** text box, and enter the taxable amounts from Employee Stock Purchase Plan (ESPP) shares or from the sale of nonqualified-employee stock options. Check with your tax professional to see if either of these options applies to you.

4. Click in each of the fields, and select or type the information that is appropriate for this expense, clicking **Next** as needed and clicking **OK** to return from any subsidiary dialog box you open.

5. Click **Next** to continue to the Interest And Dividend Income worksheet.

USING THE TAX LINE IN CATEGORIES

You have the option to include tax information when entering a new category.

1. Click the **Tools** menu, and click **Category List**.

2. Click **New** in the lower-left area of the window to enter a new category, or select an existing category, and click **Edit**.

3. Click the **Tax Line Item** down arrow to display a list of possible tax-line items. These items are arranged by IRS form number and schedule letter. Check with your tax professional if you have questions about the meaning of each tax line. Click the name of the tax item.

4. Click **Extended Line Item List** if the item you need does not appear on the standard line item list. Then click the **Tax Line Item** down arrow, and click the item you want you use.

5. Click the **Tax-Related** check box.

6. Click **OK** to close the Edit Category dialog box.

Enter Interest, Dividend, and Business Income

If you have received forms from your financial institutions, such as 1099-INTs or partnership K-1s, use the information shown on these forms. Otherwise, enter estimates in this area.

1. If the Tax Planner isn't already open, click the **Tax** menu, click **Tax Planner**, and click **Interest/Dividend Inc** in the left pane.

2. Click in the **Taxable Interest Income** text box, and enter the amount of taxable interest you will receive for the year from savings or money market accounts.

3. Click in the **Dividends** text box, and enter all the amounts reported on K-1 forms from mutual funds, stocks, partnerships, estates, trusts, or S corporations. If you have not yet received a K-1 form, estimate the amount that you received.

4. Click **Next** to display the Business Income worksheet.

5. If you have a small business, use this worksheet to enter the information from your Schedule C (see Figure 10-2) or from a profit-and-loss statement.

6. Click in the **Revenue-Self** text box, and enter the total revenue for your business. Click in the **Revenue-Spouse** text box, and enter the revenue for your spouse's business.

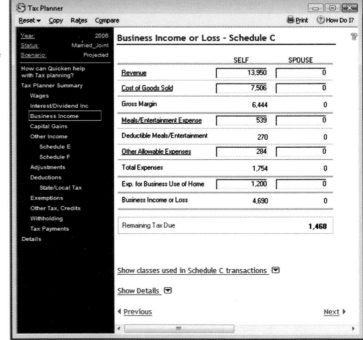

Figure 10-2: If you operate a small business, enter the data from a financial statement.

NOTE

On a profit-and loss statement outside of Quicken, what is called gross margin by Quicken might be called *gross profit*.

CAUTION

There are some specific rules about using your home or part of it for your business. Consult your tax professional for more information.

CAUTION

When you use the Capital Gains And Losses worksheet, make sure you understand which type of gain or loss, short-term or long-term, you are entering. In this, as in all areas, it is important that you consult with your tax professional.

NOTE

Unrecaptured depreciation is a special type of gain that may apply when you sell real property you have previously depreciated, as you might with a home office or a daycare center in your home. Consult your tax professional if you feel this might apply to you.

7. Click in the **Cost Of Goods Sold** text box, and enter the cost of the items you sold for each business. After you have entered the cost of goods sold, the gross margin appears. The gross margin is the total revenue less the total cost of goods sold.

8. If you have associated any expense categories with a Tax Schedule C line, that amount will appear in the Other Allowable Expenses field. Click in the **Other Allowable Expenses** text box to change the amount. After you have entered the amount for these expenses, Quicken calculates your total expenses.

9. Click in the **Exp. For Business Use Of Home** text box, and enter the amount you allot for the business use of your home. The total business income or loss amount is displayed for each business, as well as the total remaining tax due.

10. Click **Next** to display the Capital Gains And Losses worksheet.

Enter Capital Gains

Before you can enter information into the Capital Gains And Losses worksheet, you must know whether a gain is a short-term or a long-term gain. See the QuickFacts "Determining the Type of Capital Gain" later in this chapter. A capital gain is the difference between the price for which you have sold an asset and the price you paid for it. You *realize*, or achieve, a capital gain when you sell an investment for more than you paid for it. (Having *unrealized* capital gain means that an investment hasn't been sold yet but would give you a profit if you did sell it.) You may owe federal income tax (and in some cases, state income tax) on that capital gain. Capital gains are earned on many types of investments, including mutual funds, bonds, stocks, homes, and businesses. If you sell an investment for less than you paid for it, you have a *capital loss*.

1. If the Tax Planner isn't already open, click the **Tax** menu, click **Tax Planner**, and click **Capital Gains** in the left pane.

2. Click in each of the fields, and select or type the information that is appropriate for this expense. Click **Next** as needed and click **OK** to return from any subsidiary dialog box.

3. Note that long-term 28% property is taxed at a special rate. Check with your tax professional to determine if any of your property falls under this classification.

4. Click **Next** to display the Other Income Or Losses worksheet.

Work with Other Income or Losses

The Other Income Or Losses worksheet allows you to enter information that affects your tax situation but that is not covered in other areas of the Tax

DETERMINING THE TYPE OF CAPITAL GAIN

A capital gain can be either long-term or short-term, depending on the length of time you have owned an asset. Generally speaking:

- Any asset you have owned for less than 12 months and one day is considered a short-term asset.

- Normally, a gain on a short-term asset is taxed at your regular income tax rate.

- Any asset you have owned for more than 12 months and one day is deemed to be a long-term asset and is taxed at a special rate, depending on your tax bracket.

- Additional information about how to determine whether an asset is short-term or long-term can be found in IRS publications or from your tax professional.

NOTE

The Tax Planner does not determine which, if any, of your Social Security or RRA income is taxable. The instruction booklet that comes with your 1040 form has a worksheet to help you determine how much, if any, is taxable. You can also consult your tax professional.

Planner. These items include taxable state income tax refunds, alimony, taxable Social Security benefits, and so on. As with all items in the Tax Planner, review your entries and discuss them with your tax professional.

1. If the Tax Planner isn't already open, click the **Tax** menu, click **Tax Planner**, and click **Other Income** in the left pane. Figure 10-3 displays a typical Other Income Or Losses worksheet.

2. Click in each of the fields, and select or type the information that is appropriate for this expense, clicking **Next** as needed and clicking **OK** to return from any subsidiary dialog box you open.

3. Click **Adjustments** in the left pane, to display the Adjustments To Income worksheet.

Work with Income Adjustments and Deductions

After entering all your income, you need to consider those items that reduce your income before taxes. These are primarily income adjustments, deductions, exemptions, and tax credits.

ENTER ADJUSTMENT TO INCOME

Adjustments to income are those items that, while not deductible, reduce your income. They include Individual Retirement Account (IRA) contributions, health insurance paid by self-employed persons, Keogh or SEP contributions, alimony you have paid, moving expenses, and other adjustments.

Other Income or Losses	?
Taxable Refund of State/Local Income Tax	250
Alimony Received	0
Taxable IRA/Pension Distributions	600
Sched E Income - Rents, Royalties and Partnerships	0
Sched F Income - Farm	0
Unemployment Compensation	0
Taxable Social Security Benefits	800
Social Security RRA Income	0
Other Income, Gains or Losses	0
Total Other Income or Losses	1,650
Remaining Tax Due	**1,567**

Show Details ☑

◀ Previous   Next ▶

Figure 10-3: Enter other income, such as alimony, into the Other Income Or Losses worksheet in your Tax Planner.

NOTE

If you pay your real estate taxes with your mortgage payment, your mortgage company will show the amount of real estate taxes paid on the Form 1098 they send you at the end of the year.

c. Click the **Pay Period** down arrow, and choose how often each of you is paid.

d. Click in the **Withholding Per Pay Period** text box, and enter the amount of state or local taxes withheld from your paychecks.

e. Click in the **Estimated Taxes Paid To Date Plus Projected Payments Through Year-End** text box, and enter how much tax you have paid to the IRS or how much has been withheld to date as the basis for state and local taxes.

f. Click in the **Tax Payments This Year For Last Year's State Tax** text box, and enter any amounts you have paid in state income tax during this calendar year.

g. Quicken calculates what your total payments for state and local income taxes will be.

h. Click **Previous** to return to the Standard And Itemized Deductions worksheet.

4. Click in the **Real Estate And Other Taxes** text box, and enter the amount of real estate taxes you have paid or will pay for the current year.

5. Click in the **Deductible Investment Interest** text box, and enter the relevant amount.

6. Click in the **Mortgage & Other Deductible Interest** text box, and enter your mortgage interest as shown on the Form 1098 you received from your mortgage company.

7. Click in the **Charitable Contributions** text box, and enter the amount of money you have given to charity for the current year. The Tax Planner will adjust your deduction to comply with IRS regulations.

8. Click in the **Deductible Casualty Losses** text box, and enter any losses in this category. To understand what you can deduct, consult your tax professional.

9. Click in the **Misc. Deductions** and **Misc. Deductions (No Limit)** text boxes, and enter any qualifying deductions. Quicken will calculate your total itemized deductions.

10. In the **Standard Deduction** column, click any check box that pertains to your situation. The amount of your standard deduction appears in the Deduction field. If your itemized deductions are larger than your standard deduction, the larger amount appears in the Larger Of Itemized Or Standard Deduction field.

11. Click **Next** twice to display the Exemptions worksheet.

12. If you have entered the number of members in your family in New User Setup the information about your situation is already displayed. If you did not use the New User Setup, enter the relevant information, and click **Next** to display the Other Taxes And Credits worksheet. The information you entered earlier regarding your self-employment income is already included on this worksheet. If your tax professional tells you that you are subject to the alternative minimum tax, enter any relevant information; otherwise, click **Next** to display the Federal Withholdings worksheet.

Standard Deduction

☐ Taxpayer can be claimed as a dependent on another return.

SELF
☐ Blind ☐ 65 or Older

SPOUSE
☐ Blind ☐ 65 or Older

Deduction 10,300

Deduction

Larger of Itemized or
Standard Deduction

10,300

Exemptions

Number of Exemptions	
Self and Spouse	2
Dependents	0
Total Exemptions	2
Exemption deduction	6,600

10

Adjustments to Income

Allowable IRA Deduction (Not all IRA Contributions are Deductible)	2,000
One-Half of Self-Employment-Tax	332
Allowable S.E. Health Insurance Deduction	3,800
Keogh/SEP Deduction	2,000
Penalty on Early Withdrawal of Savings	0
Alimony Paid	0
Moving Expenses	0
Other Adjustments	0
Total Adjustments	8,132
Remaining Tax Due	**397**

NOTE

Quicken calculates the amount of self-employment tax for you.

NOTE

IRS regulations state that you can deduct medical and dental expenses that are more than 7.5 percent of your income. Check with your tax professional for further information.

TIP

Don't forget your eye examinations and hearing aids.

1. If the Tax Planner isn't already open, click the **Tax** menu, click **Tax Planner**, and click **Adjustments** in the left pane.

2. Click in each text box, and enter the relevant amounts if any of these items pertain to you.

3. Click **Next** to display the Standard And Itemized Deductions worksheet.

ENTER STANDARD AND ITEMIZED DEDUCTIONS

According to the IRS, most people take the standard deduction to reduce their income tax bill. However, if you pay high mortgage interest payments or have large medical bills, itemizing your deductions might reduce your tax liability even more. Quicken provides a Deduction Finder to help you with this. See "Use the Deduction Finder" later in this chapter.

1. If the Tax Planner isn't already open, click the **Tax** menu, click **Tax Planner**, and click **Deductions** in the left pane.

2. Click in the **Medical And Dental Expense** field to enter all of your medical and dental expenses for the year. Quicken will compute the amount of your deduction, if you can take one, and display it in the Allowable Medical Deduction area. If you cannot take a deduction, the Allowable Medical Deduction area shows zero.

3. If your state or locality has an income tax, click **State & Local Income Tax** to display the State And Local Income Tax worksheet. If there are figures already filled in from the paycheck detail you entered and you believe that it is correct, you can skip to step 4. Otherwise:

   a. Click in the **Withholdings** text box, and enter the state or local withholding amounts for you and your spouse through your last paychecks. This information should appear on your pay stubs.

   b. Click in the **Next Pay Date** text box, and enter the date on which you will receive your next paychecks.

State and Local Income Tax

Projected Withholdings	SELF	SPOUSE
Withholdings	750	0
Next Pay Date	10/01/06	09/01/06
Pay Period	Monthly	Every 2 weeks
Withholding per Pay Period	65	Project: Included
Projected Future Withholding	195	0
Projected Total Withholding	945	0
Projected Total Withholdings for Self and Spouse		945
Estimated Taxes Paid to Date plus Projected Payments Through Year-End		0
Tax Payments this Year for Last Year's State Tax		145
Total Tax Payments to Date plus Projected Withholding Through Year-End		1,090
Remaining Tax Due		**397**

QUICKFACTS

DEDUCTING STATE SALES TAX

The American Jobs Creation Bill of 2004 allows taxpayers to deduct state and local sales tax from their tax returns if they itemize their deductions. However, you should consider the following:

- To take the deduction, you must itemize deductions.
- If you live in a state that collects income tax, you must choose to deduct either the state (or local) income tax you paid or the sales tax deduction—you cannot deduct both.
- You can add up the sales tax you paid from your cash register and credit card receipts to determine your deduction. This requires that you keep these receipts with your income tax records for the year.
- Alternatively, you can use the appropriate amount from the sales tax tables created by the IRS. These tables are included in your Form 1040 packet and are also available online at the IRS Web site at www.irs.gov.

NOTE

The Tax Withholding Estimator helps you determine how much to withhold from your paycheck. See "Use the Tax Withholding Estimator" later in this chapter for more information.

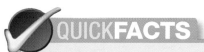

Update Your Federal Withholdings

The Withholdings worksheet may already display information you have entered, either from your paycheck setup or on earlier worksheets of the Tax Planner. If not, enter the information as needed.

In the center of the worksheet, the Tax Payment Summary displays your projected tax as well as your projected withholdings from the Total Withholdings To Date amount. Your estimated tax due or refund due has been calculated by Quicken, as shown in Figure 10-4.

Click **Tax Planner Summary** in the left margin to see the result of your entries into the Tax Planner. Figure 10-5 shows a sample Tax Planner Summary.

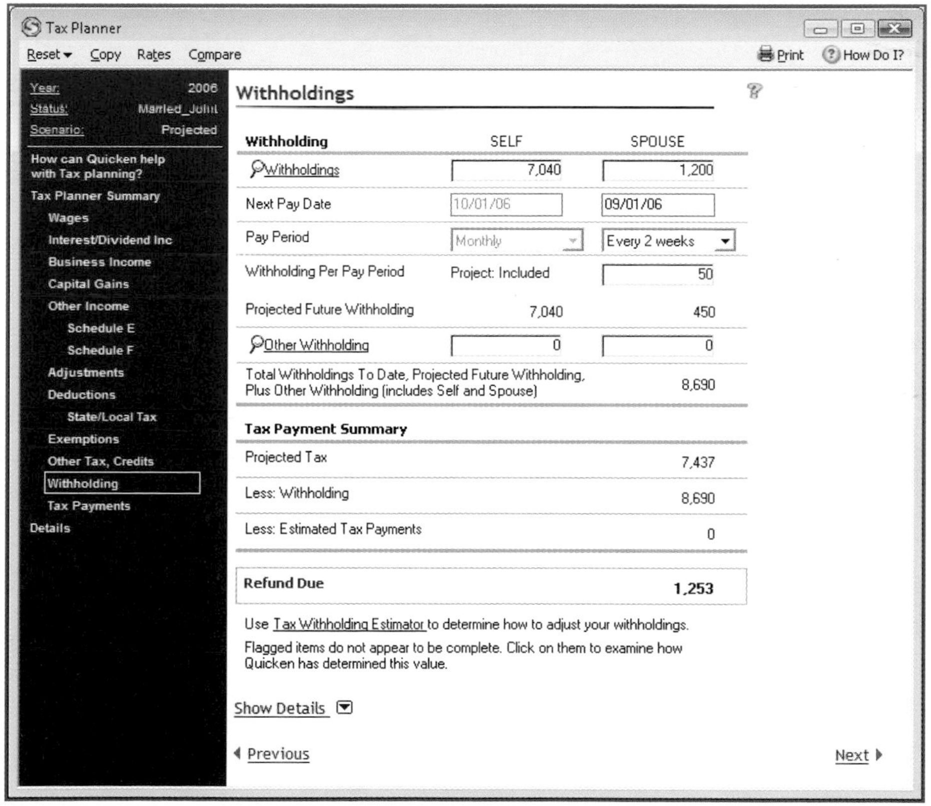

Figure 10-4: The Withholdings worksheet displays your projected withholdings as well as your current tax or refund due.

SETTING TAX ALERTS

At the top of the Tax tab in the Financial Overview Activity Center are the tax alerts.

1. Click **Set Up Alerts**, and choose from the three tax sections.

2. Click **Withholding Threshold** in the left pane, click in the **Withholding Threshold** text box, and type a threshold for your projected tax liability. For example, if you type $100 as the threshold, Quicken will alert you if your withholdings are projected to be less or more than $100 of what you will owe based on the information you entered. You should consult your tax professional to ensure you've entered the appropriate information.

3. Click **Schedule A – Personal Deductions** to be provided with information about the types of personal deductions you may claim on your taxes.

4. Click **Important Tax Dates** in the left pane to have Quicken remind of you filing dates, such as April 15. These dates are displayed in the Tax tab in the Tax Calendar section.

5. When you are ready, click **Close** to close the Alerts Center.

All alerts can be set to display as a dialog box or as text in the Alert List.

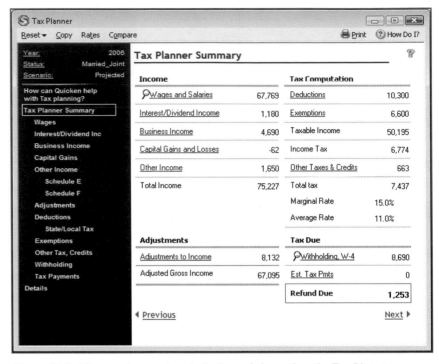

Figure 10-5: After you have entered all of your information, the Tax Planner Summary worksheet displays the results.

Work with the Tax Tab

The Tax tab of the Financial Overview Activity Center provides an overview of your tax standing at any time during the year. It shows all of your tax alerts, the tax calendar, all of your taxable income for the year, any tax-related expenses, and your projected taxes, and it offers a variety of tools to help you plan. All of this information is based on data you have entered. You can adjust this data, add to it, and create reports based on it. While, ultimately, all tax questions should be reviewed with your tax professional, Quicken provides a host of useful tools and reports to help you. To see what information is currently available in the Tax tab:

Click the **Tax** menu, and click **Go To Tax Center**. The Financial Overview Activity Center appears with the Tax tab displayed, as shown in Figure 10-6.

NOTE

The tax calendar, which appears midway down the Tax tab, displays the important tax dates for the current year in addition to any tax alerts you have set up.

Tax Calendar	Options ▼
8/15/2006	Last day to get an additional tax extension
9/15/2006	Quarterly estimated taxes are due
10/16/2006	Tax returns are due for the second extension
12/31/2006	Last day to establish a Keogh plan
1/16/2007	Quarterly estimated taxes are due
1/31/2007	You should have received W-2 forms
1/31/2007	You should have received 1099 forms
1/31/2007	Early filing deadline
2/15/2007	Last day to continue tax exemption status
2/28/2007	Forms W-2 and W-3 for household employees are due

TIP

The Projected Tax section of the Tax tab displays the information you entered into Quicken or the Tax Planner. You can click any of the links to go to the Tax Planner for that link.

Financial Overview | Net Worth | Planning | Tax

Tax Alerts	Options ▼
You currently have no tax alerts	

Show all alerts | Set Up Alerts

Projected Tax	Options ▼
Filing Status	Single
Tax Year	2006
Wages/Salary (self)	0
Total Income	0
Adjusted Gross Income	0
Deductions (Standard Deduction)	0
Exemptions	0
Taxable Income	0
Total Tax	0
Marginal Tax Rate	0.0%
Average Tax Rate	0.0%
⌕ Withholding/W-4	0
Remaining Tax Due	0

Show Tax Planner | Show Tax Summary Report

Tax Calendar	Options ▼
8/15/2006	Last day to get an additional tax extension
9/15/2006	Quarterly estimated taxes are due
10/16/2006	Tax returns are due for the second extension
12/31/2006	Last day to establish a Keogh plan
1/16/2007	Quarterly estimated taxes are due
1/31/2007	You should have received W-2 forms
1/31/2007	You should have received 1099 forms
1/31/2007	Early filing deadline
2/15/2007	Last day to continue tax exemption status
2/28/2007	Forms W-2 and W-3 for household employees are due

Set Up Alerts

Tools

Tax Planner
How much will I owe?
Capital Gains Estimator
How will that sale affect my taxes?
Tax Withholding Estimator
Am I under or over withholding?
Tax Line Item Assignment
Assign tax-related categories.

Quicken Tips

Receive free monthly Quicken newsletters for tips on your personal or small business finances

Use Turbo Tax

How do I export Quicken data to Turbo Tax?
Import Last Year's Turbo Tax Data
Prepare and File Taxes Online
Purchase Turbo Tax

Online Tax Tools

Tax Calculators
Common Tax Questions
Tax Forms
Federal Tax Publications

Go to TurboTax.com

Figure 10-6: The Tax tab gives an overview of your tax information and provides you with links to several tax tools.

Tax-Related Expenses YTD	Options ▼
Meals & Entertn	75.96
Tax:Fed	3,977.76
Tax:Medicare	556.80
Tax:SDI	0.00
Tax:Soc Sec	2,380.80
Tax:State	0.00

Assign Tax Categories | Show Tax Schedule Report

Assign Tax-Related Expenses and See Your Taxable Income

The Tax-Related Expenses YTD section of the Tax tab helps you track any related expenses. To assign a tax line to an expense category:

1. Click **Assign Tax Categories** at the bottom of the Tax-Related Expenses YTD section to open the Category List.

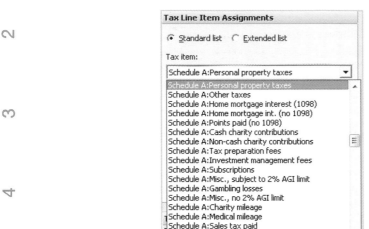

Tools

Tax Planner
How much will I owe?
Capital Gains Estimator
How will that sale affect my taxes?
Tax Withholding Estimator
Am I under or over withholding?
Tax Line Item Assignment
Assign tax-related categories.

> **NOTE**
>
> You can assign tax lines to categories by clicking the **Tax Line Item Assignment** link under Tools on the right side of the Tax tab.

2. Select the category to which you want to assign a tax line, scroll to the right, and click the **Tax** check box for that category.

3. Click **Standard List** under the Tax Line Item Assignments section on the right of the window.

4. Click the **Tax Item** down arrow, and click the tax line that is relevant for the category. If the tax item you want to assign does not appear on the standard list, click **Extended List** to include more tax items, and click the tax line.

5. Click **Close** to return to the Tax tab.

The Taxable Income YTD section gives you a link to set up your paycheck if you have not already done so.

Use the Tools in the Tax Tab

On the right side of the Tax tab are tools you can use to help with your tax planning:

- The **Tax Planner**, which is covered earlier in this chapter, helps you determine how much you will owe in taxes.

- The **Capital Gains Estimator** helps you determine the tax implications of selling assets and investments. This wizard gives you general information about potential sales but does not substitute for a financial or tax advisor. You can create up to three scenarios that combine with the information you entered into the Tax Planner. This utility is discussed in Chapter 8.

- The **Tax Withholding Estimator**, which is covered at the end of this chapter, helps you determine whether you are having the appropriate amount withheld from your earnings.

- The **Tax Line Item Assignment** allows you to assign specific lines on a federal tax form to your income and expense categories, and is covered in the preceding section.

Use TurboTax and Online Tax Tools

For additional tax tools and help, Quicken gives you links to the TurboTax Web site, several tax calculators, answers to common tax questions, tax forms, and federal tax publications.

CREATING TAX REPORTS

Click the **Reports** menu, and click **Tax**. Six reports are displayed designed specifically for taxes:

▼ Tax

- Capital Gains
- Schedule A-Itemized Deduction
- Schedule B-Interest and Dividends
- Schedule D-Capital Gains and Losses
- Tax Schedule (for export to Turbo Tax)
- Tax Summary

- **Capital Gains** creates a report that shows any gains you have realized from the sale of assets or securities.

- **Schedule A-Itemized Deductions** prepares a transaction report that is subtotaled by each item on Schedule A of Form 1040.

- **Schedule B-Interest And Dividends** creates a transaction report that is subtotaled by each item on Schedule B items of Form 1040.

- **Schedule D-Capital Gains And Losses** prepares a report of all gains and losses reportable on Schedule D.

- **Tax Schedule (For Export To TurboTax)** prepares a report of all of your tax-related transactions, and is specifically meant to be exported to TurboTax for preparing your tax return.

- **Tax Summary** creates a report of all your tax-related transactions subtotaled by category.

NOTE

Some items on the Tax menu are available only to users of Quicken Deluxe, Premier, and Home and Business editions.

USE TURBOTAX LINKS

The four links in the Use TurboTax section on the right of the Tax tab give you specific instructions on integrating your Quicken data with TurboTax:

Use Turbo Tax
How do I export Quicken data to Turbo Tax? Import Last Year's Turbo Tax Data Prepare and File Taxes Online Purchase Turbo Tax

- **How Do I Export Quicken Data To TurboTax?** opens a step-by-step Help window detailing the procedure.

- **Import Last Year's TurboTax Data** opens the Import TurboTax File window from which you can choose last year's file and follow the on-screen instructions.

- **Prepare And File Taxes Online** opens the TurboTax Online window from which you can create your tax return using a Web-based product.

- **Purchase TurboTax** facilitates ordering the product, both the online version or as a CD.

USE THE ONLINE TAX TOOLS

Click **Go To TurboTax.com** to connect with the TurboTax Web site for additional help.

Explore the Tax Menu

The Tax menu offers additional links to tax tools and planners. While many of the tools are available from the Tax tab, others are more quickly accessible from this menu.

Use Tax Menu Items

From the Tax menu, you can access the Tax Center or the Tax Planner. You can open the Category List and assign tax-line items to specific categories. You can also access a utility that allows you to find potential errors in your category assignments.

Tax	Reports Help
Go to Tax Center	
Tax Planner	
Tax Line Item Assignment	
Tax Category Audit	
Deduction Finder	
Itemized Deduction Estimator	
Capital Gains Estimator	
Tax Withholding Estimator	
TurboTax ▶	
Online Tax Tools ▶	
Tax Activities ▶	
Quicken Services ▶	

1. Click the **Tax** menu, and click **Tax Category Audit**. If Quicken does not detect a problem, you will see a message to that effect. If Quicken does find a problem, the Tax Category Audit window will open, as shown in Figure 10-7. This utility checks two types of categories:

- Standard categories that are not linked to the correct tax line

- Categories you created that may need to be linked to a tax-line item or categories that are linked to an incorrect tax-line item

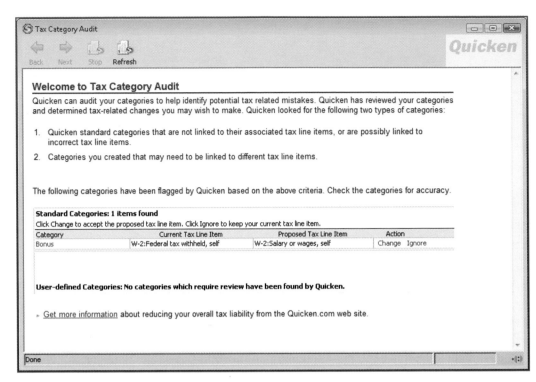

Figure 10-7: The Tax Category Audit window warns you of potentially incorrect tax-line assignments.

2. Click **Change** to open the Edit Selected Tax Audit Category dialog box, which displays a list of possible problem categories in each area:

   a. Click the **Tax Line Item** down arrow, and click the correct line item.

   b. Click **OK** to close the dialog box.

3. Click **Ignore** if you feel the tax-line assignment is correct, and the category is removed from the problem list.

4. Click **Close** to close the window.

Use the Deduction Finder

If you are not sure you have assigned tax-line items for all of your categories, or if you would just like to identify other potential deductions, you can use the Deduction Finder.

1. Click the **Tax** menu, and click **Deduction Finder**. The Introduction To Deduction Finder dialog box appears explaining how it works.

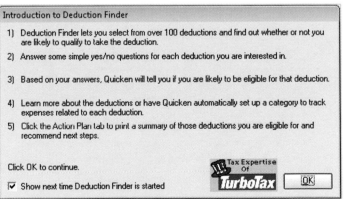

2. Click **OK** to continue, and if it isn't already open, click the **Deductions** tab to begin the process.

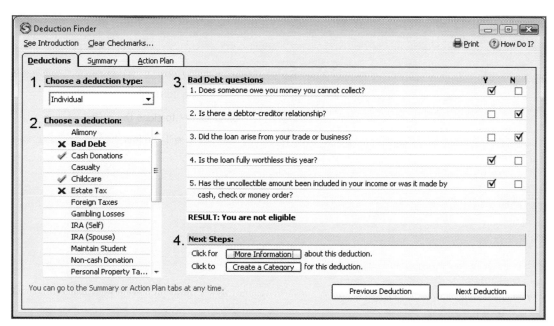

Figure 10-8: The Deduction Finder helps you find additional deductions for which you may be eligible.

3. Click the **Choose A Deduction Type** down arrow, and click one of the six types of deductions. A list of deductions appears on the left side of the window.

4. Click any item on the list to display questions about that possible deduction on the right side of the window. Click either **Yes** or **No** to answer each question, as shown in Figure 10-8.

5. After you have answered all the questions, a green check mark appears to the left of any deduction for which you may be eligible and a red X appears if you are not eligible. The result also is displayed at the bottom of the section.

6. Click **More Information** at the bottom of the window if you want to learn more about this deduction. Click **Create A Category** to display an explanation about a potential new category for this deduction, and then click **OK** to create it.

7. Click **Next Deduction** to go to the next deduction on the list, or select one that may pertain to your situation, and follow the same steps.

8. Click the **Summary** tab to see how many deductions are available for each deduction type, how many you have viewed and answered, and how many for which you are eligible.

9. Click the **Action Plan** tab to see the steps to take to use the deductions you have found.

10. Click **Clear Checkmarks** on the menu bar to clear all of your answers and start over.

11. Click **Close** to close the Deduction Finder.

Use the Itemized Deduction Estimator

You can take a wide variety of tax deductions, some of which are more common than others. Quicken provides the Itemized Deduction Estimator to ensure that you are deducting all to which you are entitled. It uses information from the Tax Planner and lets you create what-if scenarios.

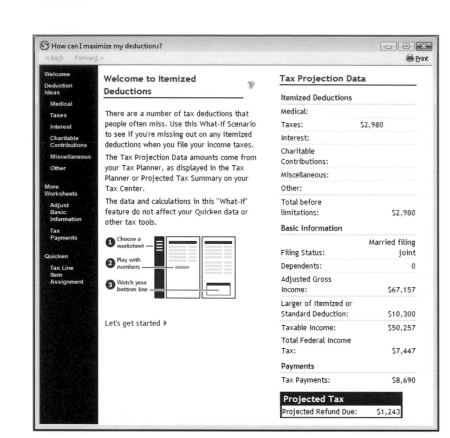

Figure 10-9: *The Itemized Deduction Estimator can help you identify less well-known deductions.*

To use the Itemized Deduction Estimator:

1. Click the **Tax** menu, and click **Itemized Deduction Estimator**. A welcome page appears, shown in Figure 10-9. The Itemized Deduction Estimator displays your projected data as you entered it in the Tax Planner.

2. Click **Let's Get Started** to begin the process.

3. The Medical Deductions worksheet is displayed. Each worksheet in this wizard displays the tax projection data on the right side so that you can see any changes. As you make entries in the scenario, your projected tax bill changes if your scenario information increases or decreases your liability.

4. Click in the **Miles Driven To And From Appointments** text box, and enter the number of miles you drove. Quicken will calculate the dollar value that is deductible, as shown in Figure 10-10.

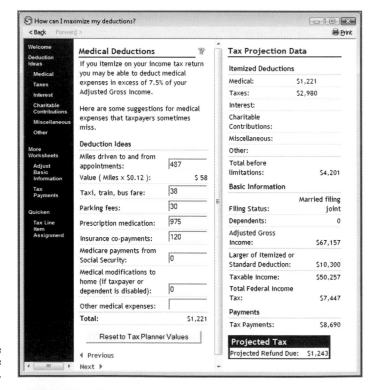

Figure 10-10: *The Medical Deductions worksheet helps you identify medical expenses you may not have remembered otherwise.*

5. Click in any of the remaining text boxes that are applicable to you, and enter any costs you incurred.

6. Enter any other relevant items in this worksheet. Your total additional medical expenses appear in the Total area.

7. Click **Next** to display the Taxes worksheet.

ENTER REMAINING DEDUCTION WORKSHEETS

The remaining deduction worksheets follow a similar pattern to the Medical Deductions worksheet. Open the sheet by either clicking in the left column or clicking **Next** in the previous sheet. Then click in the text boxes that are applicable to you, and type the amount. Close the Itemized Deduction Estimator when you are finished.

Use the Tax Withholding Estimator

The Tax Withholding Estimator Wizard allows you to determine how much you should have taken out of each paycheck. You can create a what-if scenario to ensure that you are not withholding too much or too little.

1. Click the **Tax** menu, and click **Tax Withholding Estimator**. The Tax Withholding Estimator is displayed, as shown in Figure 10-11. Each worksheet has two parts. The left section allows you to enter possible changes. The right side displays the tax-projection data reflecting the current information you have entered into Quicken or into your Tax Planner. As you make changes on the left side, the right side displays the result of those changes.

2. Click **Let's Get Started** to display the Adjust Basic Information worksheet. Select each of the fields you want to change, and either select or type the information that is correct for you, clicking **Next** as needed.

3. When you have completed all of the worksheets, click **W-4 Information** to create a printed worksheet you can take to work and use to complete a new W-4.

4. Click **Form W-4 On Quicken.com** to open and print an actual W-4 from the IRS Web site.

Figure 10-11: Use the Tax Withholding Estimator to make sure you are not withholding too much or too little from your paycheck.